Memoirs of Grassy Creek

For Gayle Winston,
my daughter

Memoirs of Grassy Creek

Growing Up in the Mountains on the Virginia–North Carolina Line

by Zetta Barker Hamby

CONTRIBUTIONS TO SOUTHERN APPALACHIAN STUDIES, 1

McFarland & Company, Inc., Publishers
Jefferson, North Carolina, and London

Publisher's note: *Not long after seeing the edited manuscript, making the final selection of photographs, and completing the pen-and-ink sketches, but before seeing the proofs, Zetta Barker Hamby died, on June 24, 1997. Our thanks go to Gayle Winston and John Stewart for seeing the book through to publication.*

Cover: The Barker family (Zetta out front) on their farm in the Grassy Creek community, ca. 1913.

British Library Cataloguing-in-Publication data are available

Library of Congress Cataloguing-in-Publication Data

Hamby, Zetta Barker, 1907–1997
    Memoirs of Grassy Creek : growing up in the mountains on the Virginia–North Carolina line / by Zetta Barker Hamby.
       p.   cm. — (Contributions to southern Appalachian studies ; 1)
    Includes index.

    ISBN-13: 978-0-7864-0416-2
    softcover : 50# alkaline paper ∞

    1. Grassy Creek (Ashe County, N.C.) — Social life and customs.
2. Grassy Creek (Ashe County, N.C.) — Biography.   3. Hamby, Zetta
Barker, 1907–1997 — Childhood and youth.   4. Mountain life — North
Carolina — Grassy Creek (Ashe County)   I. Title.   II. Series.
F264.G78H36   1998
975.6'835 — dc21   97-38307
                                                        CIP

Manufactured in the United States of America

McFarland & Company, Inc., Publishers
  Box 611, Jefferson, North Carolina 28640
   www.mcfarlandpub.com

Acknowledgments

My daughter, Gayle, persuaded me to write this book. She wanted to know about the old days. So, here it is!

To John Stewart, who has had five, six or more books published, many, many thanks for his experience and assistance in helping me add to, delete and refine the rough first draft, supplying information from his research and stored memories. Thanks to Robbie Franklin for his patience, his guidance, professionalism, and help. Thanks to the cooperative people at Grayson County Public Library who made searches and supplied information as they could unearth it on "The Wreck of the Old Ninety-Seven" and words to the song by the same name.

Thanks to Judge and Mrs. Robert Gambill for their cooperation and encouragement. Thanks to my friend and neighbor, Fanny Halsey Osborne, who is one month and seven days younger than I, and who lived and grew up about one-eighth of a mile from our home. She now lives in the house where I lived, and has lived there for many years. She has helped to refresh names and places, as have Charles and Mabel Welch.

Appreciation for encouragement and information from Harry, Isobel and Zetta Barker (my namesake), Wilma and Paul Spencer, Ola Barker and her children, Berkley and Nancy Ingram, Donald Barker, Linda Long, Gwyn and Bobby Eller, Sylvia and Jerry Hamby, Dave Stewart, Cheryl Williams, Billie Moore, Sue Smith, Olene Boyer, Dick Miller, Joe and Dixie Hart, Steve and Linda Carroll, Jay and Helen McGrady, Doris Perry, the Rev. and Mrs. Kermit Goodman, Roger, Brian, Lena and Bobby Waddell, Zetta Canliffe, Drenda and Clarence Roten, Geneva and Jack Wood, and Ada Waddell.

Thanks to the four sons of my sister, Marie, the four sons of my brother, Joe, the Bobby Hamby family, the children of Leonard Hamby and Fannie Bare, Joann Shepherd, Thomas, Reba, and Sallie Eller and the cousins in Ohio.

Thanks to Jim and Shirley Anderson, Jim and Pat Toner, Bina Orr, Georgia Dancy, Dewey Cox, Elsi Sisson, May Hale, David, Lily and Linda VanHoy, Lois Reynolds, Nancy and Jack Phipps, Paul and Virginia Pierce, Harold and Martha Young, Sandra and Wayne Bower, the Rev. and Mrs. William Burchett, Paul and

Margaret Graybeal, Fred, Wanda and Tim Rutherford, Bryan and Joyce Spencer, Calvin and Katrina Miller, and Ivan and Edna Miller.

Thanks to Martha and Harold Young, Jessie Vannoy, Jean Phipps, Betty Roland, Joe and Dixie Hart, Paulette Peterson, Linda Kelly, the Don Newberrys, the Jack McGradys, Karen and Johnny Spencer, Sally Arnold, Carrie Hudler and her children, Lou Sheets, Lois Elliott and the other children of my sister Mayme, Don and Dixie Reedy, and Charlotte Nurge.

Thanks to Earl Slick, Elizabeth Prince, Wayne Henderson, Henry and Dyann Jordan, Jim and Linda Moore, Scott, Loren and Ryan Webster, Ron Hudler, Steve Plummer, Doris and Scott Hamilton, Walter and Mary Roufail, John Siskind, an advocate for many years, Rob and Jan Noffsinger, Dave Fournier, Lucius Houghton, Billy Klein, Amy Johnson, Nancy and Nathan Hobbs, Thyia Pardo, Susan Breines, Joyce Scott, and Teré Stockwell.

A special thank you to Jackie Soderholm who made it possible for me to have more time to devote to this effort. Thanks to wonderful new friends, John and Kathy Chefas, Pete and Peggy Parish, to old friends, Dom Visconsi, whose support and caring over the years has been so important to me, Renée Landau, Blanche Rosenthal, Pete and Carlin Masterson, and Warren Schmidt.

To Ed Miller, my doctor and friend, and to Becky, Joy and Peggy, to Herb Francis, always a friend, always delightfully irascible. To Lee McMillan whose father was my classmate at Virginia–Carolina, for his support. To Dr. Robichek in Charlotte, to Dr. Tomberlin, Dr. Moose and Alice Smith in Winston-Salem, and to Joan Roan for keeping me on my feet.

Thanks to the nice lady at Radio Shack, Brenda Ballou, and to John Neaves at Carolina Printing, who repaired and kept in ribbons my fifty year old manual Smith-Corona.

Thanks to all the members of the Grassy Creek Baptist Church and the Grassy Creek Methodist Church whose friendship to me and cooperation with each other has been such a blessing.

And to all my friends and neighbors in Grassy Creek, my everlasting gratitude! I know I've neglected to mention some. Please forgive me. After all, I am ninety and a half!

Table of Contents

Foreword

When I began writing this book, I thought I was faced with the decision of whether it should be written in the first or third person; since my aim was to portray a very particular time and place, I decided, however, that I could only use first person. From 1907 to the mid–1930s, travel was extremely difficult and I had limited knowledge of families who today would be neighbors, but whom we saw only occasionally and whose experiences might be somewhat different from ours but still very similar in most respects. It seemed only feasible that I would stick to what I had actually known, experienced and remembered.

Most of this book consists of memories which I have substantiated from records culled from old papers found in drawers, trunks and boxes, yellowed from age, information from my siblings, from family Bibles, from pictures and conversation with relatives and friends of incidents of that time.

Family, home and church were the pervading values of the general residents of this area. They also placed high value on honesty, morality, citizenship, patriotism, neighborliness and politeness.

When we hear someone say "A long time ago," meaning thirty, forty or fifty years ago, I tend to think of how it was eighty-five or more years ago. I was born in 1907, and while I may not remember whether some event happened on Wednesday or Thursday of last week, there are some events that I recall well from as early as 1909!

People would often ask me (and still do) what life was like in the mountains back in those pre–World War I days, when I was growing up. When I told them, some would ask, "Why don't you write it down?" So, I was persuaded to write this book. What I have attempted to portray is not a history of early exploration and settlement of this area (that has already been done by others), but rather this is a collection of "memories" of where I grew up, the community of Grassy Creek, on the Virginia–North Carolina line. I live in Grayson County, Virginia, but "just a stone's throw away" is Ashe County, North Carolina. Our neighborhood was named for my stream, Grassy Creek, which rises at the foot of Blackburn's Knob, just up the road, and runs through my meadow about fifty yards from my house and which is fed by streams from both counties for a distance of five or six miles before emptying into the famous New River in the beautiful mountains of the Blue Ridge.

Since 1907 I have experienced a number of technological and social changes, each of which in its turn led to lifestyle changes:

* *The telephone.* A new form of communication with neighbors, and completely built and installed by our own community residents, and later leading to expansion to places outside our immediate area.

* *The automobile.* Frightening horses and farm animals. Mostly Model T Fords from Fields Ford Motor Co.

* *Electricity.* From Fields Dam on the New River.

* *Radio.* The first of which required head phones to listen to Grady Cole, on WBT in Charlotte. Later we sat over our little table set as Cole reported on the devastating Johnstown Flood of 1935.

* *Television.* First experienced in New York while attending a World's Fair and seeing ourselves on a tiny 5 × 5 inch screen.

* *The airplane.* Single engine, open, single wing and biplanes which took people for rides and blew off hats, and people would say, "If God had meant for people to fly, He would have given them wings."

* *World Wars I and II.*

But one thing has not completely changed — people helping and caring for each other in times of need. Thank goodness.

The twentieth century has seen so many changes. Take travel, for instance. Even as late as the early thirties, to travel to Independence, our county seat, or to Lansing or Jefferson in Ashe County, each about twenty miles distance by horseback, wagon or even car, would take the entire day to get there and back, to shop a bit and take care of business. Today with paved roads and modern cars, one can reach these places in little more than thirty minutes. In 1987 I left Greensboro, N.C., at 7:00 A.M. and flew to Maui, Hawaii, a distance of 5,000 miles, arriving there at 4:00 P.M. in daylight. Of course, there's the time zone difference, but to travel that far in a single day of broad daylight is breathtaking!

Each year and almost daily, there are improvements and creativity in so many fields to make life easier and better. But after all there's not so much difference in "back then" and now! We worked long hours, especially in summer. But aren't people working long hours now? And in many instances aren't both husband and wife sometimes working two jobs to make ends meet? Don't we hear "I'm just so busy" or "I just don't have time to do what I'd like to do"? There's food to buy and labels to read to see how many calories, how much fat, and what additives are in foods. We grew foods without sprays for many years, canned, dried and preserved. Today, we must get up early to jog or do our exercises. "Back then," we rarely ever saw an obese person. By the end of a day, we'd probably have walked five or more miles.

Home was a haven, a place where we had shelter, a place to sleep, food to eat, however simple, a parent to be home when we came from school or wherever to usually find a "sweet cake" or a leftover biscuit with jelly or jam for a snack. And it wasn't long before my Dad pulled the "little table" from the wall, set a kerosene lamp on it and three chairs around it and said, "Time for home-work!" I suppose most people thought of us as farmers and housewives and here let me say I have the utmost respect for those farmers and housewives. What in the world would we do without those tireless workers who have provided our food down through the years and are still trying to do it despite the difficulties and problems and restraints they face today?

Most of my working years were in the area of education — thirteen years in Ashe County, North Carolina, and twenty-two years in Fairfax County, Virginia, as a classroom teacher and elementary school principal. Before going into school work in Fairfax County, I did office work in a large department store in Washington, D.C. I had applied for a teaching position in Fairfax and was offered a position there at a salary of $500 for the year. (I had been making more than that in the department store.)

Then World War II came along, resulting in a population explosion in Washington and surrounding counties. From then on, schools popped up almost faster than buildings could be erected in nearby counties to accommodate the children as government workers moved into the suburbs. Teachers were needed, salaries improved and the Fairfax County School System became the fastest growing and most elite system in Virginia, surpassed only by the Norfolk system at that time.

Nothing I have done has been world shaking. I just tried to do whatever I was supposed to do and do it as best I could. However, two things come to mind that are especially gratifying to have done and taken part in.

During the Depression years, I was a teaching principal in two two-teacher elementary schools, in Ashe County. No schools had cafeterias at that time and some families were having a hard time feeding and clothing their families. Franklin D. Roosevelt had been elected president and, very much aware of the many, many people out of work, instituted the Welfare Work Program. Miss Ruth Reeves of Ashe County was serving as assistant in the welfare program in this county. When I presented the needs of school families, she made available certain foods, large pots, pans and implements so that these children might not only have lunches, but hot lunches! By involving the community, I managed to have a room partitioned off from my classroom, a cook stove was donated, I found two ladies who qualified for welfare aid to cook, so that not only could needy children have hot lunches but all the children in the school could too. Parents who could, took turns sharing homegrown vegetables, fruits and even money to pay for items we needed to buy.

While serving as an elementary school principal in Fairfax County, Virginia, I was asked to participate, along with six other elementary principals, in pilot-ing the accreditation of elementary schools in the state of Virginia. Colleges and high schools were accredited by the Southern Association for the Accreditation of Colleges and High Schools but not elementary schools. Some may have been accredited by the state but not by the prestigious Southern Association. The program required lots of work by the entire school personnel. Evaluation found that some employees were not certified in their field of work, certain facilities lacked requirements, and programs needed updating and improvement, and on and on. I happened to be the only elementary school principal in the county to stand to receive the certificate of accreditation for two schools when presented in Richmond, the state capital, the first elementary schools in the state to be accredited. I'm glad to have been part of this beginning program which should mean that all elementary children have equal opportunity, facilities and programs in the state regardless of where they live.

On a recent early evening in June, I went to the front porch to relax a bit. The sun was still shining on the hills but the lower areas and yard were shaded. In the blue sky some white soft clouds were lazily moving about, clinging together and pulling apart, forming different shapes. One group was a curly white dog, a French poodle, no doubt; then it changed into a long slender polar bear. Some made rows of hills covered with snow. They reminded me of how I used to slowly move the whipped cream on top of a pie or dessert trying to make it last a long time rather than gulping it down as my father and brother did. Or how I played with hot mashed potatoes making a crater in the center filled with butter to float and spread as I made hills and valleys in them before they got cold. Then the clouds moved away and my eyes fell to closer surroundings.

Across the road on the bank and along the fence of my barn lot were five or six young maple and wild cherry trees. We had had a lot of spring showers and rain lately and each young tree had new spring growth. Each tree had slender graceful branches with half-grown leaves protruding from older growth and looked as if a professional seamstress had made evenly spaced scallops. The trees had put on their summer finery — dainty, frilly, lacy gowns like those of teenage girls for their first high school prom. Just then a gentle breeze began to come along and the new branches bowed and rose as if doing a minuet or quadrille. It was all so beautiful and restful, I thought of the words of the Psalmist who wrote, "The heavens declare the glory of God and the earth showeth His handiwork" (Psalms 19).

Then I noticed the electric and telephone lines. One lone bird sat on each of them. Only a year or so ago, dozens and dozens of birds perched on these lines every evening on their way northward for the summer. Every little while a bird would fly to another spot to be closer to his friend or lover even if it meant pushing a bird out of the spot and bobbing about as if discussing where they would spend the night. And, now, two little birds, one on each line, sat on these same lines. I thought how badly we have treated God's creation. I'm afraid the whole idea of sprays, pesticides, cutting away bushes, seeded grasses, berry briars and many of nature's provisions for wildlife, done in order to grow more saleable money crops to make us richer, may have made us poorer in many ways.

Zetta Barker Hamby • *April 1997*

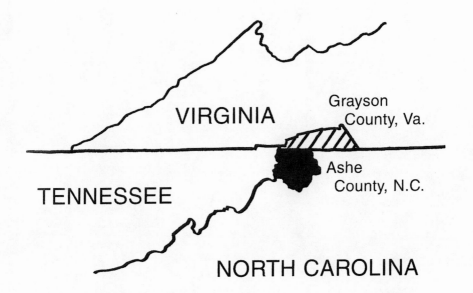

Families

There were many large families in our area when I was growing up. "Planned parenthood," I think, had not been thought of and certainly not here. Lots of children meant farm workers for land owners. Our daughter came to see Grandmother Barker after she was confined to bed two or three years before her death when she was almost 98 years of age. As Gayle asked about some relative, Grandmother would say, "He/she had thirteen children," and name every one of them. Just recently I was told that a lady I used to know said she never felt right unless she was pregnant. I had heard several times from a few elderly people that one child in a family would have the same number of children as his/her parents had. I wondered if I would be that one. As it turned out, my sister, Mayme, and brother Herbert, each had thirteen children and I had only one.

Interestingly enough, after our father had passed away, there were eight of his children living, four boys and four girls. Mayme had 12. Herbert had 13 children and both lost a child in infancy. Both had twins — Mayme had two sets of twins and Herbert one set. Joe and Marie each had four boys. Harry and Wilma had two girls each. Kyle and I only had one child each.

In the first seven years of my life, our family consisted of my parents, my sister, brother and me, and a little baby brother named Captain. One of my very first memories comes to mind out of other events and happenings. According to records of births and deaths in the family Bible and word of mouth of family members, this memory occurred in January 1909, earlier than the 19th when Captain died, when I was barely two years old. January days are short, the first days not quite ten hours long.

Evidently breakfast was over, the kerosene lamps out to save lamp oil. The only light in the room was from the flames blazing from logs in the fireplace. I was standing barefoot and in my night clothes on the fieldstone hearth beside my mother's chair. My brother and sister were standing just back of where Dad was sitting facing Mother and me. Mama was holding a little baby! This was the first tiny baby I had ever seen or recall having seen. All eyes seemed to be on me. I think I was "grinning" and not knowing quite what to do or say.

The new baby was evidently in precarious health as he was not given a

Top: My father, Charlie Columbus Barker (born 1877), and mother, Minnie Lena Spencer Barker (born 1877), brother, Herbert Schley (born 1903) and sister, Mayme Blanch (born 1900). About 1905. *Bottom:* All of the above with an important addition: I am in the middle, born 1907.

permanent name, only "Captain." He was born December 30, 1908, and died January 19, 1909. I recall nothing of his birth or death, only seeing "Little Captain" that January morning.

A few other tiny snatches of early memories come to mind. Dad had taken Mama, Mayme, Herbert and me to spend the night with Aunt Rose Shelton who lived on Solomon's Road. He went back home to milk and feed the animals. The following day when we went home, Claude, Aunt Rose's oldest son, carried me most of the way home.

We were all going to spend the night with Aunt Mega, my mother's youngest sister, who lived in Sussex. I was wrapped up in coat, toboggan and veil over my face and carried by my father. We went up our hill to the Sexton fence. Herbert crossed the fence first and I was handed over to him while Dad got over. The same also happened at the Kirk fence.

Our Immediate Family

My father and mother were both born in 1877 and married September 15, 1897. Carl Vester, the first child, was born July 23, 1899. Our spring was across the road from our house and my mother needed to get water from the spring. She put little Carl in a chair and tied him to the chair back with a soft, wide scarf. When she returned, the baby had wriggled from the chair and had fallen with part of his body in the fire. He died from burns October 2, 1900, at the age of 15 months. Mayme Blanch was born July 17, 1900. Herbert Schley came along April 17, 1902. Then Howard Hampton was born November 6, 1903. He died of whooping cough March 10, 1906. Next was the writer, born January 5, 1907, followed by "Little Captain," on December 30, 1908. So for nearly two years I was the youngest child in the family.

Thinking of memories, there are limited things I remember about my mother's funeral. I had been so close to my mother, since Mayme was seven years older than me, and Herbert five years older, and they were in school and doing chores while I was with Mama most of the seven years. I think with the shock of her death and all the arrangements, people in the house, and "goings on," I was in a daze. Aunt Ellen stayed with us a few days. When Uncle Roby came for her, she gave me a bath, combed and braided my hair, kissed me and said, "Bless your little heart. I hate to leave you."

A year later, when Dad and Etta Sexton were married, I do not recall having any resentment at all. In fact, I think I was glad that now there was someone to cook and do all the things "the lady of the house" did. Just after they were married, someone drove them to Troutdale to catch the train to Roanoke where Uncle Luther was in the hospital. While there they took a "tram" to the top of Mill Mountain which they told us about. In the many, many times I have traveled old Highway 11 and later Highway 81, passing the Roanoke area, I think of Mill Mountain and their describing their trip.

A year after their marriage, a baby, Kyle Keith, was born, September 28, 1916. Of course that meant diapers to be washed and minding the baby. After Kyle was weaned from nursing, Mayme insisted on taking him to sleep with her and me. Usually he slept between us. One night I must have been sleeping too near the edge of the bed and rolled out. This awakened Mayme and she thought that Kyle had fallen out of bed and she was saying, "Honey, did you roll out? Are you hurt? I'm sorry you're hurt!" I lay on the floor and laughed as I thought she would not be voicing all those concerns to me!

Then two years later, Joe Dent came along, followed by Harry Robert, October 7, 1920. Two girls, Wilma Juanita and Lenna Marie were born in 1923 and 1925. By this time, Mayme and Herbert had left home and were living in the District of Columbia area. But we all enjoyed these children.

While Herbert was home, he always had many farm chores to do. He began taking the boys with him to where he was working. When Harry was too little to walk the distance up a steep hill, Herbert would have Kyle and Joe carry a few small tools, he'd have the ax, mattock or heavier tools in one hand and carry Harry in the other arm. Once when he was repairing the roof on an outside building, their mother knew that wherever Herbert was working Kyle and Joe were there, but where was little Harry? She went to see and Herbert had him sitting on the roof as Harry could not climb the ladder as the other two boys could. After Herbert had gone to the Northern Virginia area and was working, Dad received a notice of a large package in the train station depot at Troutdale, Virginia, to be picked up. When he brought the package home, it was the replica of a farm wagon, green on the outside, red inside the bed, and a seat for the driver just like a real brand new farm wagon, which Herbert had had sent from Sears Roebuck! I know of nothing that gave as many hours of pleasure and use to three little country boys as that wagon.

We enjoyed the half brothers and sisters — their baby-talk and funny expressions and seeing them grow up. On a chilly summer day, when the window was open, Wilma would say, "Raise down the window." After sliding down banks, Kyle would say, "We sleed down the bank." When Harry returned from spending almost two years with Uncle George and Aunt Minnie in far away Colorado, we children would ask him all sorts of questions just to hear him talk.

Joe was the middle of the three boys and one of the sweetest people in the whole wide world. He was drafted into the army in World War II. After his discharge, he became a carpenter and a good one. He was the first of the eight living children to have his own home, a large one, built and free of debt. He worked on the Washington Cathedral in the final days of its completion. Woodrow Wilson and other dignitaries are entombed there.

When I was growing up, my stepmother, Etta, would make my dresses most of the time. When I graduated from high school, we did not have hats and gowns but the girls wore white dresses made at home. She got yards and yards of white lace about an inch and a half wide and sewed three rows around the neck, sleeves and bottom of the skirt, and used white satin ribbon for a tied sash and bow at the waist.

When I began teaching, times were hard. The Depression was brewing and money was scarce. My father lost money when the bottom fell out of cattle prices. After teaching a couple of years, I knew Etta had not had a chance to buy new clothes. At Christmas time, I bought out of a meager salary a coat and hat for her as I knew that every penny that could be spared went for clothes for the children and household needs.

I was teaching at West Jefferson and my school room was at the front of the building on one side of the hall. The room doors had glass windows at the tops. Uncle Luther appeared at the door of my classroom. When I went to the door, he said, "I've come for you. Etta is very sick and not expected to live." With that his voice broke and he cried. The principal arranged for my leave and I came home. Etta had had a miscarriage and now had an infection. She was very, very sick. Aunt Lona had always been considered the nurse among our family and relatives. As I watched Etta being given medication, water and liquids, she would become strangled. Soon, I tried giving the medicine to her. She did not get strangled. After that, I was the only one who could give her the liquids.

Relationships had been broken off between our family and the Sextons, Etta's parents, over the fencing of a right-of-way — a matter that often created frictions, it seemed, then and even now at times. Blanch, my stepmother's sister, had heard of how ill Etta was and she ran away and came over. She and I sat up at night and we proceeded to be able to do that part of her care that no one had been able to do. I had lain down one day to catch a bit of sleep when someone came and called me to get up to give Etta her medicine.

When the children's mother died, I felt so sorry for them I truly would have gladly, if possible, died in her place.

Then my father was faced with five young children to care for. Kyle, the oldest, was eleven and Marie, the youngest, was two. Grandpa Barker took Wilma through the winter months. Uncle Iredell and Aunt Vesta took Marie. Aunt Minnie and Uncle George took Harry with them to Colorado for a couple of years. Dad, Kyle and Joe remained in the home. When my school ended in April, I believe, I came home and took over the housework, gardening, laundry, milking four cows, and caring for Kyle, Joe, Wilma, and Dad. I recall cutting hair for the boys which looked as if a bowl had been placed over their heads and the hair cut closely up to the bowl. Then there were the baths to be seen about, care of clothing, and on Sunday mornings, shaving Dad's neck and getting all ready to go to Sunday School and church. A busy summer!

Again, the following fall, I was back teaching, and Wilma was back at Grandpa's with Dad and the boys at home fending for themselves as best they could with Grandmother and the aunts helping out. At some stage a Miss Blackburn and her grandmother stayed with them for a while.

In 1928, I was married. My father wanted my husband and me to take over the children until they were on their own and he would deed the farm and house to us. He felt that he had lost two wives and he didn't want to go through that again. However, I felt that would not be fair to my husband.

One Sunday afternoon, Dad, Kyle and Joe came to our apartment and Dad asked if the boys could spend the afternoon with us for a few hours. He did not tell us where he was going. When he came back and we were talking, he repeated something someone had told him that afternoon. I said, "That sounds like Mr. Jason Spencer." He had to laugh, as in truth, it was what Mr. Spencer had said. Mr. Spencer had introduced him to a maiden lady, Miss Gertie Rash, who was near my father's age, six years younger, never married, and was living with her aunt, Mrs. Marilda Kilby, as she had no other close family living in the near area. They were married March 11, 1929. We called her Grandma Gertie as we wanted our children to call her Grandma. She was the kindest most gentle woman ever, a modest and fine person. She was so good to her step-grandchildren and lived several years after my father passed away. Twice she lived in our home, sometimes with Mayme, but her very favorite was Marie who was only three when she and Dad were married and seemed like her very own child.

Why am I writing this? My father said a number of times, "I'm the luckiest man in the world. I've had three wives and two sets of children and they've all gotten along." It's true that we have all been very close. I make no difference in my full brother and sister and my half-brothers and sisters. I think stepmothers and step-children have had bad press at times, but with strong family life, training, prayer, and teaching of respect for each other, broken families could be prevented.

My father was a small farmer and any money he was able to accumulate was always needed for the many family and farm needs, but he tried to give us children as many experiences as he could. Great Aunt Caroline Davis Peak had kept a hog longer than the usual year before having it butchered. It was fed well and grew and grew and became so fat and heavy that it became a "show piece" in the community. People would stop just to see Aunt Caroline's "big hog." Dad took us to see the hog before it was butchered and to be there to watch the several men do the "hog killing." Then Great Uncle Bob Spencer had gotten a breed of swine that did not have cloven hooves but hooves like cattle, so we were taken to see those. (Perhaps that may be why some religious denominations do not eat pork but beef. Deuteronomy 14:7 and 8.)

A little tent-show came to Rugby. My mother had died and Dad took us three in the buggy to Rugby to see the show. I don't know whether it was called a carnival then or not, but it was generally called "a show." I'm sure there were clowns but the performance I was most intrigued with was three horses riding abreast around the ring, with a girl in Indian dress standing upright on their backs. No, she didn't have three legs! Her two feet were planted firmly on the backs of the outside horses, while the third horse ran underneath her. After the show, Dad bought a balloon on a stick for me, a whip (like the rider used) for Mayme and a little "Indian decorated hatchet" for Herbert. He bought cups of flavored ice for us.

We had Plymouth Rock chickens (Domineckers) for eggs to sell and for eating as they weighed heavier than Leghorns and some other varieties. Rhode

Island Reds, Plymouth Rocks and Leghorns were all the kinds of chickens we were familiar with. A few people had Bantam chickens or some showy variety. Aunt Lucy who lived at Little Helton told us that one of her neighbors had gotten Wyandotte chickens, a black and white dotted breed. Grandmother and neighbors who were always on the lookout for the best layers and heaviest chickens for selling wanted to see this new variety. One warm Saturday afternoon, Grandma and the two aunts came along and we asked, "Where are you going?"

"We're going over to Helton to see those Wyandotte chickens Lucy was telling us about."

"Dad, can we go?"

"Why, yes, I reckon so. You'll know what they look like."

So we walked the four miles to see Mrs. Porter's chickens. Grandma had lots of questions. Were they good laying hens? How heavy do they seem to weigh? Does it take more feed for them than with the hens you had before? Do they require a certain kind of feed? And on and on.

My father often pointed out the Big Dipper, the Little Dipper, the Milky Way, and Dog Star to us when we'd be walking home from church or visiting a neighbor at night. Sometimes, when a family member happened to walk in from outside and say, "It's sure a starry night out there," or "The sky's sure full of stars tonight," we'd walk out to look and maybe sit down on the porch steps and just quietly look in silent awe!

Dad had seen Halley's Comet in 1910 and would tell us about it. Then he'd tell us about the Aurora Borealis, streams or bands of colored lights in the northern sky at certain times at night, help us say and spell the word. After we were in bed and Dad would blow out the kerosene lamp, he'd look out the window and around as if seeing if everything were all right outside. Once in a while he'd say, "Get up. See that white spot over there in the edge of the woods."

"What is it?" we'd ask.

"It's fox fire."

Of course it was a fungus on a damp log but he wanted us to know what it was. Should we happen to be out at night sometime alone and be afraid, we'd know what it was.

Outside the town of Troutdale, a section of road bank had purple slate-like flat rocks. A time or two when Dad was coming home in the wagon, he stopped and picked some up and brought them for us to see. We admired and kept some for a long time.

Grandpa's

As children, we were limited in visiting friends and neighbors, so as not to become nuisances. But our grandparents lived on the farm next to our place. In fact, their land on one side was only about 300 yards from our orchard. To go by road was perhaps one-tenth of a mile from our house. There was hardly a day when someone of our family did not go to their house or someone of their family was not at our house.

Grandpa had lived at Silas Creek in Ashe County until his house burned. Looking for a place to move his family, Grandpa heard of a house and farm for sale at Grassy Creek in Grayson County, Virginia. He looked and bought the two story house with about seventy or more acres of land. The place had belonged to Mr. David Spencer who was having another house built at that time. The house they moved into was a two story house with seven rooms, upper and lower porch all the way across the front, and a porch extending from the kitchen across the back of the house.

Grandpa was born in 1844 to Alfred and Katherine Blevins Barker, and was married to Cynthia Katherine Smith. They had two sons, Ira and John Barker. While the boys were quite young their mother died. Later, Grandpa married Amanda Howell and they had seven children, of whom my father was the oldest. Uncle Ira went to Kansas to live with a relative of his mother, married and spent the rest of his life there. Uncle John married and lived near Grant, Virginia, raised a large family and later moved to Maryland.

My earliest memory of my grandparents' family consisted of Grandpa William Poindexter and Grandma Amanda, and aunts, Minnie, Lona, Uncles Roscoe, Luther, Iredell and Aunt Lucy Waddell (married to Joe Waddell). Uncle Roscoe was married to Lucy Spencer. The other uncles and aunts were single. To me, they seemed very grown up, but I suppose their ages ranged from around twenty to the early thirties. One of my earliest memories of Uncle Roscoe was that he was in a room at Grandpa's and I could not go into the room because he had typhoid fever. However, I recall passing through the hall, the room door was slightly open and I could see him lying in bed. He and his family were living in a small three room house and he was brought to Grandpa's to be isolated to protect his family of wife and three children. The oldest, Carmie, was what today would be called Downs Syndrome.

Poindexter was a name too hard to say and write, so Grandpa was called not Poin but "Pine," in fact, "Big Pine" as he had a nephew named Poindexter but called "Little Pine." Little Pine was the son of Grandpa's brother, Uncle Monroe. Even now, in 1997, I find there are a lot of relatives of "Little Pine Barker." The name Poindexter was later divided by my grandparents, and Uncle Luther was given the name "Luther Dexter" and Uncle Iredell was "Iredell Pine."

Grandpa was one of the sweetest and finest persons I've ever known. My father told us of a revival going on in the Silas Creek community where they were living. Since Dad was the oldest of the children at home, he was to look after the younger children while Grandpa and Grandma attended the revival. One day a neighbor said to Dad, "Your pa has quit cussin', hasn't he?" When Grandpa became a Christian, he became a Christian in word and deed! Several times he told us that when he was baptized, some men used their canes to move "mush ice" (soft ice beginning to form) in the creek, but Granddad believed that when one becomes a Christian they should be baptized and not let a little

mush ice stand in the way. When he read in the paper of a good deed that someone had done, or someone told him of charitable or helpful activities, tears of
joy ran down his face and he'd say, "Isn't that wonderful!"

Grandpa had fought in the Civil War along with others in Grayson County
and nearby areas. For several years these men would set a date, put on their old
uniforms (as long as they could get in them), or any part of their war gear and
meet for a day-long reunion. Aside from Grandpa, the only other old soldier I
knew personally was Uncle Marion Handy. Grandfather really looked forward
to this event. I asked once, "What do you men do at those reunions?" He said,
"We march. If there's an officer, he gives orders to see if we remember them. If
anyone has decorations or any relics brought home, we take them to show." Of
course, a mid-day meal and talk of remembrances of places, events, people and
present day homes and families were discussed. They learned who had passed
away, the health of those who couldn't come. The last reunion Grandpa attended
was held at Volney, Virginia, with only three present. One by one they went to
the great Confederacy in the sky or became otherwise unable to attend. Grandpa
spoke sadly of his comrades and regrets of no more earthly reunions.

Grandpa would hire my brother and sister to help hoe corn and I would
go along and would want to help and earn some money, too. I was always given
the row next to the one Grandpa was hoeing, and he'd cross over and hoe a few
hills to help me keep up. He'd say, "Hurry up. It's going to rain." We'd look up
and not a cloud in the sky. At the end of the day I was paid a nickel!

Grandpa became ill with what was diagnosed as colitis and died a week
later. When asked what hurt, he'd say, "Nothing. Isn't it awful to be so helpless
when nothing hurts?" He had said many times, "I don't want one of them store
bought coffins. I'm a large man and I'm afraid the bottom might fall out. I want
my coffin made by a good carpenter — made of strong wood." And so it was. A
man at Grant made caskets and so Uncle Iredell took needed information to Mr.
Redford or Rutherford who made a beautiful casket with dark outside fabric,
carrying handles and shirred white fabric lining. Grandpa was 88 when he died.

No visiting minister, regardless of how hurried he appeared to be, got away
from Grandpa's without having prayer. Granddad always knelt for prayer, at
home, church or wherever. In later years he had rheumatism in his joints. To a
minister who was known for his lengthy prayers at church, Grandpa said,
"Brother _____, don't pray so long. My knees hurt." My grandparents inter-
preted the Bible as they understood it and heard it preached as the ministers
understood it. The family was closely knit and expected to be generous, thoughtful and always polite. Aunt Minnie said, "We never jawed our parents!," meaning they never talked back to their parents. Grandpa had a sense of humor and
would play with us grandchildren. When a few of us were spending the night
with them, he would let us tie springs of his hair with cloth strings until his head
was covered with tied bows and he'd say, "Now I'm an Indian." When he'd get
tired, he'd say, "Now let's play Old Folks at Home."

"Grandpa, how do you play that?" we'd ask.

He'd say, "Let's sit down and be still."

Grandpa called me Little Kate for several years. I asked him why he called me that. He said, "My mother's name was Kate, my first wife's name was Kate and our oldest daughter's name was Lucy Kate. I like that name."

Today, as I think of Grandma, I see her as a matriarch. She was sensible and wise, was listened to and respected. I never knew her to spank, slap or shake a child. Yet all she had to do was tell us or speak to us if she saw us doing anything we shouldn't be doing. Adults seemed to ask her advice and she visited the sick and was always ready to share with those who needed help (certainly those who worked and helped themselves; she had no use for those who wouldn't work).

I thought Grandpa was rich. Grandpa had served in the army in the Civil War and drew a small pension — I really don't know how much, seems to me that I had heard about $50.00 a month. Anyway they hardly ever bought sugar by five pounds, but in hundred pound bags and lard in five gallon tin cans. When someone mentioned "lard can," we knew what that meant. Of course, my grandparents had been accumulating things for years with nine children to help and being conservative and knowing how to manage what they had.

With four grown-ups, single and of "courtin'" age in the house and lots and lots of kinfolk, Grandpa's place had a lot of visitors. Even with walking only three or four miles in those days, it seemed silly not to stay over night. They had nine or ten beds and many weekends all of those beds were filled. This required food preparation and cooking. Dad used to say, "Pa fed out a fortune." Dad and his siblings called their parents "Pa and Ma." At church on Sundays, Grandpa went around inviting everyone there to go home with them for dinner (mid-day meal). On Saturdays, two cakes and as many or more pies had to be baked. A pot of beans and maybe a pot of cabbage cooked to be ready. Irish potatoes and sweet potatoes washed and ready to be peeled, a couple of chickens killed, plucked and cut up — and maybe partially cooked or ham sliced to be ready for frying. Even on week and work days, three daily meals were prepared.

No such stuff as a sandwich and a bowl of soup for lunch and cereal for breakfast. There might be rice or oatmeal for breakfast but they were appetizers only. A big pan of Aunt Lona's biscuits, sausage or ham or fried "streaked side meat," a bowl of cream gravy, sometimes "red eye gravy," two of three varieties of jelly, jams, apple butter and honey and even brown sugar on hot buttered biscuits made up farm weekday breakfasts. I don't know why my parents allowed me or Grandpa's family let me spend nights there when the house was already full of people. If they minded, they never let me know it. Sunday mornings there were fried or scrambled eggs cooked in the long cast iron griddle which was 16 or 18 inches long — long enough to cover two "stove eyes." (Cook stoves had removable lids to allow the cast iron kettles and pots to be placed nearer the fire for faster cooking.) The table was usually loaded with ever so many different dishes and people urged to "taste this or that" or everything. "This is honey that Cousin Eva brought. Do taste it. That is strained honey Luther bought from Mr. Jones when they robbed the bees. Try some of that on a hot biscuit."

Getting up time at Grandpa's was four o'clock every morning. While the women prepared breakfast, the uncles fed the horses and cattle. Breakfast was eaten, dishes washed, beds made, floors swept, chickens fed, hogs slopped. Then they sat down and waited for daylight to come, especially on winter mornings of long nights. If a trip were planned to Troutdale or Lansing or Helton to the flour mill, the team was harnessed, the wagon loaded and ready to move with the first ray of daybreak. After the uncles married or moved away and Grandpa had died, Grandma and the aunts found it difficult to have wood for the stoves and fireplaces and they didn't get up so early.

Grandpa had passed away and Grandma and the two aunts were now the sole occupants of the house and farm. Although Grandma's health was not as good as much earlier, she continued to be in charge. She complained that, "The girls are so puny," although they were in their seventies. But Grandmother still made decisions. Aunt Minnie wanted to grow celery but Ma said, "I'll not have that stuff growing in my garden." When Aunt Lona wanted to keep a calf to grow and sell later for money for her personal use, Grandmother said, "No, it'll cost too much to feed it. Go ahead and sell it now."

A neighbor was to mow the hay fields and the orchard needed to have the grass cut. Grandma would not let that horse-pulled mowing machine in her orchard, skinning up the trees. So she used a scythe. The girls said the day she finished, they had to meet her at the gate leading into the orchard and help her into the house. She was ninety or older.

Some years later, the daughters were working in the garden one cool spring day and Grandmother was cold. She couldn't find kindling or the right kind of wood for a bit of fire, so she walked out to a wooded area near Mr. Halsey's house to pick up some wood. On the way to the house she fell and fractured her hip. So, she had to stay in bed and would do so most of the rest of her life. Gayle wanted to visit her while she was still lucid. We'd hear them laughing and she'd be telling Gayle some funny story. As Gayle would ask about some relative, she'd say that So and So had thirteen children and name everyone of them. She died in March. She would have been 98 in June, and still lucid. A most remarkable woman!

After I had taught school one year — the school term of 1925-26 — I went to spend the night with Grandma

The blade had a three- or four-inch metal stem that was inserted into the wood handle. The blade was removed for sharpening. A little metal clamp then held the blade in the handle.

A wood hand plug to use when mowing is difficult.

Mowing Scythe: A long, slightly curved blade for mowing grass.

Letter from my grandmother, Amanda
Howell Barker (written in the 1940s).

and Aunt Lona. They treated me as if I were special company. They didn't want me to help do the dishes, make the bed or sweep the floor. Aunt Lona would be doing the chores and say to me, "Go sit down and talk to Ma!" And Grandma would talk to me as if I were someone special.

After my husband, Gayle and I had moved to the Washington area, I had a letter from Grandma. My parents' school year consisted only of three months and they finished only seventh grade. I have no idea how much schooling my grandparents had. In Grandma's letter she spelled as the word sounded.

Although sisters, Aunt Minnie and Aunt Lona were quite different. Aunt Lona was serious, not afraid to try almost anything that had to be done, and ready with a quick gingery retort. Aunt Minnie was more reserved and ladylike.

Aunt Lona was the alarm clock. If someone wanted to get up at any ungodly hour, she got them up. She was chief cook, seamstress, broom maker, medical advisor, child psychologist and nurse on call when the lady of a home was sick. She was never married but had had two serious beaux. One was killed by a falling tree. Norman was taken ill and died.

One day as Aunt Lona was going through the hall, she was mumbling and someone said, "What's wrong? What are you mumbling about?" She answered, "I'm going to change my name. It's Lona this and Lona that. I'm going to change my name to something that's harder to say!" She never did change her name, but she remained single and cared for her parents as long as they lived.

Mr. George Plummer who had grown up in the Grassy Creek area, had left and settled near Fort Collins in Colorado, and met and married a lady there. His wife died leaving him with five children — some of whom were already married or grown. But he was seeking a wife. He came to visit his brother, Mr. Bob Plummer and we heard that this man was "well fixed. He has some oil wells in

1. William Poindexter Barker, my grandfather (b. 1844, d. 1932). 2. Amanda Jane Howell Barker, my grandmother (b. 1858, d. 1956). Enlargements of these pictures, taken shortly after their marriage, hung in the living room of their house for almost a hundred years. 3. About ten years later. 4. Shortly before his death. 5. In her front yard, in her "plush" chair and black taffeta dress, about 1950.

Left: Aunt Lona Barker with my sister, Mayme, about 1906. Note the embroidered quilt used as background. *Right:* Uncle Luther Dexter Barker in front of the photographer's "classical" backdrop.

Colorado!" His brother had just the lady for him, one who knew how to work, cook and do just about everything a woman was supposed to do! So they came to visit at Grandpa's to meet Aunt Lona. But after tactfully arranging a number of "get-togethers," he picked Aunt Minnie, married her and took her to Colorado.

Aunt Minnie and Uncle George came to visit several times, driving in Uncle George's Velie automobile. Once while they were here, the hydraulic brakes of his car needed fluid. Local auto shops had no experience with that kind of brakes. My future husband was working in the Ford Garage in West Jefferson and my father took Uncle George to him. He and mechanics, garage owners and people at the drug store consulted and came up with a solution that seemed to work. But when Uncle George and Aunt Minnie stopped in St. Louis on the way home, Uncle George went to a Velie dealership to trade for a later model car. They didn't have on hand the one Uncle George wanted but they could order it. So they took the train home and he went back to pick up the new car when it was ready.

We always looked forward to the visits of Uncle George and Aunt Minnie. They brought gifts and things we did not have or hadn't seen. They brought and even mailed beautiful feathers of "wild chickens" or pheasants, alfalfa honey, little polished rocks done by Indians and made into bracelets or pendants.

Aunt Minnie had such pretty dresses and coats, such as the plum colored satin dress, the fur Kolinsky neck piece of two minks biting each other's tails, and a real pearl necklace. They seemed to love each other very much. When either one was out of the room and came in, they would pick up a chair and go sit beside the other.

One day, as Uncle George sat in a bank president's office in Fort Collins, to co-sign a note for a young neighbor to replace worn-out farm machinery, he had a massive stroke. Aunt Minnie and a step-daughter-in-law cared for him until he passed away a month later. After the estate was settled, Aunt Minnie came back to live with her parents and sister. When she went upstairs at night, we'd hear her just weeping her heart out.

Being the youngest and smallest child, until I was eight or nine years of age I could be spared from work and chores more than Bubby and Sissy. Grandmother would take me with her to visit

Uncle Iredell Poin Barker with his wife, Vesta Osborne. Luther and Iredell shared their father's middle name.

sick neighbors. We went to visit Mrs. Jennie Blackburn, wife of Preacher David Blackburn. Mrs. Blackburn was in bed sick. We walked across the Halsey hill and down Mr. Granville Spencer's field. The Blackburns lived in a tiny three room, board and batten house. When we got to the house we entered the kitchen door as it was more convenient. On the little flat topped kitchen stove was a tin wash pan filled with pennies and water. The saved pennies had stuck together and they were being heated so they could be taken apart.

Nelia lived with Mr. and Mrs. Blackburn. I think she may have been a niece of Mrs. Blackburn. I don't know what became of Nelia after Mrs. Blackburn died. Reverend David moved to a house in the Volney area. He had been very conservative and spent little money. People speculated that he had money. Once after he had been away from the house to which he had moved, he found that his house had been ransacked, even the strawtick on his bed had been opened and searched, evidently by someone looking for money.

At times Uncle Luther would bring me on trips to Troutdale and Lansing. He was courting two ladies who happened to have younger sisters about my age. He would take me along, thinking if I were visiting these young girls, the parents of his date would be more lenient toward his spending the night. We went in high style in a buggy drawn by two horses to the home of the one who lived the farther away. He dated this lady for twenty years but never married her. In fact he never married at all. When he and the other lady "broke up," he asked me to go ask her for the gifts he had given her. He said if I would do that, he'd give me the jewelry. When I asked my father if I could do that, he said, "No. Emphatically no. If he wants to get them back, let him get them." He must have gotten them or she sent them to him, for he gave me a bracelet which he called a Friendship Bracelet.

Uncle Luther began having attacks of what appeared to be indigestion. The attacks became more frequent and lasted longer until he became "bedfast." The family had every doctor in the surrounding area try to find the cause of his illness and to treat him: Dr. Osborne, Dr. Pennington, Dr. Jones and others. One doctor tried pumping out his stomach with a tube inserted through his mouth and throat. I left the house when this was being done. Finally Dr. Waddell recommended that he go to the hospital in Roanoke. Dad arranged for someone to drive him and Uncle Luther to Troutdale to take the train to Roanoke. As they were leaving the house, Grandmother and the two aunts would not have sobbed any louder had he been carried to the cemetery. Evidently "going to the hospital" was thought to be the final act! He was in the hospital several weeks and they did careful observations but were unable to determine his problem. He had learned that some foods seemed to bring on those attacks and when he was brought those foods, he would not eat them. Finally it was decided to do an exploratory surgery. What did they find? Appendicitis! They put his appendix in a vial of bromide and he brought it home.

Uncle Luther had been to the city and had experiences he had never had before. He found that asparagus could be eaten rather than just grown in a little spot in the yard for feathery-like fern to be used in floral arrangements. Country people called it "spar grass." Grandmother sometimes fussed that her "spar grass" would be ruined by Uncle Luther cutting off the six or seven inch spears as they came out of the ground. No other members of the family would eat that "weed." Uncle Luther introduced us to the first grapefruit we had ever seen, much less eaten. He planned and arranged the first Ice Cream Supper we had heard of and had a chance to taste.

Uncle Luther took me along with him on a trip to Lansing — I suppose to have someone to talk to or remain in the wagon to keep watch over things while he went inside to make purchases. The wagon bed was full of fertilizer, sacks of feed and a lot of small purchases and it was getting dark before we got home. There was the Sheets' Hill to cross with some steep places and curves which he dreaded with a loaded wagon and tired after a long day. We stopped at Uncle Roscoe's. Aunt Lucy and the children had gone to visit her parents, so we spend the night with Uncle Roscoe who lived about a mile or a little more from our home. The next morning we had corn flakes for breakfast — my first. He had gotten two boxes and paid ten cents a box for them.

Uncle Iredell was the youngest of Grandpa's children and my father's youngest brother. He was the musical member of the family. All of his brothers and sisters sang in church and in get-togethers but Uncle Iredell was a song leader and played the organ. In fact he bought and played the first organ I recall seeing. He taught school one year at least and I suppose that was when he bought the organ. In fact that organ is still in the house Uncle Iredell last lived in and can still be played.

Uncle Iredell and Uncle Luther, when work permitted in winter and on weekends, would saddle up a horse and go to visit relatives in other communities, visit churches, make acquaintances and get to know quite a number of people. Despite the muddy dirt roads, they would don their leggings and oil cloth or rubber slickers and go to visit newly made friends and, of course, invite friends to visit them.

Uncle Iredell dated and married Vesta Osborne, daughter of Dr. Fielden Osborne. They eloped. They had no children but had two foster children, Pauline and Freda.

Sometimes we'd get warts on our hands or especially, it seemed, on fingers and thumbs. A wart is a growth of thick, hard skin over a small area, probably caused by pressure on a particular spot from some activity just as corns may be made on the feet from shoes that do not fit properly. Uncle Luther had heard that they could be removed by inserting a thin sewing needle through the wart and holding a burning match to the end of the needle. He used this method on a wart on my hand one time. I don't remember whether I gave credit to this procedure or not. However, in doing some research, I found that warts were sometimes removed "by burning with nitric acid."

Someone suggested they could be removed by using the milk from the plant called milkweed. So, when I'd go to drive the cows to the "milking place," I'd break off a piece of milkweed and rub it over a wart.

I had spent the night at Grandpa's. While Aunt Lona went to milk the cows and put the milk away, Grandma and I washed and put away the breakfast dishes. Drying my hands, I noticed on one of my fingers the wart that had been there for a few weeks and of which I was embarrassed, for I was now a teenager and had boyfriends. Grandmother went to sit in the "sitting room." Now, what had I heard? "I'll try it," I decided. Aunt Lona had a brand new dishrag she'd made from a portion of a man's cotton knitted union suit that had been discarded because of holes in the elbows and knees, but washed and boiled to snow white. I went to the kitchen, got the new dishcloth, rubbed it over the wart, went outside, looked for a flat rock imbedded in the ground, lifted it and put the already damp dishrag under it and placed the rock back to look as it did before being moved. When the rag rotted the wart would be gone! This had to be a secret.

When Aunt Lona started the lunch meal, she looked for her new dishrag. She said, "Ma, what did you do with my dishrag?"

"Why, I hung it on the nail where we always hang it."

"Well, it ain't there. I've looked in the cupboards, in the oven, under the dishpans and everywhere, and I can't find it."

"I told you I hung it where we always do," Grandma answered.

"I bet you threw it out with the dishwater," Aunt Lona said as she went outside and looked over the yard fence where they always emptied the dishwater. She fussed about the dishrag she'd only made a couple of days earlier, saying she couldn't depend on Ma to put things where they belonged. I felt guilty about Grandma getting the blame for the dishcloth.

A few weeks later the wart was gone!

Uncle Charlie

My mother's oldest sister was Aunt Rose Ann Spencer who was married to Uncle Charlie Shelton. I don't remember very much about Uncle Charlie. He had a mustache, was a photographer, had eight children, went to the World's Fair in St. Louis, and had the first phonograph I had ever seen. I remember the Victrola in a cabinet with a horn speaker and a little white dog on the side of the speaker with its ear cocked for listening.

I knew of no other Sheltons in Grayson County at the time other than Uncle Charlie and a brother and sister. I understood that they came from Marion, Virginia. I have an old picture of my mother with Uncle Charlie's brother, Oscar, and his sister, "Mittie." This was taken before my mother and father were married. Uncle Charlie may have been the photographer.

Uncle Charlie was looking for a wife and Aunt Rose had inherited a sizable piece of land (land now owned by the Robert VanHoy family on Solomon Road). He met and married her, built a five room house and had six children while living there: Claude, Lena, Brian, Burl, Kline and Harry. Looking for a place where his photography would be successful enough to support his growing family, he took his camera and went to Washington, D.C. He evidently found that area fertile ground for his work as he wrote Aunt Rose to sell the place and plan to move to Northern Virginia. Mr. and Mrs. Marsh Sexton bought the place and Aunt Rose began planning for the move. She must have sold the household furniture, all except a wardrobe (a tall cabinet with two doors for hanging clothes and a drawer underneath for folded clothing or other articles). This piece of furniture was brought to our house until arrangements were made for the family to leave and the cabinet to be shipped from Troutdale on the same train the family would travel on. I thought that wardrobe was the tallest thing I had ever seen.

I cannot be sure of the year these events took place, but Aunt Rose's children assured me that they moved from Grassy Creek in 1909. If that is true, I would have been only two years old. Their youngest son, Harry and I were born the same year. When the closing was made on the farm, and household things sold, the family of seven moved into our two bedroom house until they were to leave. I recall an argument that Harry and I had. We were both wearing hand-knitted stockings that reached above the knees and were held up by elastic garters made from webbing about an inch wide. Our garters of black background had designs made with colors and we each insisted ours were the prettiest.

Uncle Charlie bought a farm and house on Pope's Head Road in Fairfax County and moved his family there. He made a picture of the house with the family arranged in front of it, except Brian (the nonconformist) was sitting on the roof. (Later, Brian left home and the family never knew what became of him.) Virginia and Margaret were born in the new house.

Claude, the oldest son became a park policeman in Washington. Lena, the oldest daughter found a job in southeast Washington at St. Elizabeth's Hospital for the mentally ill. She wrote to her cousins, my sister and Susie Pugh, Kate and Zella Spencer, that there were openings for work.

Cousin Susie Pugh, Aunt Ellen's oldest child and only daughter, responded first and added her urging to Lena's. Well, cousins Zella and Kate Spencer, daughters of Uncle Aris, talked to my sister, Mayme, and finally after much persuasion and pleading, parents gave permission for the girls to go. After all, even though St. Elizabeth's provided living quarters, Uncle Charlie's family and mother's other brother, Uncle Byers and family lived nearby. So the girls were put on the train in Troutdale with tickets to Washington where a relative would meet them at Union Station. These girls wrote to friends that they had left at home and soon Callie Ballou and Tena DeBoard joined them.

Within a year or two, my brother Herbert decided to leave the farm and go to Northern Virginia. My mother's brother, Uncle Byers Spencer, was a successful carpenter in Ralston, a suburb of Arlington, and Herbert worked with him until he went out on his own as a carpenter.

With Mayme and Herbert gone, I was the oldest at home and although I stayed in school when school was in session, a lot of work fell on me. I helped Dad stack hay. He would pitch a fork of hay to me and tell me where to place it around the stack pole. I did a lot of day dreaming as I hoed corn, cleaned house, washed clothes, fed the animals — day dreaming about Washington or some other city — having pretty clothes, living in the big buildings, taking the street car that used to run from D.C. to Fairfax and Clifton to visit Uncle Charlie's and Uncle Byers' families, going to Glen Echo Amusement Park to ride the merry-go-rounds, roller coasters and other rides, eating hot dogs and cones of ice cream, and going up in the Washington Monument and all the other things my sister wrote about and sent pictures of and wondered if I'd ever have those experiences.

My sister married Odell Blevins whose family came from Whitetop, Va., and whom she met when visiting Uncle Charlie's. Cousin Susie married a Mr. Green in D.C. and lived there with husband and children. Cousin Lena married a Mr. Chaillet of French descent; they had a large number of children and lived in D.C. until her husband died and the children grew and were out on their own. Then Lena bought some of her father's land and moved to Pope's Head Road where she died about 1991. Zella and Kate came back to Grassy Creek and married in this area.

Pope's Head Road was off the road between the towns of Fairfax and Fairfax Station — a distance of about 2 or 3 miles. Trains from Alexandria and Washington passed through and stopped at Fairfax Station, hence the name.

Neither Mayme nor Herbert finished high school, but after Mayme stopped work at St. Elizabeth's, she took an exam from the Board of Education in Fairfax County, where Mr. Woodson was Superintendent of Schools for thirty years, and taught school two years at Fairfax Station Elementary School and boarded with Uncle Charlie who lived on Pope's Head Road not far from the school.

Herbert worked with Uncle Byers and became an excellent carpenter and built a home for himself and family at Fairfax Station where his wife and children still live.

Uncle Charlie's family and mine kept in touch. Once Uncle Charlie sent a large barrel of pears from his farm to us by train to Troutdale. They were the large pears like the ones we buy in the grocery store today and which he knew did not grow here.

One winter, my father's sister, Aunt Lucy Waddell died and we got word that Uncle Charlie had passed away as well as Little Blair, Uncle Roscoe's son, all in the same week.

All of Uncle Charlie's family has now died except grandchildren. His daughter, Lena, Virginia and Margaret (the youngest) died within a few weeks of each other.

Politics

Many summer evenings after supper, Uncle Luther or Uncle Iredell came to our house and they and Dad would sit on the front porch and discuss politics. I don't know what the issues were at the time but although both were registered Democrats, they seemed to differ in their views on the prevalent governmental problems to be voted on. It seemed to me that if one of the uncles argued in favor of a particular issue, my dad would be "the devil's advocate" and point out the opposite sides of the problem, even though I knew my father had supported the issue. Once, I asked Dad the difference between Democrats and Republicans and he said, "Democrats support the poor and Republicans support the rich."

My father was registrar in our political township for many years. He liked to get to Independence, our county seat, as often as he could to talk to county party officials. These same officials sometimes came to our community seeking votes. The Nineteenth Amendment to the Constitution was passed giving women the right to vote. One night my elementary school teacher and her husband came to our home for her to register. The registrar was supposed to ask three or four questions of the person to ascertain whether the person was literate (could read or not). Since she and we were all in the living room, he wrote out the questions on paper with room for her answers to be written out. All at once, she stood up, went to the fireplace, kicked a log into it, and half crying angrily said, "Mr. Barker, it is grossly unfair of you to ask a question which I am not supposed to know." With that she and her husband hurriedly left the house. Dad picked up the paper which she had thrown down and looked at it. We asked, which question did she not know. He said, "What is the Nineteenth Amendment?" We dreaded to go to school the following morning, but the teacher was just as friendly and sweet as ever. I don't know when she learned what the Amendment was.

My grandmother and aunts scoffed at the idea of women voting, and despite my father's urging, steadfastly refused to vote. "That is a matter for the men to take care of. Women have no business going out to voting places where all kinds of men hang out with all kinds of filthy talk and drunks stagger around. It's no place for decent women and what do we know about politics anyway? That's men's business." It became known that a lawyer in Independence who was seeking office for himself and other party members and who was making a tremendous effort to have his become the leading party in the county, had started giving nonregistered voters $2 if they would register and vote. Well, the opposite party could not let this practice go unnoticed. So when Grandmother and the two daughters learned they would get two dollars if they registered and voted, they registered and became voters.

At one time in the early thirties when I was teaching in Ashe County, it became known that political dues were to be collected to support candidates running for office. We knew that if we wanted to be appointed to our positions for another year, although salaries were very low, we must contribute $5 to this fund. There was a town election held in mid summer once and I always thought voting was to be by secret ballot and it not be known how one voted; evidently Professor Nye had voted for the wrong person. He was dismissed from principalship of the school. All schools' openings had been filled and he and his family had no work for the following winter. That was extremely hard on this family as the oldest son was working on his medical degree in a university in Philadelphia and needed financial support from the family. However they moved to Grassy Creek and he became principal of Virginia-Carolina High School the following year.

Race Relations

I never thought of or heard of such a thing as "race relations" when I was growing up. It is true that I knew of only one black family in our immediate community when I was small. There was one black family who lived for a time on Cousin Felix Davis' farm. A few times when my mother was not well, Dad would get the lady of this family to come to do laundry and housework. She would bring her son and he and my brother would play together, and that family would eat at our table with our family. I never heard a single word from any member of our family indicating any thought of segregation until many years later when my father remarked that he didn't think that there should be racial intermarriages. Both our daughter and I were shocked to hear my dad make that remark!

There was a black community that lived in the Crumpler area of Ashe County. One family who lived at the foot of Pasley Hill on Old Highway 16 had the most beautiful American Beauty roses when my husband and I were dating. I commented on the roses once when we were passing. My husband stopped and asked if I might have a bouquet from their rose bush and they generously gave me one. We developed a deep friendship which continued as long as we lived there. There was a Negro church in that area and my husband, Gayle and I were invited to an all-day meeting there. We went and had dinner with them and enjoyed the day. Once when Gayle and I were coming to visit my parents at Grassy Creek, my car had a flat tire near to where four black men were sitting under a tree, taking a rest from the hot sun. Without being asked, they saw the situation, removed the tire, repaired it and put it back on. That was no easy task in those days on the old cars.

My husband told of a family of blacks who lived near his family and when he was allowed to go along with the adults in wagons to Wilkesboro, a two-day trip each way including camping near Wilbar or Deep Ford Hill, he always slept with Uncle Bud Whittington (the black) as he would keep this little boy warm and covered from the cool night air.

When my daughter was little and I had been away from teaching for a time, I was called back to teaching. I had to find someone to care for my child. Someone told me of a family named Boyden who had a grown daughter who might be available. We went to see her. The family lived in a large two story house in Clifton and they agreed to allow Margaree to be a live-in member of our family. We thought so much of the Boydens. This was a time when Golden Delicious apples were popular. The Boyden family had a tree of them which could have been the envy of Stark Bros. who were promoting this variety of apples. We had the Boydens for Sunday dinner once. Margaree got married and another daughter, Susie, came to live with us as long as we needed her. After we moved back to Grassy Creek, my husband and I tried to find the Boydens, but roads had been changed, Clifton had changed and we couldn't find them.

When desegregation came to schools, I had two black teachers. One teacher was somewhat tense about being thrust into a situation where the community had no black children in school. The other teacher was very open and free in the surroundings. Once when she was trying to help the students understand the term "race," she said, "Johnny is white, Emily is yellow, I am black." The class all said, "No, you're not!"

Only two families in an enrollment of 700 children showed any objections to having black teachers, and when they asked to have their children moved to another classroom, I objected strongly because of what this would do to their young children. However I pointed out that it would be no problem since the vast majority of parents were asking that their children be allowed to have these teachers when possible because of their reputation as teachers and the respect of students and faculty for these two people.

Homes

While a number of homes were quite small and modest, the people in our community liked pretty things — pretty clothing, pretty home furnishings, and pretty surroundings. While home owners might make their own houses and furniture, they used ideas learned from friends, neighbors and relatives. Those whose forefathers had emigrated from Europe had seen some beautiful pieces of household furnishings they had brought with them. Others had visited relatives in cities or had grown up in or near towns, and had seen things they did not have and could not afford at the time. As they could, they made pieces of furniture, varnished or painted. While this furniture was not the highly polished pieces from the famous makers, Chippendale or Duncan Phyfe, it was sturdy and practical.

My grandfather, with a helpful carpenter, made several oak pieces. One piece in particular, I suppose could be called a dresser. There was a mirror in the center of the upper part. On either side of the mirror were cabinets with doors to hold hats. Under those cabinets were small drawers about six inches deep, eight inches long, to hold ladies' gloves and handkerchiefs. The lower part of the piece was deeper by probably ten inches, had two doors in the center with shelves for sweaters or folded clothing, and drawers on both sides for underwear, hosiery and other pieces of wearing apparel. Then Grandpa had made a more practical or ordinary piece which they used in the "sitting" room, with drawers and shelves behind two front doors. These two pieces would have long since been sold except that these solid oak constructions were too heavy to be moved! Grandpa made two pie safes in which to put pies to cool and also to keep other foods away from flies. The doors had tin panels with intricate patterns pierced by small nails. Of course, a number of men made kitchen and dining tables — long tables to accommodate lots of children and visitors.

Now, while the homemade furniture was not highly polished and gleaming, the women in the household made pretty embroidered scarves and doilies, crochet pieces and drawn-thread hemstitches to enhance the looks and also for protection from spills or staining.

Flowers, lots of different flowers, were in the yards to look at, for passersby to see and to have for bouquets inside the house. Of course, we did not have formal flower beds or flower gardens, but in every available spot that did not have to be used for something "more useful" such as a grape vine or bee hives, flowers grew. I remember the beautiful and fragrant sweet peas by the garden or yard gate in shades of blue, white, purple and pink. Most yards had snowball bushes and hydrangeas — the big bushes that grew and grew, producing large white blooms that toward fall developed pinkish tinges before turning brown, to be gathered, the leaves stripped off, hung upside down to dry before being made into winter arrangements. At Grandpa's, the big hydrangea bush at the end of the front porch was so tall that one could go to the upstairs porch and pick the flowers. It is still going and growing strong today. I've seen some of these bouquets last for two or three years. Then there were the smaller, more fragile type of hydrangeas in white and pink. Sometimes people would pour laundry bluing around them for blue blooms. Lilacs blooming early in the season with their purple or violet colors threw out delightful fragrances for rooms, corsages, and even just passing the shrub. Light and dark blue, pink and white morning glories climbed porch posts or garden fences, while cinnamon vines ran up twine cords from ground to the porch ceiling, giving off its cinnamon aroma in the late evening and early morning dampness. Then there were hollyhocks, Sweet Williams, bleeding hearts, and dahlias, bachelor buttons, and roses — all perennials — and placed where they would grow year after year. Then annuals, seeds saved and shared with neighbors and some new ones bought from the seed rack in the store, were planted at spots in the yard or in a row in the vegetable garden. Asters, zinnias, cosmos, marigolds, touch-me-nots and pansies and sunflowers. In Grandma's vegetable garden there was a strip at the upper side about three feet wide and sloping that tended to wash in a hard rain, so she planted Sweet Williams and in a year or so that was such a beautiful bank of solid blooms of reds, whites, pinks and mixed and variegated colors and this bed provided beauty year after year with practically no work except pulling out a few weeds, but the plants crowded out weeds and grass.

Also, almost everyone had red rambling roses which really did ramble unless pruned to contain in a spot or area. Again, Grandma had a weeping willow tree near her spring house and had set out a rambling rose bush near the willow tree when both were small, but both grew. In summer there was that green graceful tree with red blooms throughout the draping branches. People would stop in the road to look and walk or drive the 200 yards to ask what kind of unusual tree this was. Incidentally, in Winston-Salem in the late teens and early twenties, these red rambling roses were widely grown in the city — along fences and streets.

When I was perhaps four or five years old, one Sunday morning my mother had bathed and dressed me for church and while she was getting herself ready, I wandered around in the front yard in my white eyelet embroidered dress and I thought there should be some color to show through those dainty eyelets, so I picked some large yellow marigold blooms and dropped them inside the waist of my dress. When my mother saw what I had done, I was certainly a candidate for a spanking but fortunately they didn't leave a stain.

There was a plant, a perennial, called Ladies' Wash Bowl — why this name, I don't know — with narrow leaves about four inches long and pink blooms. It was not grown especially for its floral attributes but it was thought that the crushed leaves had some medical uses. We'd apply the leaves on light burns, abrasions and any open sores.

In some of the wooded areas there appeared orange, bright yellow and pink flowers on bushes which we called honeysuckles, but they are now known as wild azaleas. These shrubs had many little branches growing close together making the bushes look like almost solid flowers. These began appearing in some yards. On some of these there would appear after the blooms an occasional fruit which we called "a honeysuckle" and after the deep green began to turn less green or whitish as tomatoes do, we'd pick and eat them. Obviously, they weren't poison.

In early spring and into late fall, one of the weekly chores and usually on Saturday, the yard was to be swept. Carrying wood from the woodshed, bits of bark, sawdust and little splinters had been dropped, and wind had blown dried grass and leaves onto the yard and walkways. We seldom had rakes that removed all of these things, so we went to the woods and gathered honeysuckle bushes for brush brooms. These bushes had lots of tiny limbs close together and we'd break them off to about 30 or 36 inches long, tie perhaps six or eight together with twine. These brooms would sweep bare walkways and flirt debris out of grassy areas to be collected and carried away. One year we were very ambitious. The barn lot was pretty well covered with corn stalks. The cattle had eaten the dried leaves from the stalks during the winter leaving the ground covered with the stalks. We raked these into piles for my father to haul on the farm sled to barren spots on the farm. People today carry tobacco stalks for the same purpose — to hold the bare spots from washing in hard rains. Of course, one hardly finds corn stalks today as the whole corn crop is ground into ensilage. There are no corn shocks, no corn shuckings, no saddling up the horse to carry a bushel of corn to Little Wiley's or Mr. Robbins' grist mill to be ground for the week's cornbread!

Another weekly chore, except in cold, cold weather, was cleaning the spring. Our spring, across the road from the house, had a cemented square box surrounded by a flat cemented area on which to set water pails and lower than the spring box to prevent ground soil and water from getting into the spring. To clean, the water was dipped out and the inside of the box scrubbed with a little broom. Then water was dipped out until the water bubbling up in the bottom was perfectly clear. Then the wooden cover was replaced. The area around the spring box was scrubbed and rinsed. Gravity water soon refilled the spring box. Saturdays were busy days. Along with sweeping the yard and cleaning the spring, buzzing was going on inside the house. In the kitchen, loaves of potato yeast sour dough light bread were in the baking and a cake or a couple of apple or custard pies made as there might be company for Sunday dinner. The glass lamp chimneys were washed, the lamps filled with lamp oil, the wicks trimmed and rounded, fireplaces cleaned of ashes and the andirons wiped with an oiled rag, and furniture dusted. A rest period meant that one loaf of bread, hot from the oven was cut and eaten. Each one had his own spread to go with the fresh bread. Dad would go to the springhouse for a cup of sour cream for his, others wanted jam or jelly. I just wanted lots of butter on my slices. By four o'clock, we'd usually have our jobs finished and take a rest if inspection showed a passing grade. The next task was to see that lots of water was carried and heated for Saturday night baths.

Sunday meant going to church and rest. If we didn't have company for noonday dinner, we knew we'd have something special to look forward to for our own dinner and evening supper.

There were several large houses, two story with 5 to 8 rooms, in our community, but more one story with four or five rooms and some with one, two, or three small rooms. Land was quite cheap. Some had been acquired by land grants issued to encourage newcomers to settle in the area, and some inherited from families who owned large acreages and some that could be bought for five cents to a dollar per acre.

Some of the two story houses nearby were those of Mr. Granville Spencer, Lyda Robbins, Mitchell Spencer, David Spencer, Lee Reeves, Billy Reeves, Grandfather Poindexter Barker, Dr. Osborne, "Big" Wiley Spencer, Robert Plummer, Isham Thompson, Bob Pierce (Sussex), Steve Sexton, Robert Waddell, Avery Wood, Felix Davis and the Perkins families of Helton. Aquilla Greer had the first brick house in this area. A number of houses started out as small log houses and were later added to with more rooms. Of course, none of the houses were air-conditioned other than by open doors and windows and cracks from wood in walls and floors that were not completely dry when built. It was not uncommon to have snow blow through room cracks, around doors and windows. Those who could afford it had their rooms wall papered and this made for warmer houses. Some of the very small houses had the walls covered with newspaper, paper from the catalogs, store packages and even any cardboard on hand to keep the houses warmer. Uncle Luther became a paper hanger, and was kept quite busy. The first thing he did was to cover the walls and ceiling with cheese cloth held on with carpet tacks. Why? I don't know unless it kept the wall paper over the uneven cracks from tearing or pulling loose. The spaces between the boards still showed through the wall paper. The paper strips were measured, designs matched, the back side of the paper covered with paste and hung on the wall or ceiling. I liked watching Uncle Luther handle the paper by folding it, letting it out as needed, brushing and smoothing out the wrinkles. It was quite a challenge for one person to hold the paper strips and do an overhead ceiling perfectly by oneself. Some people had oil cloth covering put on the walls. That was the first wall covering in our house. It was wider than regular wall paper and could be wiped clean with a damp cloth. While I lived at home, only the dining room was papered and it with oil cloth. I admired the papered walls of those who had them, but then in later years I had the old paper pulled off the walls of our country farm house, the carpet tacks removed, the walls washed to show, in some cases, the wormy chestnut or bird's eye maple wood in the rooms that did not have wallboard nailed over the wood.

The neighbors who had the large houses and could afford it, had rugs or carpets on their floors or had beautiful highly polished hardwood floors. I was never in many of those houses as we did not have overshoes or protection from mud for our shoes and did not want to walk on those floors with our old patched and weather-worn shoes. Too, we felt uncomfortable with those who had finer clothes and houses than we had. The large houses were mostly for families with a number of children — girls and boys — who were reaching the age to need their own rooms for themselves and to have visiting friends of their own age. The first floor rooms likely had fireplaces for heating. Thimbles in the chimneys made it possible to have stoves in the second floor rooms for heat. (A thimble was a piece of tin or terra cotta inserted into a hole in the chimney left by the mason when building the chimney, and into a room for a wood burning stove.) Mortar or a fitted metal plate was placed around the thimble in the room to keep out drafts and protect the wall from excessive heat. (Terra cotta is a kind of hard, brownish-red clay or earthenware.) These chimneys were usually of brick, often made in the vicinity. Many smaller houses had only one fireplace with a chimney of field stone and held together with mud for mortar, and built on the outside of the house, thus letting a lot of heat escape.

Some of the small houses (one, two or three rooms) might have only one fireplace and a stove for cooking. A few had only a fireplace for heating and cooking, by placing an iron pot or skillet on carefully fixed logs or over coals on the hearth. Stoves were not always available locally, so one might have to, if he could afford to, buy one from Sears or some catalog. In addition to regular cookstoves there were flat topped iron heating stoves with two removable lids which could be used for heating and cooking. Then there was a small tin stove for heating with such thin sides that would get red hot quickly and cool off very quickly. These little stoves were very dangerous and required careful watching.

A number of families consisted of parents, grandparents and ten or twelve children, and lots of beds were needed. Large, medium and small houses had one or two beds in the living (sitting) room in which the parents and youngest children slept. At my grandfather's there were two double beds in the "setting" room, one in the parlor, four beds in each of the upstairs bedrooms and a corded bed in the original kitchen along with a fireplace and cook stove. (A corded bed had a framework of ropes attached to the bed sideboards on which to place the strawtick instead of open or box springs.) This kitchen was later torn off and the back porch made into a new kitchen. Sometimes all the beds were filled with overnight visitors and Aunt Lona slept on the corded bed in the original kitchen as she was the one counted on to get up, build a fire and start a big breakfast.

The large houses of four and five rooms were usually painted on the outside and had front and back porches with banisters. The smaller houses, quite often were board and batten (upright boards with two inch wide strips covering the cracks) and hardly ever painted.

I do not know how my great grandfather, Solomon Spencer, accumulated land. Perhaps by buying, selling or trading, but he had owned quite considerable acreage in the Grassy Creek area. Along the Grassy Creek road between what is now route 745 and New 16 Road, he gave a number of acres to my grandfather, John Spencer, down to the now Solomon Road and back to the Reeves line and along the Grassy Creek Road past the Mabel Welch place. From the Solomon Road, he gave acreage to Aunt Martha Davis Francis, and to another daughter, Aunt Caroline Davis Peak, to the Lee Anderson line. Across the hills and along the Charlie Spencer Road from the S. B. Sexton place almost again to New 16 Road to his son, Robert (Uncle Bob Spencer, father of "Big" Wiley, Frank and Joe).

My grandparents, John and Martha Jane Anderson Spencer, lived in a log house on Grassy Creek Road near the barn now owned by Johnny and Karen Spencer. In this house their six children were born: Aris, Byers, Rose Ann Shelton, Ellen Pugh, Minnie Barker (my mother) and Mega Hash. I was told that Grandfather John had died and that Grandmother Martha had begun to have a larger house built but died before it was finished. Uncle Byers finished the house and lived there for a time. It was later owned by Mr. Arthur Graybeal, the Rev. Oscar Spencer, and Gilmer Spencer and is now owned by Johnny and Karen Spencer who moved it from the original location to a spot along and back on Solomon Road. Uncle Aris built a two room house with a porch and an attic entered by a ladder from outside. Aunt Rose received land and built a house on land now owned by Mr. and Mrs. Robert VanHoy. My mother, Aunt Ellen and Aunt Mega sold their lands — my mother after she was married to help pay for land bought from Mr. David Sheets. Mr. Sheets had purchased the land from Mr. John Reedy who had received the land as a grant on July 31, 1845, from James McDowell, Esquire, governor of Virginia.

And so it was that land owners who had large parcels of land passed it on to children and on to grandchildren. Some large houses were found to have been started as log houses and added on to. When Grandpa Barker's house was to have insulation blown into the walls it was found to have some room walls covering log walls. The Cox house, I was told, had once been a four room log house, but later a beautiful 12 room two story white frame house with porches. The first brick house in the area was built and owned by Aquilla Greer who is reported to be a brother of my great, great grandmother, Sarah Greer Pugh.

Our House

Our house consisted of four rooms — kitchen, dining room, living room and parlor. A hall separated the living room from the other three rooms. There was a front porch with banisters and a back porch. My father had meant to build

other rooms and had the lumber on hand but the night before the carpenters, two Badger brothers, were to start work, some of the lumber burned. He always thought that arson was the cause. There seemed to be a lot of jealousy, at that time, between neighbors over who possessed the most material things. My parents were devastated when the lumber burned. The carpenters would be there and now plans had to be changed quickly. A youngish couple whose heart was set on having a parlor, but now would have to use the room, more or less, as a bedroom. But they continued to call it "the parlor," thinking "One day, we'll still have a parlor." Later, Father added another room.

The living room, called the "sitting room," contained a fireplace which was the main and most used source of heat in the house in the winter months. Over the fireplace was a mantel which held the clock, the two kerosene lamps, matches, and always, a pin cushion.

We had four beds — two in the living room and two in the parlor. My parents, my sister and I slept in the living room and my brother slept in a single bed in the parlor. We did not have a sofa or overstuffed chairs in that room at that time, but there was an organ, our best bed with matching dresser, a wash stand with china bowl and pitcher, lace curtains, carpet of woven strips sewn together and straight chairs. In fact, this room was more of a bedroom than a parlor at that time. A trundle bed was kept under one of the beds in the living room and when cousins, uncles and aunts, or neighbors came to visit, several of us children slept in the trundle bed. Sometimes we children slept four in a bed, two at the head of the bed and two at the foot.

One bed in the parlor was called the "Preacher's Bed." We had services at our church only one weekend each month. The minister usually rode horseback or in a buggy and preached on Saturday morning, held a business meeting, and had services again on Sunday. Since he came a distance of several miles, he spent Saturday night with parishioners, and usually, I thought, with our family. Also, at times, traveling salesmen, cattle buyers, relatives or neighbors who lived some distance away would spend the night. "Some distance away" might mean three or four miles of walking or riding horseback.

Opposite: Our house, ca. 1913. Evidently, my father was proud of what he and my mother had accumulated and wanted as much shown in this photograph as possible. My mother and my sister, Mayme, are standing on the front porch. Dad and Herbert are holding the team of horses. Herbert is standing on the stile, a wood platform about 24 inches square and about 30 inches tall, attached to the outside of the yard fence, to be used by ladies and children for mounting and dismounting horses. I was holding an ear of corn and tossing grains to the chickens, turkeys, guineas and geese to keep them in the picture. The white gander seemed to be posing.

Photographs were printed on postcards which could be sent through the mail. There was space for a message, lines for the name and address of the receiver and a spot where the one cent stamp was to be placed.

Probably, my father would send a picture to Uncle Ira in Kansas, one to Uncle John in Maryland, one to Uncle Byers in Arlington, Va., and to acquaintances with whom we exchanged photographs.

Cast iron bar in old kitchen fireplace on which to hold pots for cooking meals.

The kitchen contained a table, stove, "meal chest" and cupboard and chairs. Our first stove was a flat topped, wood burning stove with an oven and four cooking plates called "eyes" which were removable to allow for black cast iron cooking pans, fry pan or tea kettle to be placed closer to the fire or heat. Under the fire box was a pan to catch ashes and any coals that might fall through openings in the bottom of the fire box. Later, we had a better and bigger stove which was shipped from a factory by train to Troutdale, our nearest railway station. This stove had a warming closet which protruded out a bit over the cooking area with doors which opened and closed and was used to place some foods to keep warm. Next to the oven on the right hand side was a reservoir which held about ten gallons of water to be heated for household use.

The dining room had a long wood table, I suppose made by my father. It would easily seat eight people and sometimes ten or more. On the side of the table nearest the wall was a wooden slatted bench with the wall serving as a back rest. The bench was the length of the table and became very smooth and satiny from diners slipping in and out of their places at the table. Chairs were used at the other side and ends. There were two smaller tables about 20 inches square to hold water or milk pitchers, desserts or extra foods. We never had an ice box or refrigerator when I was growing up. Milk and foods that needed to be kept cool were kept in the springhouse in a trough made of concrete or heavy wood with cold running water flowing into one end of the trough and out the other end.

The windows and doors had no screens and flies were a constant menace. A bush branch with lots of leaves would be cut and waved back and forth over the table while a meal was being served to keep the flies from the food. Sometimes we took a few sheets of newspapers, put them across a round stick or rod, tacked or pasted to the rod, sliced the hanging paper into strips about an inch wide and moved this back and forth while people were eating. These paper gadgets, too, were called "fly bushes." My grandfather had a large contraption consisting of a wooden framework that held several of the newspaper covered rods — enough to cover the length of the table — and manipulated by a treadle that rested on the floor operated by someone's foot. This person, seated nearest the treadle, could eat while keeping the flies away.

Our house had no indoor plumbing. Water was carried from a spring — the spring, at first, was across the road from the house and flowing from a spring higher up between two hills. Later a pipe was laid underground and water ran by gravity to a spot in the yard near the house. A cement box was built large enough for a water pail to dip up two or three gallons at a time. A house was built beside the spring with a porch and a roof covering the spring.

In the hall of the house we kept a wash stand. This piece of furniture held a large china wash bowl and water pitcher and soap dish for visitors to wash hands and faces. A rod over the stand held towels. Extra towels and soap were stored in the cabinet in the bottom section of the stand. Usually hung on a nail over the wash stand was a "comb pocket." Some of these were made of tin and carried in stores and some were made of cardboard and covered with wall paper by the home owners. More affluent homes might have complete sets of these facilities in each bedroom. A complete set would be washbowl, large water pitcher, smaller pitcher for drinking water, a still smaller pitcher to use when brushing teeth, soap dish, shaving mug, and chamber pot. Some of these sets were elaborately painted with flowers or other designs and are now collectors' items. Poorer families had enameled chamber pots, later replaced by combinets or slop jars with lids. For farm and family workers, there was usually a wash bench or shelf on the back porch with tin or enamel wash basins, bars of hand soaps, pails of water and towels hung on a rod or nails. Water carrying was a nonstop chore in those days.

Regardless of the poor condition of the existing dirt roads with their ruts, mud holes and unbridged streams crossing them, people built their houses near the roads. This saved precious land of small farms, meant shorter distances to walk to wherever one was going, and to mailboxes. If one could afford them, front and back porches were necessary parts of houses.

Porches are for sitting! With no air-conditioning, how could farm families enjoy the cool evenings after a hot day's work

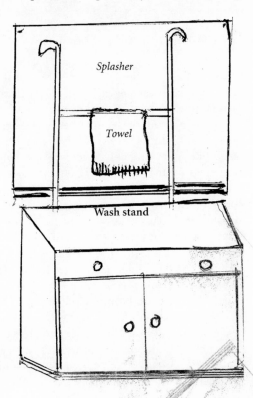

Splasher

Towel

Wash stand

Comb pocket

without a front porch? But more importantly, the front porch was a place where passing friends and neighbors stopped to talk and possibly "sit a spell" to exchange news of family health, crops, community news and gossip!

Our house had a front porch the length of the hallway and most of the length of the living room with balusters around the outside edges except for the exit over three steps down to the field rock walkway to the front yard gate. There were always a few chairs there for just "sitting" and the steps also served for sitting, especially for youngsters who often tumbled down them and ended up with swollen knots on the foreheads!

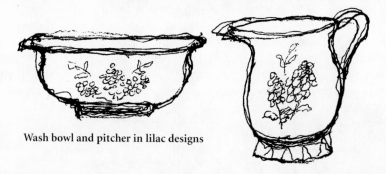

Wash bowl and pitcher in lilac designs

Then there was the back porch, an essential place for so many activities of farm families to prevent "mussing up" inside rooms. Our back porch had the "wash bench"—not the laundry bench but where we washed our hands and faces daily. About four feet from the floor and attached to the wall, Dad had built a bench-like affair, probably four feet long, eighteen inches wide with a two inch wood strip around the front and one end edge, with the other end sloped slightly to let water drain off to the ground. The bench was lined with tin to protect the wood bottom. In the bench floor were two or three tin wash basins and dishes to hold hand soaps. Above the bench was a wood shelf to hold three zinc or enamel two and one-half gallon water buckets and dippers. At the end of this shelf were nails on which to hang towels, to dry hands and faces. Water buckets were to be kept filled with water for drinking, washing up, to use in cooking and dish washing. Here, also, vegetables were washed for peeling and made ready for cooking and canning.

An old wood table held the two wash tubs for doing family laundry before we had a "wash house." Wood for the fireplace and cook stove was stacked for winter use here and nails in the walls held various old rain and snow everyday wraps. Later, when we had more outside buildings, Dad partitioned off part of this back porch for a bedroom.

Some winter mornings we'd awaken to a deep silence and wonder why there were no sounds. On getting up we'd find the ground, trees, fences and outside buildings, in fact our whole world, covered with a blanket of white pristine snow, so beautiful and pure looking as if daring anyone or anything to break this majesty. Too, Jack Frost had been busy painting mystical scenes on the outsides of the windows. I would try to figure out what the figures or scenes were but when I moved to another spot there would appear differently formed patterns as if watching a kaleidoscope. Old Man Winter had left long icicles hanging from the porch roof and, in spite of our parents' warnings we'd slip and break off some to suck, all the while thinking "wouldn't these be good to put in our lemonade in summer!"

Then on hot summer nights, we'd sometimes awaken to a strong electric storm when the house seemed almost to shake from the loud thunder as lightning bolts lit up the rooms, and we'd cover our heads to try to shut out the lightning. So glad when the storm was over and we could go back to sleep. Sometimes when we'd get up in the morning after the storm, rain drops might be hanging from graceful drooping tree branches and when the sun hit the trees, they'd look as if they were wearing breathtaking diamonds and other varied colored precious stone necklaces.

Electricity

Around 1931 electricity came to our area! Fields Manufacturing Company at Mouth of Wilson, Virginia, about four miles from where we lived, had built a dam on the New River, a few miles east of their woolen mill, to provide power for the mill and electricity for residents nearby. My father had bought and moved to an eight room house, originally owned by Mr. David Spencer. After many discussions with Mr. Cam Fields concerning costs and advantages, he decided to have electricity put in the house. He had heard that Gwyn Denny, son of Cousin Rev. Edgar Denny was wiring houses, so he had him do the electrical work. A one bulb light with a short pull chain was put in the center ceiling of each room and the front and back porches. A double electric outlet was put in the living room for a radio and electric iron. I'm sure the "radio" was a deciding factor that led to Dad's agreement to join the "Electric Association."

Mr. Denny pointed out the need for kitchen and room outlets, but my farmer father could see no real need to spend good money for extra lamps and kitchen gadgets when there were "good lights to 'see by' and a wood burning cook stove."

After the wiring was completed and tested, Dad wanted Grandpa to see the house all "lighted up." He sent Kyle with the car to bring Grandpa down after dark so that when they came in sight of the house he would see light through the twenty windows and on the porches. Of course Dad was proud and Grandpa couldn't believe his eyes and said, "It must have cost you a lot of money!"

Outside Toilets

No one had inside plumbing and certainly, everyone needed a toilet or "two seater outside john." Some of these toilets were just built over the ground, but ours was built with the chair height seat over a dug pit of about 36 inches deep and the size of the seat. The floor, roof, sides and door were of wood. The door had a wood button on the outside when not in use and another on the inside for privacy. Sometimes these buildings were called "privies," the plural of privy.

None of the local stores carried such a thing as toilet tissues as we know them today. So, we saved the big "twice-a-year Sears catalogs" and the many small sale catalogs that came from the mail order houses to use to make rolled lamp lighters and to use in the toilets. When telling city cousin, Velma, this, she asked, "How in the world did you use those glossy stiff colored pages?"

"Why, honey, the catalog pages in those days didn't have the glossy stiff pages — just black and white regular newspaper pages. I told you we saved everything back then, any newspapers (which we didn't always have), paper that came around things in the packages we had ordered and old mail stuff left in our mail box." Sometimes the men would place a pail of dry corn cobs in the john. At school if we knew there was no paper, on the way we'd pull large leaves from bushes or trees.

Some toilets I've seen and known of were over a branch or creek until there were laws with specifications for these buildings. One can still see some of these old outdoor privies — some falling over or being used to store junk or something. I know of some still being used. Although churches now have indoor plumbing, the outside johns may be used when there is an "all day affair with dinner on the grounds."

Beds

Up until around 1926, no one I knew of had mattresses as we know mattresses today. Of course, there were homes I was never in but we visited friends and neighbors and relatives and knew rather well how they lived. I was about twenty years old before I slept on a commercially made mattress and this was in West Jefferson while boarding in a dormitory for teachers.

In our county and surrounding counties, farmers grew wheat for flour and in late summer the threshing machine went from farm to farm to thresh the wheat. The straw was separated from the wheat grains and thrown out on the opposite side of the thresher box and one or two men would stack the straw into what we called a straw tick or stack. Everyone looked forward to having new fresh straw for the bed ticks as after a year's use the straw had become very worn and thin and the new straw made the bed feel and smell so good! Straw ticks were made of unbleached muslin, often called "domestic" as it was a fabric widely used in country homes for bed ticks, sheets, pillow cases, bed spreads, furniture covers but also for underwear for the family. In the 1951 Comprehensive Desk Dictionary, Thorndike and Barnhart define "tick" as heavy cloth to cover mattresses and chairs. Straw ticks were made with allowances for refilling with lots of straw. If a family did not have straw for the ticks, they might fill the ticks with corn shucks. Newly filled ticks made a high bed which not only looked beautiful but felt comfortable and each household tried to have one bed kept for special company and for visitors to look at and rate the lady of the house highly for the full bed with the white bedspread or a special quilt and pillows covered with embroidered pillow shams. (Pillow shams were flat pieces of cloth, hemmed all around and embroidered with turkey red thread with flower, bird or word designs [HOME SWEET HOME] and stiffly starched to cover the pillows that were stood up and leaned against the headboard.) Since pillow cases were usually used for a week before laundering, the chief use of shams was to hide soiled and wrinkled pillow cases — hence the name "shams." On top of the straw ticks was a feather tick. Most feather ticks were filled with goose feathers, but if people did not have geese the ticks were filled with chicken feathers. The ticks to hold the feathers were made of very heavy blue and white or green and white striped cloth — heavy and closely woven to keep the feathers from sifting out. Every morning after breakfast, the beds were to be made. This meant removing the feather ticks and fluffing up the straw until the bed was smooth. The feather tick was then fluffed and smoothed. A yard stick or round rod was kept in each bedroom for moving across each bed to make it smooth or even.

Embroidered pillow sham with letters embroidered in satin stitch, surrounded with flower and vine design.

The bed frames in country houses were more often than not made by local carpenters or by the home owner. The headboard of the frame was usually tall to protect the sleeper's head from night cold air that seeped through cracks and under doors. These headboards were sometimes decorated with notches, varied shapes made with whatever tools were at hand. One of our tall headboards that a Mr. Gaultney had helped my father make was decorated with round wooden pieces set in a design. The beds were rather short and narrower than those of today. I've often wondered how large and tall people managed to sleep comfortably in those beds. Average size mattresses would not fit on those beds and if used these days, they would have to have longer sideboards. Bed covers were almost always quilts rather than blankets and the comforters of today. Winter time found the women piecing quilts. Most of the family clothing was made in the home and scraps were meticulously saved to be pieced into quilts. Ladies also exchanged dress scraps and quilt patterns. Mrs. Reedy might tell you that

"That was from Mrs. Baker's gingham dress and that one is from Dora's new skirt." The pretty quilts were on beds where they could be seen and admired. A thrifty woman was known by the quilts she owned. Coverlets, as they were called, were woven from wool that had been spun and some of it dyed. The colors most used in these covers were red and white, blue and white and green and white. Today, these coverlets are very scarce and are collectors' items.

I recall that in a bedroom upstairs at my grandmother's, a double stack of quilts reached from the top of a table to the ceiling. When visiting my grandmother and the weather was cold, she placed so many quilts over me that my arms and shoulders ached.

Quiltings were popular in those days. There were at times and places quilting bees, but neighbors usually knew when someone had a quilt in the "frame" and would go with a thimble and favorite needle and quilt until time to go home to do the evening chores and prepare supper.

Coverlets were woven on looms by older ladies who had learned the process from mothers or grandmothers and they might pass the knowledge on to their daughters. They learned that warp was the long threads fastened in the loom and woof or weft were the threads on a shuttle that passed over and under the warp threads in the loom. Patterns in the cloth were made by having a certain number of woof threads of one color and changing to another color to make the design. My aunt told me that once in church when there was a lull in the minister's sermon, a lady could be heard counting the colors of warp and woof in the design of the dress of another lady in front of her. Housewives of the early century wove blankets for the beds. My husband and I spent a night with his grandparents and found one of grandmother's wool woven blankets over our bodies rather than a sheet. We pushed it down to the foot of the bed for the night but made sure it was pulled back up before grandmother came to wake us up the next morning. After we had moved to Northern Virginia and had bought a home of our own, my in-laws packed our things for the movers to bring up for us. Everything reached us just fine except a handwoven coverlet and a handmade Dutch Girl quilt for our daughter's crib, again, collectors' items.

A set of pillow shams in our house had peacocks embroidered by my mother with turkey red thread as this kind of red dye did not fade.

Later, cotton woven bedspreads could be ordered from one of the mail order houses and every household tried to have at least one white spread for the special bed. Then chenille bedspreads became available, and ladies learned to make their own spreads with white muslin and a tufted design in a color — tufting made by pulling thread from underneath and leaving a couple or more inch lengths close together on top. Then the long threads

Pillow sham with pea-fowl

were clipped in the center, and fluffed by hand into a soft fluffy pattern. Later French knots were used to make designs on bedspreads. Neighbors shared designs or patterns and sometimes the designs could be traced by pressing a hot iron on the material over the French knots.

Brooms

In addition to growing our foods, we made an effort to grow or make as many of the things we needed as possible. We grew broomcorn for brooms. Each year we kept seeds of broomcorn to plant the following year. Broomcorn was a tall plant resembling corn with stiff stalks with flower clusters on the many spreading straws or fine branches at the top of the stalks. When the flowers had dried the fine branches or straws were covered with the seeds which were combed out before making brooms. The stalks were cut off near the ground and hung upside down until completely dry or until made into brooms.

Aunt Lona would make a batch, maybe 6 or 8, fireplace brooms. She cut the long stalks, leaving about 20 or 24 inches next to the fine branches. The seeds were combed out by using a strong comb, a curry comb or a wooden comb made by Grandpa. When the stalks were cut to the length Aunt Lona wanted, the stalks were stood in a tub of warm or hot water to make them soft and pliable. Then starting just above the bushy branches, the stalks were tied tightly together with several rings of twine. Then with the twine she would go over and under each stalk, draw the stalks tightly in the row and move with this process, each row about an inch apart, until she had reached the end of the stalks. Then she would trim the top to be even and use several wraps of twine to hold the ends together. Lastly, the straws were cut to make the broom even. Sometimes she would insert a little wood stick, or rod, in the top end so one would not have to bend so far. These brooms were used to brush up hearths of ashes or dust from firewood but they were often used to sweep porches or whole rooms. Sometimes these were the only brooms a family might have. Aunt Lona might dread to get into broom-making but she was an expert and always made several at one time.

We usually grew several rows of broomcorn. We learned that Mr. Elbert McCarthy, a blind man of Lansing, made brooms like the ones we buy in the stores today. Dad would take a goodly bunch of broomcorn to Mr. McCarthy to have made into brooms. Mr. McCarthy would make them for half of the broomcorn or to be paid for each one. Mr. McCarthy also made caskets. If we were to wait until the brooms were ready, we'd visit Cousin Effie Childress who lived a few houses from Mr. McCarthy. I've heard that people could never cheat Mr. McCarthy. I don't know how he could distinguish the denominations of money but he could.

My father grew up at Silas Creek and was in school with Mr. McCarthy at least one year. He said the boys would go to a field near the school to run races. There were hay stacks in the field. He said they would line Mr. McCarthy up

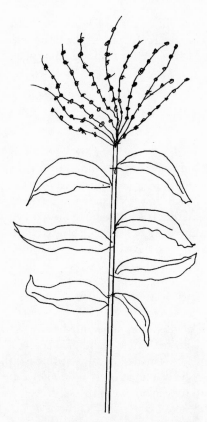

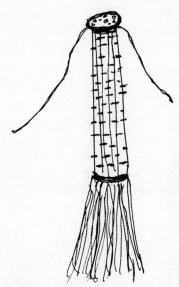

A number of stalks were selected and tied together with twine just above the fine branches then with the twine she went in and out alternately to the top drawing the stalks tightly and tying them with several rings of the string.

Broomcorn grew on tall stalks and when matured had lots of seeds at the top of long slender branches or fibers. The seeds were combed away when dry before the brooms were made.

A finished broom

where he would be in direct line with the hay stack and run into it. Dad said the blind boy would invariably avoid the hay stack.

There was also a man in the Grant, Virginia, area who made brooms from the corn carried to him. I do not remember his name, but when we were going to Troutdale, we'd leave the broomcorn at his place and pick up the brooms at a date he'd give us.

Growing broomcorn was a good deal like growing sorghum cane. When the seed first came up, the leaves looked so much like the little grass blades, we'd have to be very careful to pull out the grass and leave the broomcorn plants, especially in the first hoeing.

Spring Cleaning

After a long, cold winter of living inside with doors and windows closed and despite efforts to keep the house as clean as brooms, mops, feather dusters and dust cloths could help, we knew that the time was fast approaching for spring cleaning. We tended to look forward to having the house clean again, and yet with a certain amount of dread of all the work involved. The type and amount of work were influenced by the interior of the rooms. If rooms were papered and carpeted, the walls and ceilings could be carefully wiped with a soft cloth or wet mop and mild soap and water. Some rooms at that time might be covered with oilcloth which could be safely washed with wet cloths. Rugs, instead of carpet, could be hung outside and whammed and beaten with a broom stick or wood paddle. Small throw rugs could be washed. All rooms were likely to have dust from sweeping and have smoked surfaces from fireplaces and stoves when an errant wind or wet wood poured smoke into the room.

Along with many others, our house had wood walls, ceilings and floors. We tried to find a warm sunny day to clean one chosen room. To do an adequate job, it required a full day. Chairs, tables and furniture were emptied, cleaned and carried out of the room. Cushions and small rugs washed and hung out to dry. Water, lots and lots and lots of water heated outside in the big copper kettle or black cast iron pot to use for the job. The ceilings and walls were scrubbed with hot water and lye soap with a broom and rinsed by throwing water over them and standing well back out of the water running or dripping from the ceilings. By this time the floor was pretty wet, but more water and lye soap were thrown over the floor and it scrubbed with a scrub broom. In each room, a hole had been made with an inch auger in the lowest spot in the room (if any) to let the water run out by being pushed by the broom. After the scrubbing was finished, the floor was rinsed with warm or cold water until the rinse water was perfectly clear. Windows had already been cleaned and opened to let the room dry.

A man, Johnson Reedy (known as Jonse), made scrub brooms & baskets, and bottomed chairs with splints. He would take a medium-size hickory, maple,

Scrub broom as made by Johnson (Jonse) Reedy

oak or other hardwood tree, cut about a four foot length, peel off the bark, start at one end and shave strips one-half or three-fourths inch wide down to near the opposite end. The shaving was done until a handle was left that would feel comfortable in the hand. Then all the strips were gathered together at that end of the stick and tied with another strip several times. Now the shaved strips were cut to eight or ten inches in length and even. This made a very good broom to scrub wood floors. (One could not rush Jonse. He seldom made a promise of when he would have an article ready. The best way to get an order filled right away by Jonse was to joke with him and invite him to stay for a good meal.)

In the bedrooms the quilts, blankets, straw and feather ticks and pillows were taken outside. Quilts and blankets were inspected to see if they needed to be washed. If not, they were hung on the clothes lines along with feather ticks and pillows to be aired and sunned. Feather pillows and ticks really fluffed up plumply and soft when exposed to warm sun. The straw ticks were inspected and if there was still straw left in the straw rick, the straw was replaced in the ticks. At night, after the day's procedure was finished, the room might have a bit of lingering odor of dampness and soap, but the scent of cleanness and the aired and sunned beds were so pleasant to tired bodies that we fell asleep hoping this would last until fall cleaning time.

The Wash House and Laundry

Everyone needs clean clothes and clean bedding, especially farm families, and it was necessary to have a spot where the family laundry or "wash" as it was called could be done. Without indoor plumbing, thought was given to deciding on the best place to do the laundry. There would be dripping water buckets, splashing from the wash tubs, and from wringing by hand the wet articles, which could result in damage to wood floors and certainly meant mopping up, putting away the wash tubs, wash board, boiler, soap holder and other pans used, and other chores added to already tired persons who had done the wash. Large houses might have a room for this purpose while smaller houses would select a back porch, an outdoor shed, a spot in the yard (in summer) or the kitchen.

There was not room in our house, other than the kitchen for the weekly wash, so our father built a "wash house," using one side of the wood shed for one wall, and near a pile of wood used for heating water. In this building with a dirt floor was a built-in table to hold two zinc wash tubs, wash board, container to hold lye soap, pans for "wash by hand" articles and for bluing and starching. Water for the laundry ran through an underground pipe from the spring house to a water box attached to the outside of the wash house. A black oval shaped cast iron pot was on a furnace built of varied size field stones held together with mud as mortar.

The white articles were washed first — white shirts, blouses, sheets, pillow cases, table cloths, handkerchiefs and underwear. They were scrubbed on a washboard with homemade lye soap. Handmade wooden washboards had carved horizontal ridges from side to side on a board about 1½ inches thick and attached to posts or legs about six inches longer than the ridges to rest on the bottom of the tub. Store-bought washboards had zinc or tin ridges on a wood background.

Articles to be washed were gripped with both hands and rubbed up and down over the board until all parts of the item had been rubbed. The dirtier the garments, the more rubbing and scrubbing was required with extra attention to the most soiled areas, such as collars, cuffs and sweated underarm parts. Knuckles were often skinned and sore after two of three hours of scrubbing in warm water with strong lye soap. After the white articles were washed, they were boiled in the black iron pot with some of the lye soap added to the water. A smooth rod, such as a broom handle, was used to punch the things down into the boiling water from time to time to make sure all parts had been boiled. While this was going on, the colored articles were scrubbed. Then the tubs were emptied, rinsed and filled with fresh, warm clean water and the clothes put through two rinse waters, to make sure all the soap was washed out. Some of the white items were put through a bluing water to make them look whiter. White articles tend to turn yellow after a few launderings and bluing overcomes this tendency. Store-bought bleach was unheard of but powder or liquid bluing could be bought in the stores. Only a few drops or a small bit of the powder was needed for a tub of clothes, and if too much was used, the items came out with blue streaks and had to be washed again. Materials used in making bluing are soluble Prussian blue and coal-tar blue. Men's shirts, separate collars, dresser scarves, doilies, pillow cases and some articles were starched. Stores carried powdered starch to be mixed in water, but many families often made their own starch by mixing wheat flour in boiling water and straining the mixture through a fine sieve or cheese cloth to remove any lumps. Those doing the laundry regularly, after a few experiences, learned to judge the amount of bluing and starch needed for the particular use.

After the white things were finished, the colored things were put through the two rinses and all were hung on a clothesline to dry. If the weather was sunny and dry, everything smelled fresh and pleasant. But if the weather was cold, windy or rainy, that was the "washer's nightmare" — will they be blown off the line, might the line break and land them all on the ground, or when will they get dry? When the weather is cold, hanging out a wet wash is mighty cold work. Laundry for a family of five, seven or more people was usually a good four or five hour job for one person.

In this period of time in our community, the word "wash" implied the family laundry. When one spoke of washing, they were not referring to bathing, washing dishes, shampooing hair, mopping the floor or cleaning any other thing. They meant strictly "doing the laundry."

"We always wash on Monday."

"Jane is doing the wash."

"Have you washed this week?"

"I will bring in the wash."

"We had a big wash."

A Mr. Caudill came around with what he called a washer — sure to take the drudgery out of doing laundry. He, with some hired help, had made the washing machine of wood for the most part. It had two wooden rollers with carved ridges like a washboard, except wider from side to side with a crank for turning the rollers. The contraption would be on top of two wash tubs filled with water and soap, the clothes fed between the rollers back and forth from tub to tub until the articles were supposedly clean. When all had been run through, tubs were emptied and filled with clean water for rinsing. He certainly had the right idea, as some of the earliest washing machines used the same principle. I knew of no one who bought one. However, I have a smaller version bought in an antique shop and the maker had gotten a patent on it. The following appears on it:

Made by T. F. Adams in Erie, Pa.
Patented May 28, 1877 or 1887
The year is hard to make out but is 1877 or 1887.

Ironing

Ironing followed washday as surely as night follows day. The clothing and cloth items in the homes were made of cotton without the addition of other fibers of today and wrinkled after washing. Men's shirts, ladies' blouses, pillow cases and any starched articles were sprinkled with water to make them damp so they would iron without wrinkles and were rolled up and wrapped in a towel or sheet so the dampness would penetrate the entire item. Flat irons, heated on the top of the stove or in front of the fireplace, were used. The dampened clothes caused the irons to cool rather quickly to be replaced with hot ones. The more irons one had meant a shorter task rather than having to wait while one heated. The temperature of the iron was tested by putting the end of a finger to the tongue for moisture and then touching the iron. If it sizzled, the iron was hot.

Even cotton sheets, handkerchiefs and everyday clothes were ironed. Some people starched bed sheets. What a chill one got when crawling between starched sheets on a cold night! Starch from the starched things tended to stick to the bottom or face of the iron. Salt on a cloth or white paper beside the ironing surface to rub the iron over helped to remove the starch. Most people did not have an ironing board and ironing was done on a folded bed sheet on the kitchen table or some other flat surface. Neighbors often borrowed irons when there were lots of things to be ironed.

Iron

Men's white shirts were not to have a wrinkle showing, especially on the front and collar. Many white dress shirts did not have attached collars and the collars were heavily starched and had to be perfectly ironed. Sometime later, there were celluloid collars that could be bought and attached to the shirt at the back of the neck and at the front with collar buttons.

Of course, there were wool and linsey or linsey-woolsey fabrics that required special cleaning and pressing. Linsey-woolsey was a strong coarse fabric made of flax and wool or of cotton and wool.

A few people grew some flax to be spun with wool for men's suits and ladies' skirts and jackets.

Shingles

All the buildings at our place were covered with shingles — the house, barn, woodshed and other out buildings. Now my father was planning to build a spring house and would need shingles. Too, he noticed that a few shingles had blown loose on the barn and might have to be replaced. "Seems like there's always times when a few extra shingles are needed," Dad said, as he and Mom talked of how helpful it would be to have a spring house since the water was pumped from across the road to the yard.

"Shingles are handy to use to level things like hanging that door at the end of the hall and when we put in the new stove," he added.

"Where'll you get more shingles?" Herbert asked.

"We'll make them," was the reply.

"How?" Herbert wondered.

"I've got to go to Cicero," Dad said.

As he walked up Sheets' Hill he would glance at the woods to see which hardwood trees he could spot and where they were located. When he reached Cicero's house, Cicero and Mary were working in the garden. After health, weather and crops were discussed, Dad said, "Cicero, I need some shingles. How about making some for me?"

"Why me?" Cicero asked. "Lots of folks can make better shingles than I can."

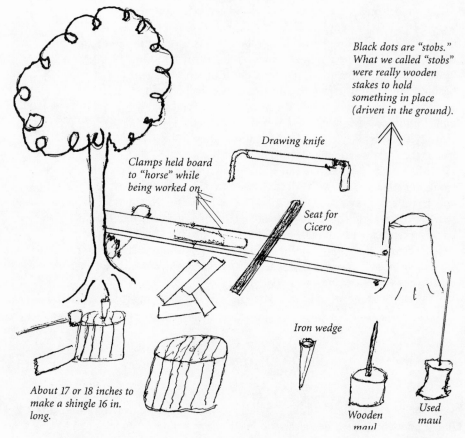

Black dots are "stobs."
What we called "stobs"
were really wooden
stakes to hold
something in place
(driven in the ground).

Drawing knife

Clamps held board
to "horse" while
being worked on.

Seat for
Cicero

Iron wedge

About 17 or 18 inches to
make a shingle 16 in.
long.

Wooden
maul

Used
maul

"Now, Cicero, you know you are the best shingle maker in the country. How about it?"

Cicero dug up a stubborn root of dock, shook off the dirt and threw the root across the garden fence before answering. "When do you want them made?" he asked.

Dad told him about two or three hickory and maple trees he had cut down while building a new fence recently. He told Cicero they were in good condition and he had a medium size maple tree that was shading part of the garden which he planned to cut. Cicero asked about equipment. Dad told him that the Badger brothers left some good boards from building the house and that one could be used to make the "horse." "I've kept them in the granary loft out of the weather. One or two are about two inches thick and six feet long."

"Do you have a good drawing knife?"

"Yes, the one I use when shoeing horses."

"Old woman, do you think I could spare a day or two?" he asked.

Mary said, "Well I reckon. The garden is in pretty good shape for now. You'll be home every night, won't you?"

"I reckon, unless they're going to have fried chicken every night for supper and chicken gravy and hot biscuits for breakfast," Cicero assured her.

Dad added, "He'll be home!"

Two or three evenings later, after supper, when the July days were at their longest, Mary, Cicero and the two children walked over to our house. While Mary and Mom chatted on the front porch and we children played outside, Dad and Cicero inspected the trees, selected a board for the "horse" and a place to set up the contraption. "What about this spot?" Dad asked.

They looked around and Cicero said, "How about here? We could put one end of the board against that stump and the other end against that tree. That looks like about six feet, doesn't it?"

"You're right," Dad agreed. "Herbert and I'll saw blocks about 18 or 19 inches long and haul them here. In the meantime, I'll have the ax and drawing knife good and sharp. When can you be here?"

"I guess about Tuesday and Wednesday of next week, if you can be ready then."

The next three or four days, Dad and Herbert were busy sawing the trees into blocks after cutting off all the branches and hauling the blocks on the farm sled to the selected place. The ax and drawing knife were sharpened on the grinding stone, iron wedges collected, the iron clamps found, some wood "stobs" made and everything in readiness. The tree bark had been peeled off the blocks and some blocks split to 2½ or so inches thick.

Cicero arrived early and he and Dad set about setting up the "horse" as planned and, using stobs, made sure it was secure and not wobbly, with one end against a strong stump and the other end slanted by being held up with a log underneath making it about 18 inches off the ground and held tightly against a tree. Mary had covered a board, that was probably eight inches wide and ten or twelve inches long, with some parts of old worn out sweaters for Cicero to sit on. He was frequently called on to make shingles and had found that a padded seat helped when working long hours astride the "horse." Cicero placed his seat about three feet from the tree, placed the clamps where he wanted them, and then with the drawing knife would rive one end, turn the board around, rive the other end, turn the board over and do the same. His shingles came out very

Wooden maul

Wooden maul after much use

Wooden wedge

Iron wedge

Ax or axe

uniformly, but if he later saw one he was not pleased with, he put it back under the clamp and reworked it until he was satisfied with it. While he was riving the shingles, Dad was kept busy splitting more boards and tossing or carrying them to where Cicero could easily pick them up.

In the meantime, we children carried bark out into sunny spots to dry for kindling. We would also carry the finished shingles to a place where Dad would arrange them in a way that allowed them to get the most sun and the air could pass through the stack.

If the July and August weather was mostly sunny, dry and hot, they might be dry enough for use in about two months. (There was plenty of waste material from shaping and sizing the boards, and Dad used this. He would first make a ring of boards about ten feet in diameter with the thick end of the shingles to the outside. Then a row over the first row, held apart by placing waste strips between and alternating the shingles in each row to allow air to pass between the rows as well as between shingles.)

In spite of toting and carrying, we children enjoyed the process, not only because of the transformation of the wood blocks, but also because of Cicero's sense of humor in answer to our many and silly questions. Too, it was also nice to have a visitor on week days.

There would also be something special for dinner or lunch, perhaps a "sonker" pie or a dessert of peaches with cream and sugar and Mom's lemon pound cake.

When the shingles were dry and ready, the carpenter or homeowner began placing the shingles in a row over the already horizontally placed boards at the lowest edge of the roof, with each succeeding row overlapping about midway along the row, and alternating the sides so that there were no long seams. The uniformity and placing the shingles without bulges or cracks would not allow rain or snow to seep through.

Telephones

I'm not sure of the year when we had our first telephone — it must have been 1912 or early 1913. I tend to date some events by the year my mother died in 1914 and things that happened while she was living.

Meetings must have been held and informal talks as families visited or met at the store or in the road. But 12 or 14 families decided they would like a telephone and the only way to have one was through their own planning, financing and work.

Of course, poles were needed — the size and kind of wood agreed on. Those who had suitable timber gave it and those who didn't volunteered extra time and work — felling trees, stripping off bark, getting poles out in the sun to dry, digging post holes with post hole diggers and stretching wire. I suppose the poles were set at approximately the same distance apart, so they could know how far a roll of wire would reach. How the wire was joined, I don't know. I don't recall hearing of soldering at the time. After the lines had been run to poles near each house, wire was joined to the main line and run to the spot in the house where the phone was to be placed.

The phones were purchased — I suppose in a lot, as all appeared to look the same. The wooden box, about 18 inches tall and 10 or 12 inches wide, was attached to the wall, held two batteries, had two bells that rang with every call, a crank on the right hand side for ringing the calls. A speaker stood out on the front to talk into and the receiver or ear piece was on the left side and when not in use, rested on a Y-shaped metal lever. The phone or wires, evidently, were not grounded. Sometimes during an electric storm, the phone would pop and crack and sometimes fire would run off the phone. Finally, a cut-off was attached to the phone and wall and we'd "cut-off" the phone during a storm.

Each family with a phone had their own ring. Our ring was a long, a short and a long. On the wall near the phone was a paper or cardboard that showed the rings of all phone owners.

C. C. Barker _____ ____ _____
Grandfather _____
Mr. Reedy _____ ____ ____
Mrs. B. Jones ____ _____ ____
Bob Brown ____ ____ _____

Everyone heard all the rings and if they wished, would pick up the receiver and listen. No one thought of this as eavesdropping. That was the way we kept up with who was sick, when any catastrophe occurred, news and events, or just a friendly visit with neighbors.

Dad and other men would congregate at the store at Grassy Creek at times when weather was too bad for farm work, and at times when a community problem needed to be discussed. The store, while located in Ashe County, was only a hop, skip, and jump from the Virginia state line, Grayson County. Men of both counties would be at the store and found problems common to both areas. Ashe areas needed to contact people in the Grayson area and the other way around, especially places of business in Troutdale, Grant, Jefferson and Crumpler. A telephone connection was needed. After much discussion, a telephone line could be run from Mrs. Pasley's little switchboard in Crumpler to one in Grayson in the Grassy Creek area if one were placed there. My father agreed to let it be placed in our house. It was a simple affair — a box on the wall with two bells attached to the big phone batteries and using the receiver and mouth piece on the regular phone. A little lever was pushed from one slot to another to connect, hold and disconnect. Later, a more sophisticated switchboard was set up in Mr. Lyda Robbins' home and operated by Mrs. Robbins. Since we did not have electricity, batteries had to be replaced after much use.

The telephone wire used with our first telephones was a single strand of galvanized or steel wire with no outside covering. Glass insulators were put on the poles and a strand of wire wound around them in a groove made when the insulator was manufactured to keep from losing or transferring electricity and sound with nonconducting material. On very cold nights, we'd hear a kind of sound, a rather continuous sound and when we asked what it was, Dad said, "It's the phone wire singing. When the wire gets real cold, it tends to tighten and makes the sound you hear."

Weddings and Funerals

Weddings

I suppose I was eighteen or older before I attended a formal or church wedding. In fact, even the first formal wedding I recall was that of a cousin who came from Maryland to marry the sweetheart he had left behind when his family moved north. The wedding took place in the bride's home with invited friends and relatives. Some couples went to the minister's home to be married but many couples eloped or "ran away to be married." If the bride's parents didn't approve of the prospective groom, the couple would elope. This meant that any pre-planning was kept "hush hush" until the ceremony was over lest the bride be held hostage by her family or the wedding interrupted by an angry father, maybe accompanied by a couple of stalwart brothers or even the sheriff. When either of the couple was under the age of eighteen or the legal age (whatever it happened to be in the state), they would often go to another state, where a license could be obtained without a waiting period. Also, if they wanted to keep the marriage secret for a time, they could, because locals hardly ever got an out-of-state newspaper. For this area, Tennessee seemed to be the state where couples eloped to.

A friend told me once, "I've only stolen two women in my life, my wife and your sister, Wilma. When she and Paul were married, I slyly 'snuck' them to Tennessee."

The oldest daughter of a neighbor and her husband eloped and after they were married dreaded to face her father's ire. I don't know if he really didn't like the groom, thought no one was good enough for his daughter, or wanted to keep her home for the help she could be in his large family.

My mother had died in 1914, and about a year later, my father had his eye on a younger sister of the above mentioned bride. Single and wanting to get in the "good graces" of that family, he planned a get-together with single members of his family and of the newly married couple. One Sunday evening this group rigged up two wagons to be drawn by horses, and the wagon beds filled with a goodly amount of soft hay to sit on, went to where the couple was staying and told them they had come to take them to the bride's home. The couple resisted but the group playfully tied the bride and groom with ropes they had taken along and told them, "We're kidnapping you and we'll tell the family we had found you all tied up and we rescued you and brought you home!"

In this group were my father, my sister and brother, two aunts and two uncles, and some brothers and sisters of the bride who were in on the prank. The parents could hardly be unfriendly in the large group, so everything turned out fine. I was too young to be a part of this escapade. I was sent to Grandpa's for the night. At nine o'clock Grandmother took me upstairs to sleep. The weather must have been coldish for she piled so many quilts on me that I could not turn over and my shoulders ached, and I couldn't get to sleep. I felt lonely and afraid! Afraid of what? I don't know. I still missed my mother and had not been alone in a dark room so far away from anyone. Of course, my grandparents were just downstairs but on the other side of the house. I think that was the longest night I ever spent.

One day my sister and I went to visit our friends just across the hill. My sister told me she had a letter my father had given her to deliver secretly to the object of his affections. After we were out of sight of our house, Sissie took the letter out of her pocket and getting my "cross my heart I would not tell," opened and read the letter. How she managed to open the envelope and close it without it being apparent, I can't understand. In the letter, my father had written, "I can neither eat, nor sleep, nor work for thought of you!" Romantic? A farmer with three children!? Years later I told my daughter Gayle about this letter. About 1985, a friend who had bought the house and was restoring it, found this very letter, which had been stuck in back of a window facing. He gave it to Gayle.

Well, I suppose the young lady knew her father would violently oppose his daughter marrying a man fifteen years older than she, and with three children besides. Their mailbox was only about 150 feet from our house, and someone from that family came daily to pick up their mail. She managed to slip some of her clothing out of the house, and hide it in a hollow stump in the wooded area. One Wednesday night, Prayer Meeting night, she and some of her sisters and brothers were, as usual, going to prayer in the local church. She and my father met at the "stump," she changed into her white seersucker dress, her black and white high top, laced shoes and they proceeded to a minister's home which had been prearranged and were married. While all this was being planned, Aunt Lona stopped in to ask me if I could go with her to visit Aunt Lucy Waddell. Of course, this had already been planned although I didn't know it and it was as we were on our way home a few days later that Aunt Lona told me that my father had married and "I had a stepmother."

Uncle Iredell had been "sparking" Vesta Osborne, daughter of Dr. Fielden Osborne. She had enrolled in Virginia-Carolina High School and traveled to and from school on horseback. She had stored some of her clothing and personal items in the saddlebags which usually carried her school books. This was a perfect situation for them to elope. They arranged for Curtis Sexton to take the horse back home. I don't know what excuse he gave the father for returning the horse, but after he was safely out of reach of physical harm, he began yelling, "A wedding! A wedding! A wedding!"

There was lots of talk about serenading newly married couples. Groups would find out where the couple was staying, the first night if possible, and when it was thought the couple had gone to bed, they would take pots, pans and anything that would make noise and serenade the bride and groom for an hour or two—also hollering and whooping, rather than soft music.

When Grandpa heard of a wedding, he'd ask, "Did they ride the groom on a rail?" What about the bride? We'd ask and he'd say, "Oh, they take the bride for a ride in a wheelbarrow."

Etta Sexton in her wedding dress, 1915

Evidently, these people liked to have fun and tease whenever they could. And from what I gathered from my grandparents who were born in the 1840s, this kind of thing had gone on for years.

Johnny, the oldest son of Uncle Aris and Aunt Sarah Ann Spencer, married Dora Plummer, daughter of Mr. Bob Plummer, around 1918. Aunt Sarah Ann planned a "wedding supper" for the newlyweds at her home one Sunday evening. She had invited just relatives of the couple as their house was small.

The house had two rooms plus a small "meal room," a front porch and an attic which could be entered by an attached ladder from the outside. The largest room had a fireplace, cook stove, a long dining table, a double bed and chairs for sitting and using around the dining table. The other room had two double beds, a bureau or chest of drawers, and what was called a "little table" for a lamp, and three or four straight chairs. The attic room served as a little sleeping room for the boys in summer or when needed. The bed was a "pallet" (a sort of mattress on the floor and quilts or covers when needed).

The selected day for the wedding supper was a cloudy, coolish threatening evening, but we donned our Sunday clothes and started, Dad, Mayme, Herbert and I. On the way a few soft snow flakes started to fall as we walked and we took the short way across the hill instead of the longer route. Aunt Ellen and her family did not come from Volney, nor did Dora's family from Long Branch, evidently discouraged by the snow and the distance.

Johnny's two sisters, Zella and Kate, teenagers, although the event was to be just a family affair, had told a friend or two, who told some of their friends, all of whom were always looking for an excuse for a "get-together" for fun and something unusual. Well, several young men arrived. By this time the snow was getting heavier and the wind beginning to blow. We and the later arriving guests had hung our coats and hats on nails on the porch walls and were enjoying Aunt Sarah Ann's chicken and dumplings and other special delicious foods. Then it was time to cut the wedding cake — a large chocolate pound cake with a thimble and collar button hidden inside. After the bride had cut the first slice, Aunt Sarah Ann made sure that a girl got the slice with the thimble and a young man the collar button, to see who would be married next, as a bride throws the bridal bouquet today. Much teasing, laughter and fun was going on at this stage, everyone unaware of the wild blizzard with fierce winds blowing and drifting the now heavy falling snow and of the freezing temperature outside. Then the horrible realization that guests were faced with going home. Late arrivals found that some of their wraps, coats and hats, had blown away. Despite trying to find where the wind might have dropped them, some were not found until after snow drifts had thawed days later. I'm sure that a few young fellows ended up with frostbite. Since we were the first arrivals, our wraps were still on the porch. As I was young and little, I was left to spend the night. When Dad, Mayme and Herbert got home, Herbert's ears were so frozen, he was in great pain for a long time.

Now Aunt Sarah Ann was faced with making sleeping arrangements for the family. The dining table had been cleared and she made a bed for the groom and Uncle Aris to sleep on the table. (After all, heat rises.) Zella and the bride slept in one bed in the other room. Kate and I slept in the other bed. Aunt Sarah Ann, Vernett and Tom used the bed in the "sitting room." Vernett and Tom were the two youngest children in the family.

I'm sure some of the young men spent the rest of the night with a buddy whose home was closest by.

Mr. David Spencer's first wife, Lutitia, (called Tish by close friends) had died. His children were grown up, some married, and he realized that he might soon be left alone. Some time in the middle 19 teens, Mr. Spencer took a new wife and she was from Winston-Salem. We knew her as Miss Sallie. With the dirt and muddy roads of that time, travel was slow and difficult, it taking possibly two days to get from Ashe or Grayson counties to even Wilkesboro, I wonder how in the world Mr. Spencer got to Winston-Salem and met Miss Sallie. Whether he spent some time there or they carried on a correspondence, I don't know. He may have had a friend or relative who knew Miss Sallie and maybe they wrote and exchanged pictures for a time and he went "down the country" (as people called any place below the mountains whether toward Winston, Greensboro, Charlotte or even Wilkesboro or Norfolk, Virginia). Anyway they were married and he brought her to Grassy Creek, where she lived until after Mr. Spencer's death. Then she sold the place to my father and returned to Winston-Salem. A relative of hers stopped at my house around 1977 and told me that her Aunt Sallie was still living in Winston at that time.

Then before I was seven, I went with my mother to visit my great Uncle, Robert (Uncle Bob) Spencer who lived on the road now known as the Charlie Spencer Road. Uncle Bob was sick. He, too, after the death of his first wife had gone "down the country" and married Miss Lena. I don't know where she was from, but she was a handsome lady — tall, straight, had brown eyes and dark hair.

As for Mr. George Plummer and his courtship of Aunts Lona and Minnie, this story is told in an earlier chapter. Aunt Lona was known as a good worker, conservative but gingery, and would make any man a good wife! But Minnie was prettier, I guess, softer, at least, and was more reserved and ladylike. So Uncle George chose Aunt Minnie! He stayed a few weeks and he and Aunt Minnie were married after only a brief courtship and then Aunt Minnie was on her way as a bride to Colorado. I suppose Aunt Minnie was likely in her forties when they were married. I don't know the ages of Miss Sallie or Miss Lena but I suppose neither of the three wanted any longer to be labeled as "old maids." Aunt Minnie always called Uncle George "Mr. Plummer," and I think Miss Sallie called her husband, "Mr. Spencer."

It seems coincidental that each of these three men had five children but in each case only one or two still at home. Some of Mr. David Spencer's relatives, grand or great grandchildren or nieces or nephews still stop by to see me at times.

Funerals

There were no funeral homes or mortuaries in our area or nearby communities in the first two and a half decades or this century. Had there been, roads and methods of travel at that time would have made it impossible to take advantage of those that might have been in Jefferson or Troutdale. So communities took care of burying their dead.

To hear of the death of a relative, neighbor, friend or even of someone people had never met but knew of, sadnesses and sympathies were aroused. All the proceedings, from the last breath drawn until the funeral was over, were seen to by the families, friends and neighbors.

A place was selected to "lay out" the body until burial. In summer, a cool room or porch was used. In winter, if there was a spare bedroom, it might be used. If not, often the living room or parlor was selected. Carpenters' saw horses or four chairs were chosen to hold boards the length of the deceased, the body placed on them and covered with a sheet. Immediately after death the arms were crossed from the elbows across the chest. Eyes were closed and quarters placed over them to hold them closed. A strip of soft cloth might be put under the chin and tied over the top of the head to make sure the mouth was held closed. Usually, before the body was removed from the bed, it was bathed and if burial clothing was on hand, it was put on the body. If not some suitable clothing was used. Women bathed the bodies of women and men bathed the bodies of males. It was inconceivable that men would bathe the body of a female or a lady the body of a man.

While the casket was being made, soft cloths were saturated in wood alcohol and placed over the face to prevent discoloration. Of course, today undertakers take care of this with embalming and their secret methods.

Some elderly people or others expecting to die at any moment, kept burial clothing on hand. One elderly relative had all her burial clothes ready to the point of having pins in the bands of the skirt and any other place where they might be necessary. When mortuaries or funeral homes and travel permitted, they kept ready burial clothing called shrouds.

Caskets were made by carpenters or cabinet makers nearby. Measurements were made of the bodies — of length and width — and approximate weight. Lumber in wide widths was obtainable and usually the sides, bottoms and cover of coffins were in one piece. Coffins slanted from the head part to a wider width where the folded elbows were and then tapered to the opposite end. The lid was one piece the same shape as the casket. Some were varnished and lined with white cloth and later some were padded with cotton and a trim of lace might be used. A few carpenters kept materials on hand for caskets and I saw three small caskets for children in the bedroom of one wood worker. Also, a few elderly people had their caskets made and kept in their house.

While the casket was being made there were other activities going on. The grave to be dug (by neighbors), bringing in prepared food for the family and visitors, sitting up at night with the body and family, selecting the cemetery and a minister, and place where the funeral would be held. There were not many churches nearby and the distance of one, two or three miles over muddy or dusty roads made travel difficult, and after all, most people walked to the funeral. Often the funeral was held in the cemetery, in the home if there was room, on the front porch — if a porch, or under a tree in the yard. I attended several funerals on front porches and in yards, or in cemeteries. In a radius of about a mile or less, there were ten cemeteries. Those who had land to spare set some aside for a family burial place and since many families were related, there was hardly any problem of having a place for burial. If you did not have space to bury a family member in your own cemetery, you would have no problem finding a plot in someone else's! Some of the ten cemeteries are now neglected, a few completely abandoned. Families are using cemeteries which communities pay to have cared for, or the large ones which sell plots and have perpetual care.

Caskets were always opened at the cemetery for viewing by those who came only to that part of the proceedings. My grandmother told of attending a burial and viewing the body of a lady. Some days later she remembered that when she was looking at the body, there was perspiration on the lady's face! Grandmother wondered how many others may have been buried alive.

The first funeral I attended was that of a little girl, three or four years old who choked on a coffee bean. I was very young, maybe four or five years old. My mother, sister and I along with a few other people walked by the Halsey house, up and over the hill to the Granville Spencer cemetery. Likely the small casket was carried by a couple of men to the cemetery from the home as the family lived nearby. As we viewed the body, I saw a beautiful little girl, dressed in a white dress and she looked as if she was asleep. The family and relatives were sobbing and crying loudly. I didn't understand the crying and asked my

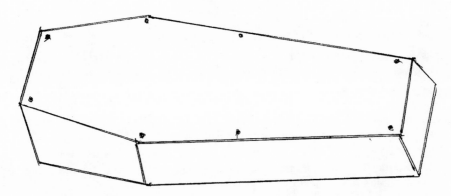

Carpenters made caskets of wide wood boards or wood planks. They were sloped to the spot about where the arms were placed across the chest, then sloped to the end. The top was the same size and shape of the coffin and fastened on with screws.

mother why, and she said, "Because their little girl has died and will no longer be with them."

Some years later I attended the funeral of a young woman, perhaps about 20 years of age, held on the front porch of the home. We stood in the yard while the family and minister sat and stood on the porch. Later a son of the same family died in Arizona and the funeral was held on the same front porch. Then my Aunt Lucy died in winter and her funeral was held in the living room of Mr. Irving Young, a relative, and she was buried in the cemetery on his place. Much later, a high school classmate of mine and close friend, died in childbirth and her funeral was also held under the shade of a tree in Mr. Young's front yard. When the deceased was near the burial site, men carried the casket to the grave. Sleds or wagons carried the caskets to the cemeteries when there was some distance to be covered.

My Mother's Death

When I was seven, I was told I could go and spend the night with my friend, Blanch, who lived across the hill. I was elated as I never had the opportunity to visit Blanch as much as I liked. Too, they always had some foods we didn't have, such as ground cherry preserves, or something prepared differently. The next day I stayed on cherishing not to be called home. In the afternoon, Mrs. Sexton, Blanch's mother, told me she had been called, and that I had to go home. As I neared the house I heard crying and my first thought was that someone had been hurt. My sister met me and said, "Our Mama and the little baby are dead." I had had no idea that a baby was expected, in fact I had no idea how babies got "there" except that doctors seemed to be connected somehow with new babies.

Two of my aunts were there and shortly my mother's youngest sister, Aunt

Mega, and Uncle Tom came from Sussex. After a bit, Uncle Tom was leaving and I asked why he was leaving and was told he was going home to make the casket for my mother. Some men were busy arranging a place on the front porch on which to put the bodies. The bodies were covered with a sheet. The next day, Aunt Ellen came from Volney. After a white embroidery-trimmed night gown was put on my mother, Aunt Ellen would take me to look at my mother and take my hand and put it on her face. I didn't like that as my mother had always felt warm to me. I don't remember the funeral at all or the burial. Dad had a team and wagon and so did Grandpa and neighbors and I'm sure they were taken to the cemetery where her parents, John and Martha Ann Spencer and grandparents, Solomon and Nelly Spencer were buried.

When there was a death in the community, whether everyone knew the deceased or not, friends and neighbors and resident men dug the grave. It was a hard job to get a grave dug whether in hot weather, frigid, rainy or whatever the weather might be. "Death does not wait for any man." Graves were dug with farm shovels and mattocks to loosen the soil, picks to pry under any rocks that might be there and axes to cut roots. So it was hard work. I have heard the saying: "When a person dies, the only land he needs is three feet by six feet." But at that time more land was needed. After the depth was decided on, the width was more than three feet, allowing near the bottom to have a ledge or about 10 or 12 inches all around above the space for the casket for four men to stand on to receive the coffin when handed down by four other men. Then it was lowered into the space into which the coffin was placed. Then men used shovels to fill the grave with the soil which had been removed. Most of the dirt was used and the grave would be heaped up above the level of the ground but would gradually sink to practically ground level.

How different now when funeral homes have the graves dug with machines. However, when I came back to the area twenty years ago, there was still some hand digging of graves. The earlier preparation was free but morticians now charge for this service.

In the early 30s a young woman, perhaps in her late twenties or early thirties, died after being "bedfast" for about three years. Three other ladies and I were called to bathe the body and get it ready for the undertakers in Jefferson to pick up. As we walked to the home, the ladies told me that the body had bed sores and there would be an odor. They said we would need to dip snuff during our task. We broke off birch branches and chewed the end to use to put snuff in our mouths. I had never dipped snuff and wondered how I would fare. The family asked us to bathe the body and put the clothes they already had on hand on their daughter. The parents did not want men dressing their young lady. Sure enough, there were huge bedsores on her back which drained excessively as the body was moved. One lady held the snuff box, while we worked with the body, and we would take the chewed end of our toothbrushes and put them in the snuff and back in our mouths. The family brought out the clothing to be put on the body — all brand new white clothing, panties, bra, hose, a slip, and pretty white, lace trimmed dress. Then they were ready to call the morticians. How sad! They didn't realize that all those nice white clothes would be taken off, possibly stained from the bed sores, while the body was made ready to be placed in the casket, and for viewing.

Grandfather "Big Pine"

In 1932, Grandpa fell ill and after a week passed away. He had always said he wanted to have his coffin made rather than buying one of those "covered things that's become available at funeral homes." He didn't trust those, and since he was a large man was afraid the bottom might fall out. There was a gentleman in Grant, Virginia, who made caskets to order and he was taken the needed information and made Grandpa's coffin. It was the first casket I had seen that looked like those we see today — covered with a felt-like covering, handles for carrying and inside padding, white lace trimmed lining.

Grandpa was 88 years old and was buried in the Grassy Creek cemetery. His was one of the earliest burials in this cemetery which serves our community today.

The custom of a body being kept in the home before burial, and of the family sitting up with it, is rarely observed today. But one custom is still observed — the kindness and caring of friends and neighbors who prepare and take lots and lots of food to the bereaved family, send flowers, attend viewings, serve as pall bearers, send sympathy cards and attend funerals. Certainly travel and automobiles and funeral homes have changed the whole funeral process. Viewings are attended more than the day time funerals because many more people work than used to.

A Mr. and Mrs. Davis lived in a little board and batten house beside the road about where Basil Kilby's house is. My grandmother took me with her to go there as she had heard that Mr. Davis had died. He was "laid out" in the main small room. In the same room, Mrs. Davis was in the bed very sick, and she died before her husband was buried. I do not know whether there was a double funeral and burial. Mr. Davis may have been in the casket as I recall seeing the entire body with no cover on it. Coffins in those days had covers in one piece and were removed for viewing.

My parents and I attended a funeral which was held in a yard near the cemetery where another man was to be buried. I think this man had been very ill for some time and may have been having breathing problems because his mouth was wide open. The family forgot to close the mouth until too late. For the longest time I could see that face. I was perhaps thirteen years of age.

I was told of people who appeared to be dead, were laid out and later began breathing and lived. We had heard on the telephone that a Mrs. Peak had died. Eventually preparations were made to "lay her out" but when the body was moved, she revived.

Cousin Martha's sister had died and was "laid out" on the back porch. The next morning, Cousin Martha started to the spring to get a bucket of water. As she started off the porch she bumped against the corner of the boards on which her sister was lying. When she came back from the spring, her sister was sitting up.

A few years ago there appeared an article in a Virginia newspaper of a lady who was struck on the head by a falling tree branch under which she was standing. All the preparations for burial were made and the body was taken to the church. While the viewing was going on, someone noticed an eyelid moved. The "dead" lady said she had heard everything that was going on but could not move a muscle. We had read this article in the paper while living in Northern Virginia and Myrtle Gambill here in Grassy Creek had also read the same article at the time of the occurrence.

I can understand how this could happen some years back, especially when bodies were not embalmed. After my baby was born, I had lain down to have a nap. My husband had come home from work, supper was on the table. I heard them talking, saying I was sleeping a long time. I was hearing all the conversation but could not move. I wanted so much to have someone touch or move me a bit. Finally, after trying to move an arm or foot, I was able to get up. A strange, strange feeling!

Murder

"Where's Benjy?" Aunt Ellen asked as the family sat down for supper, as they waited for Uncle Roby to ask the blessing. "Benjy, Benjy, Come on." Benjy came reluctantly and slipped into his place on the bench. Grace said and Uncle Roby took out some potatoes and passed the bowl. Benjy helped himself to some potatoes, a piece of cornbread and butter but refused the green beans, tomatoes and slaw. He ate slowly and played with the mashed potatoes.

"Why aren't you eating, Sonny?" Aunt Ellen asked.

"I'm not much hungry," he answered.

"Don't you feel good?" she asked.

"I'm all right," he said. That's strange, she thought, as he usually was hard to fill up like most growing eleven-year-old active boys. But, of course, she reasoned everybody has some days when they don't feel like eating and this day had been a hot one — more like a "dog day" than a fall September day.

When the boys started upstairs to bed, Aunt Ellen wondered if their beds had been made. She and Susie had been canning tomatoes and corn and shelly beans for goulash and hadn't checked upstairs today. She followed up to see. Booker and Spurge were already making their bed. She and Britt straightened the sheets and covers on the other bed, she fluffed the pillows and turned the covers down. Benjy had taken his shirt off, dropped his pants to the floor and started to get in bed. "Benjy," Aunt Ellen screamed. "Did you get sunburned today? Your back is blood red! Why, no. That's not sunburn. You've got red streaks across your back. And there's some on your legs. What happened?"

"Kemp and I were hitting each other with switches. Just playing around," he answered.

As she looked closely and touched the raised, red welts as Benjy flinched, she said, "Why, you wouldn't do that to each other — hurt each other like that! That's crazy."

She went to the head of the stairs and called, "Roby, come up here. Would you look at this boy's back! Did you whip him?"

"Why, no. I haven't whipped him. Why he's not been with us where we were fixing fence in the upper place. Just Booker, Fred and me. And I don't beat the kids. You know that. What happened, Boy? How'd you get all messed up like that?" he asked while looking closely and noticing Benjy wince as he ran a finger along a red streak. "You boys wouldn't beat each other like this, just playing. Did you get in a fight?"

"No." Benjy answered.

Aunt Ellen went downstairs and got Susie's cold cream and gently spread some on the swollen red streaks. "Honey, I know you hurt," she said consolingly. Benjy was her youngest, and still the baby, not only to the parents but to the older brothers and his only sister. He had been such a handsome little tike with deep brown eyes and dark brown hair which his mother would not have cut until he was old enough to start school. When he was five, Aunt Ellen and Benjy attended a school function with our family. Benjy was dressed in his yellowish-tan Norfolk suit with his hair in corkscrew curls hanging down to his shoulders. Some older boys were snickering and pointing at this little "strangely dressed" boy with the "girly" hair. If Aunt Ellen noticed, she didn't let on, and was not about to cut that beautiful hair.

In the meantime, Booker had gotten out of bed and he and his dad looked and talked and decided something just wasn't right about this. Uncle Roby went downstairs and called Kemp's home. Mrs. Michal finally answered. She said, "We were in bed. My husband went to Marion today and is spending the night with his cousin and we went to bed early." After hearing Uncle Roby's story, she said, "Wait a minute. I'll ask Kemp. He didn't say anything about what they were doing this afternoon." When she came back to the phone, she said, "I looked on Kemp's back and legs and he has red streaks, too. He looks like he's had a switching. He stammered around and told us two or three different tales. He didn't say they were playing. He finally said Mr. Berk whipped them. I asked him why and I've got to get the gist of that story together."

"You mean he said Berk at the store did it?"

"Yes, that's what he said. When Jim gets home he'll get to the bottom of what's going on."

"Thank you, Miz Michal. I'm sorry to wake you up," Uncle Roby said.

Back upstairs, he said, "Benjy, I want to know how you got them streaks on your back and I want the truth and I want it now!"

Hesitantly, Benjy said, "Mr. Berk did it."

"Berk. Why?"

"He said we stole his eggs," was the reply.

"Stole his eggs? Why did he say that? Did you steal his eggs?"

"We were hunting bird nests out in our woods and we found a hen's nest under a bush. It had four eggs in it. I guessed it was Mama's hen or Miz Jenkins', who had stole her nest out. We didn't have any money and said we'd like to have some candy or those new crackers at the store. Kemp said he knowed where there was another hen's nest. So we took three eggs and left one for a nest egg. We got two eggs in the other nest. We went in the store and asked Mr. Berk what they came to. He asked where we got the eggs. We said we brought them from home and he said we didn't. That we stole them outta his hen nest out at a hay stack. We said we didn't but he said we did. He said we were robbers and liars. He said bad things about our parents, too. He said we needed to be learned not to steal and lie. We started to pick up the eggs and leave but he wouldn't let us."

"What do you mean, he wouldn't let you?"

"We picked up the three eggs to leave but he beat us to the door and shut it and locked it."

"What did he whip you with? Did he have a switch in the store?" Uncle Roby asked.

"He didn't use a switch. He got a whip — one of them buggy whups he has in that milk can at the end of the counter."

"Oh, how awful!" Aunt Ellen gasped. "You poor baby. Roby, what are we going to do about this?"

"Let's try to get some sleep. We'll see about this tomorrow morning," he answered.

The next morning at the breakfast table, Uncle Roby said, "Booker, help your mother with the milking and we'll go see that butcher." They waited until they thought Berkley Yancey was at the store. They took the short cut in the well-worn path through the little wooded area and down through the Jenkins' field next to the fence, ending at the road in front of the little store. (This way was used by walkers on their road saving considerable distance rather than going to the highway and turning north as used by wagons and cars.)

Mr. Yancey was sweeping the wooden floor when they entered. He looked up and said, "Morning. What can I do for you gentlemen?"

Uncle Roby answered, "You better ask what can we do for you? Berk Yancey, what do you mean beating up my boy?"

"He told you, did he? Somebody needed to teach those boys not to steal and lie," he replied.

Uncle Roby answered, "I'll do the teaching of my kids and I'll tell you right now, nobody'll whup my children and get away with it."

"Well, you parents haven't taught them and somebody had to do it. They've got to know we don't put up with that kind of behavior."

"When my kids do something they shouldn't do, all anybody has to do is tell me or my wife and we'll take care of them. And you'd better know we don't put up with folks like you beating our children."

Angry words went back and forth and Uncle Roby started to reach for one of the buggy whips as he retorted, "Yancey, I'm going to use one of these on you right now, like you done to those boys."

Booker stopped his father's hand, "No, Dad. That's not the way to settle this. He's admitted he did it and I heard him. We'll let the court settle this and everyone will know what he did. He'll lose more than a couple of eggs."

"All right, but I'd like to wallop the stuffing out of him right now," he answered. "Berk, this is not over. You'll pay for this. You remember that."

Booker was a handsome young man, clean, upright, sensible and respected in the community. He had been elected to be superintendent of Sunday School in the local Methodist Church despite his youthful age of twenty-one years. Everyone liked Booker.

Sunday School was held on Sunday afternoons at the local church for the convenience of some families in the community who attended morning services in another church.

The Sunday after the confrontation with Mr. Yancey, my brother and a cousin attended Sunday School with Booker and family after having spent the weekend with them. After Sunday School, they walked along with Booker and his girlfriend as he accompanied her home until they reached the road to come home. Mr. Yancey was standing on the little porch of his store at the edge of the road as the walkers passed by. Booker left his girlfriend's home just before dusk to go home. He took the short cut as they usually did.

Monday morning Uncle Roby called up to the boys to get up and get ready for breakfast which Aunt Ellen and Susie had almost ready. As they assembled at the table, Aunt Ellen asked, "Where's Booker? Wasn't he up?" Spurge said, "He was already up, I reckon. He wasn't in the room when I waked up. Ain't he down here?" Nobody had seen him.

"I guess he went out to see about something," someone volunteered. Everyone went about the morning chores as usual expecting Booker to walk in any minute and eat his breakfast which Aunt Ellen had put in the oven to stay warm for him. She had an uneasy kind of feeling when he didn't show up after an hour or more.

The party phone rang and she picked up the receiver to listen for any community news, if any. It was Mrs. Jenkins and another neighbor. Mrs. Jenkins said, "You know, Betty, it looks like a man is laying on the ground down here in the path. I've not seen it move."

"Maybe it's a scarecrow somebody was moving and laid it there until they could move it," Betty suggested.

"I don't know," Mrs. Jenkins said. "When Andy and the boys come in, I'll send one of the boys down to see."

Aunt Ellen felt a pang in her chest as she heard this. She called Uncle Roby, grabbed her bonnet and ran toward the path. As she ran, her breath came in gasps and her chest ached. What if, she thought. "Oh, Lord! Oh, Lord!" It seemed those were the only words she could get out as she ran — not waiting for her husband whose arthritis wouldn't let him keep up. Mrs. Jenkins, seeing Aunt Ellen and Britt and finally Uncle Roby, started down there, too. Britt reached the body first and saw that it was his brother Booker! He was lying face down. The back of his jacket was covered with dried blood. Aunt Ellen screamed and cried as she tried to get out words. "Who did this to my boy? Oh, my poor, poor boy. Out here all by his self!" and on and on. "Daddy, Daddy, who did this to our boy?"

"That butcher down there. He did it. He did it." Uncle Roby kept saying over and over. People began gathering as they came along the highway and the short-way path and the word spread on the party phone line.

Someone called the sheriff. The store wasn't open. Mr. Yancey was not at the store nor at home. Neither was Mr. Yancey's son, Dr. Yancey. Dr. Yancey, who had a car for making his rounds could not be reached for three or four days.

There was never a minute when Booker's death was not on his mother's mind. She kept thinking if only we could have been with him if it had to happen. "How long did he have to suffer all by himself out there? So near his home and family! If only I could know!" Booker was twenty-one years and one month of age when he died. He was buried in the cemetery started by his great grandfather, Solomon Spencer, of Grassy Creek. His headstone bears the inscription: Booker Gray Pugh, Twenty-one years and one month of age.

Aunt Ellen kept his bloody jacket hanging on the wall of the front porch for a long time. When she passed away she was buried beside her beloved son.

Mr. Berkley Yancey was missing for about three years when there appeared a small article in the newspaper that he had surrendered to authorities in Roanoke, Virginia. As far as I know, he was never found guilty as there were no witnesses.

A young life snuffed out, a family left hurting, a life under suspicion — over a few eggs — stolen or otherwise!

It was perhaps the school term of 1926-27 that two young men with a rumble seat car came to the dormitory where another teacher, Cecil Campbell, a boarding student, Ruth Vannoy, and I were living and asked to take us for a ride. Cecil and I rode with the driver while Ruth and her friend rode in the rumble seat. It was a sunny afternoon and we drove out to Glendale Springs, turned around and came back to West Jefferson. While the sun was shining where we were, we could see dark, heavy clouds in the southwest, some flashes of lightning and hear low rumbles of thunder. Someone mentioned that there was an electric storm brewing somewhere. The following morning when we arrived at school, the principal, looking grave and sad told us that the father of Mr. Lester Segraves had drowned in a flash flood the afternoon before. We, and everyone in town, knew Mr. and Mrs. Lester Segraves who both worked in the First National Bank in West Jefferson. As the event began to unfold, on that hot afternoon, people in the Grassy Creek and Little Helton areas shuddered at the ear-splitting peals of thunder which seemed to get louder and louder followed with blinding flashes of lightning reaching to the ground, sending chills up and down the spine and a sense of numbing fear in the heart. All at once the clouds opened and water began pouring as if a dam had burst. Those who had not already sought shelter inside from the impending storm, started to do so at the closest point. We heard that two people who were working at the Segraves farm, unhitched the team of horses and started to the barn and house. By the time they reached the barn, the little stream which started at the foot of Sheets' Hill and fed by small branches into Helton Creek, a bit south of the Segraves house, had spread out of its banks to such a depth the men (probably Segraves sons) saw no chance of getting to the house where Mr. and Mrs. Segraves were in the house alone. Mrs. Segraves was confined to the bed because of some illness. Mr. Segraves was unable to walk and was in a chair — it seems I had heard a wheel chair but it may have been a rocking chair or an overstuffed chair. The water rose so rapidly that neither could escape from the first floor room where they were and no one could get to them. The mattress on Mrs. Segraves' bed began to float and finally came to rest on top of a bureau or chest of drawers. She lived but Mr. Segraves drowned.

There was a rather small yellow house along Long Branch, as we knew that little stream and which was owned by a family as I remember by the name of Handy. Every time I passed the house, I admired it as always looking so neat, freshly painted and well cared for in a well groomed yard. This house washed away.

In this downpour, the little stream in front of our house began to rise so rapidly that Dad took the children to the apple house, which had a double wall filled with sawdust as insulation. I suppose he thought that if the stream continued to rise that the sawdust between the walls would absorb some of the water and would be the safest place for the family. My stepmother had died, leaving five children, the oldest of whom was ten or eleven years old. Dad had gotten a young lady by the name of Blackburn to keep house, cook and look after the young children. Miss Blackburn's grandmother came along with her and they were with the family while this cloudburst was occurring. After it was safe to leave the apple house, a survey was taken of the surroundings and there were mud slides on the steepest hills. Each side of the little stream was littered with brush, fence rails and anything that happened to be in the path of the swift water.

Mr. Paul Plummer's father lived a mile or more from the Segraves place. Paul told me that, even though there was lots and lots of farm work to be done to save crops and get ready for winter, his father assigned Paul and a hired worker to do nothing but clean the debris and repair the banks of Long Branch on their farm.

The Segraves house is still standing at the same location — a two story white house that appears to be well cared for and lived in.

Religion

After my mother died, my father realized his responsibility of raising three young children, gathered us around before bedtime at night, would read the Bible and we'd all kneel at our chairs and he'd pray for our new family — wisdom or guidance for himself and blessings for us. It was quite a task for my fourteen year old sister, Mayme, to be faced with all the housework, cooking, laundry, gardening, taking care of a seven year old and the many, many chores of a farm housewife.

When I was growing up, there were only two religious denominations in our community: Baptists and Methodists. Nearest to our home, both groups met in buildings used both for elementary school and church, and both groups attended church services, Sunday School and revivals interchangeably. Most Baptist ministers in rural areas pastored four churches and would come to our church one Saturday each month, hold a business meeting and sermon Saturday morning from 10:30 A.M. to noon, have dinner (midday meal) with a parishioner family. If he lived some distance away (four or five miles or further), he would spend the night with a family church member and have Sunday dinner with another family. All services were held in daytime since the buildings were not lighted for nighttime activities. Later, some churches gradually began to get some types of lamps that were placed on little shelves on each side of the sanctuary, beginning with kerosene lamps, and later another type of lamp with a fragile filament that was not too dependable. If either of these lights failed during services, people would get their lanterns hanging on nails in the back of the church, brought to light the way home, light them and set them around, hoping the lamp oil would last until they walked home. Attendance was better on Saturday night since men could not always leave pressing farm work in day time.

Religion was extremely important to our people, especially Baptists, who were adamant in their belief of religious freedom. They selected their pastors, and church officers, and all church business was mandated by voted approval of the majority of church membership. Our particular branch of Baptists was known as Missionary Baptist, according to Jesus' command, "Go ye into all the world and preach the gospel to every creature"(Mark 16:15). Then there was the

72

"Old" or Primitive Baptist denomination, which I am told holds to "predesti-nation," and also the Union Baptists, who (and once again, this is only what I've been told) had opposed the separation of states during the Civil War.

Methodists in upper Grassy Creek met in the two room school and church building. There was and still is a Methodist church in lower Grassy Creek where residents attended services, funerals and special events when weather, roads and distance permitted. This church building has walls and ceiling of tongue and groove wood with beautiful stained glass windows bestowed by family members in honor of deceased relatives.

Church attendance was the social event in the area. It was at church that everyone had the chance to meet friends and acquaintances not often seen other-wise, to catch up on what was going on in their families, in their immediate com-munity and church, see what everyone was wearing. Even teenagers and young people looked forward to church gatherings as this was the perfect opportunity for an additional date other than Saturday night and for others who hoped a young man might ask to walk them home.

My earliest memory of church was in a little building at Long Branch as it was called then, but now is call Brookgreen. The tiny building, which is now falling down, was used as a Baptist church and an elementary school, but has been replaced with a brick building. We walked a distance of a mile and a half or more for Sunday School each week and for preaching when the pastor came. When there was to be preaching, my mother always had in her "satchel" (pocket-book) a "sweet cake" (sugar cookie) or a slice of lemon flavored pound cake for me, as the service was apt to be long. Any visiting preacher in the congregation was asked if he'd like to say a word, and any or all took advantage of the oppor-tunity to speak and sometimes, it seemed to me, to preach a sermon.

I recall a communion service in this little church. Following the example of Jesus with his apostles at the Last Supper, the congregation observed foot washing. Wash basins, water and towels were brought. The ladies sat on the left side of the center aisle while the men sat on the right. The very front pew on each side was kept for altar calls or "the mourners' bench" or for visiting min-isters, but was also used for the foot washing ceremony. When the minister had read the appropriate Bible section, he asked that those who felt worthy to par-ticipate in the Lord's Supper come and sit on the front pews. Of course, each pew would accommodate only five or six people at one time. A deacon would get the basin, water and towel and wash the feet of the first person sitting at the end of the pew. A lady did the same on the ladies' side. Then those two people washed the feet of the next person. As each member had completed his or her duty they went to their seat to make room for others to go forward. When this ceremony was completed, little squares of unleavened bread (baked by a lady in the community) were passed, followed by a glass of wine or grape juice, each person taking a sip from the same glass. Incidentally, gender-segregation applied here too.

As my grandfather got older and the roads no better he wanted a Baptist church nearer to where he lived. Land was either donated or bought from Mr. John Waddell at the top of Sheets' Hill, a building erected and named "the Gap." I suppose the materials were purchased by contributions of the members and people who wanted to help. Sometimes a strong church would help financially for new churches. The work was done by church members and anyone who offered.

The outside of the building was weather boards and the inside tongue and groove. The church had a center aisle, and was heated with a wood burning stove in the center of the sanctuary. The pews were made by the men in the community — the longest ones at the front and back and shortest ones near the stove, allowing heat from the stove to be better distributed. Aside from that, the occupants could see better. There must have been a master carpenter who did the planning and made the lectern for the raised pulpit. Over the front door facing the road there was a glass transom. Grandpa Barker purchased the bell which was housed in a belfry and rung by a rope which extended from the belfry to a spot just inside the front door. My father was elected to be the sexton whose job was to ring the bell to let people know that services were to be held that day and later to inform those standing around in the yard and visiting, that services were now beginning.

One Sunday the minister stopped preaching in mid-sentence and the congregation looked at him — perplexed and so silent one could hear a pin drop. A couple of minutes later he finished his sermon. After church he told my father that through the glass transom he saw a man floating through the air! As he then looked through the window in the direction the man was moving, he saw a man on top of a wagon load of hay passing the church!

Sometimes people were dismissed from church membership — for drinking, "cussing," stealing, working on Sunday, infidelity and carousing. Dancing and playing cards were frowned on. As late as 1926 or '27, I was teaching in West Jefferson, and a new couple in town had a dance to which some teachers were invited. Very shortly the local school board sent a form to all the teachers to sign a pledge that we would not attend dances. People in our area were, for the most part, kind, helpful and empathetic, and thoughtful of those in dire need (if the person worked and tried). At times a wagon would come by collecting for a family whose house had burned or had had some disaster, it mattered not if one did not know the party, people gave quilts, household items, vegetables, corn, food, and clothing or some money.

But there existed grudges — sometimes forgiven and sometimes not. Line fences and family inheritances seemed to be the main reasons for grudges. In one church two brothers had a "falling out" over their line fence. They attended the same church, would shake hands with everyone except each other.

Ladies were not to wear short hair, as the Bible stated that long hair was a "glory" to a woman (I Corinthians, chapter 11). I had heard this over and over from my grandmother and two aunts and at church. Aunt Minnie, one of the aunts, married and moved to Colorado. She and Uncle George came back to visit and Aunt Minnie had had her hair "bobbed." Then it was all right for ladies to have short hair and the other aunt had Uncle George cut her hair. My hair was never ever cut until after I was teaching. I was attending summer session at Appalachian Teachers' College and wrote to ask my father if I might have my hair "bobbed." Before I received an answer, I went to the barber shop and had my hair cut. Then a letter came from Dad in which he said, "No. Absolutely not." The damage was done and I asked my boyfriend to take me home and stay the weekend, thinking I might not be severely reprimanded. And I was not! We ladies in West Jefferson at that time went to the only barber shop in town to get our hair cut or trimmed. This shop was owned and operated by Mr. Bracket Grayson and his brother-in-law, Mr. Perkins.

After our church, the Gap, was ready to be occupied and there were new members who had not been baptized, Grandpa would build a pond in the little stream in his barn lot several days before the baptizing date so the water would have time to be nice and clear and deep enough for the rite. When I joined the church, I was baptized in Grandpa's pond.

In the 20's and 30's word would make the rounds that a minister "from afar," along with a song leader were coming to hold a "protracted" camp meeting in a central area. Farmers tried to get pressing farm work to a stage where it could be left pretty much alone for a week or so, and wives and children hurriedly gathered, canned and preserved garden stuff and fruits and berries, and hoed the garden to be ready for the camp meeting. Friends and neighbors came considerable distances by horseback, by buggy, wagon or on foot. Sometimes these meetings went on for ten days or two weeks — singing, sermons in the mornings, prayer meetings in the afternoons and gathering together again at night. These meetings provided fellowship, and entertainment as well as spirituality.

Baptist churches held associational meetings once a year, usually in August, when each church sent three or four delegates to represent their church. Ministers from each church and interested lay members would attend. At the close of the meeting, a church would volunteer or one would be urged to have the "'Sosation" next year. These gatherings lasted three days, in day time because of lighting, and with the same church because of travel. Delegates and visitors who traveled several miles stayed in homes in the host parish. Weeks before the designated date, feverish activity was at a high pitch. Houses must be completely cleaned, lists of needed food made, recipes exchanged, butchering decided on, bed linens, table cloths and towels laundered, baking, preserving and pickling done. In the meantime, men were selecting beefs and sheep to be butchered and deciding how much they might sell to those who didn't have animals to kill, getting together framework and boards for the long tables to set up outside for dinners-on-the-grounds.

Gap Baptist Church had closed, but the Grassy Creek Baptist Church was completed and opened for services in 1927 and our family became members of that church. Two years later, in 1929, this church hosted the annual session of the Ashe Baptist Association for three days with members, delegates, ministers and visitors over night and providing lunch on the grounds on August 30, 31 and September 1.

Of course, big preparations had to be made and lots of food provided for this three day event.

My father planned to butcher a beef. If we did not need all of it for the association event, there would be no problem selling some to other families. Butchering, if done properly, required the services of an experienced butcher. A black man who lived down the Grassy Creek way toward New River was known to be a good butcher. Dad put my nine-year-old brother, Joe, on a horse, gave him questionable directions to see if Mr. Taylor (if that was his name) would come and butcher a beef. Mr. Taylor came on the designated day and good humoredly told my father that Joe rode up to the house and very politely asked, "Are you Mr. Taylor?"

Mr. Taylor answered, "Yes, I am."

Joe asked, "Are you the nigger that butchers beefs?"

In the meantime, for this event or any other special occasion, rivalry among housewives ran high for the most variety, the most attractive and the most delectable foods for the long tables which would be loaded with platters piled high with fried chicken, home-cured ham, roast beef, mutton, and vegetables — green beans, creamed corn and fresh garden peas, cole slaw and chow-chow. A section for pickles galore — beet pickles, crisp cucumber and dills, pickled peach and pear in half gallon glass jars and home baked "light bread," rolls and biscuits, along with desserts. Pies of apple, peach, egg custard, chocolate, coconut with meringue along with highly decorated cakes of three or four layers with various frostings — seven minute white frosting, brown sugar seafoam, coconut, swirled chocolate and many layered molasses stack cakes with spiced, cooked dried apple filling between the layers.

Today these gatherings use catered meats, chicken and fish along with potatoes, and slaw from fast food providers. Families may bring salads, pies, cakes and Jell-O desserts. Today's associational meetings are divided between two churches and people come and go in fast automobiles, eliminating the hosting of overnight representatives. There are still the loaded tables with wives' special delicious foods and desserts.

One summer day, a wagon stopped at Grandpa's and someone came to the house to say that the driver was ill and could they stop long enough for him to have some cold water and rest a bit. Of course they could. This was a Reverend Banks, his wife and three children who had come from some place in Tennessee. It turned out that the father was quite sick. He was put to bed at Grandfather's and his wife and two boys were to stay there and Eunice, the daughter, who was about my age, was to stay at our home. I don't remember where this family was headed but the father was not able to resume travel for some time. Meanwhile it was determined that this family needed a place to live. Of course, Grandpa always thought that ministers were needed in the community and that they were to be cared for. It was found that there was an empty house in the Sussex community and it was made available to this family. They had with them only a few household items so word was spread around that there would be a pounding held for the Banks family on a certain date. The area well knew what a pounding was since many pastors were paid very little or no salaries but "poundings" were given for them. I suppose that the term "poundings" was because sugar, flour, salt and many store items were sold by the pound. Any other household items that families could spare were given — such as quilts, towels, linens, food stuffs, kitchen items and tools and clothing.

I knew a minister who pastored a country church about 10 miles from his home, and he mentioned to a deacon in the church that he had noticed that that particular church was not on record as having given anything to missions. The deacon, who was well fixed financially, said the church could not afford to spend for missions. The minister then asked if it would be all right if he gave his salary for one month to missions so the church would get credit for the contribution. That was all right with the deacon. Then the records showed that that church gave $1.25 toward missions. I knew the minister well and he passed away only a year or so ago (1993).

As to the generosity of our people, they worked hard and had respect for others who worked hard, but were not so generous with those who did not appear to show effort to take care of their family or themselves.

The oft told story went the rounds of the man who was too lazy to work and about to starve. People got tired of his begging or stealing and told him if he didn't work they were going to bury him alive. Two neighbors put him in a wagon and were on the way to the cemetery. Another neighbor asked what they were doing and when they told him, he said, "Isn't that a bit too harsh? I'll give him a bushel of corn." The lazy man raised up in the wagon and asked, "Is it shelled?" The neighbor answered, "No." The lazy man said, "Drive on."

In 1918 when World War I was going badly for our allies, President Wilson called for a national day of prayer for the peaceful end of the war. He named a day for this event — to be observed by all Americans, regardless of location or work. I think the day may have been a Wednesday — not Saturday or Sunday which today would be considered handy and maybe result in a long weekend. And I believe it was in either July or August and at eleven o'clock. My father and brother were working in the fields but came in with sweaty bodies and shirts, took a quick "wash up," put on clean shirts and shoes, and we all, elders and young went to our church, the Gap, at eleven o'clock for prayer.

At the eleventh hour of the eleventh day of the eleventh month the war came to an end. Power in prayer? Who can doubt it?

For ever so many years thereafter, this event was celebrated on the eleventh of November and was known as Armistice Day. When I was teaching at the West Jefferson Consolidated School, the principal, Professor Nye, called the entire school to the auditorium at eleven o'clock, November 11, to give thanks for the ending of the war and to honor the dead, wounded and living men and women who participated in that war. Mr. Bower Duncan, a high school teacher in that school, told the assembly of his experience of Armistice Day. He was on an allied front line that day. They knew something important was in the air but the soldiers reported to their stations as usual. At eleven o'clock all firing was stopped and the German soldiers began marching to a designated spot and laying down their guns. He said they mingled some, smiled, some shook hands and spoke. That night there was a huge bonfire as ammunition and certain war supplies were set on fire.

The Gap Church had been closed for religious services. Uncle Iredell had started to tear down the building. One very hot day he was working on the roof, evidently the part to be removed first. He came home for lunch and was stricken with a massive stroke. He was in a coma for twenty-seven days, I believe. At that time people thought a stroke was inevitably crippling at best, and that the only hope even for survival was what a doctor might prescribe. Exercise or physical therapy was not considered it seems. I suppose that Dr. Osborne, Uncle Iredell's father-in-law felt he had done all he could do and suggested that they might call another physician. They called Dr. Ray in West Jefferson, but evidently the diagnosis was the same, I don't really know.

Uncle Iredell told me that all at once he woke up and it seemed as if he had just awakened from a night's sleep. He got better, and although he had quite a limp and used a cane, lived many years thereafter.

Some folks thought that this was God's punishment for starting to tear down the church!

The Kirk family had sorghum cane and frost was expected on Sunday night. Mrs. Kirk insisted that the cane must be stripped, cut and gotten in, although it was Sunday. A short time later she died suddenly. Again, some said it was God's punishment for working on Sunday.

Sunday School

My first memory of Sunday School was in a class for youngsters six years old and younger. Each Sunday we tots had a card with a picture of a Biblical character or event on the front and the "memory verse" underneath. A short story and questions were on the other side. The memory verse was to be memorized and my mother or older sister made sure I could recite it before the next Sunday. Then we received a new card.

While the Gap was being used by the Baptist Church for Sunday School, one Sunday each summer was set aside for "Children's Day," when the young people from kindergarten age to teenage, put on a program, planned by the Sunday School superintendent and teachers. Classes sang newly learned songs, recited poems and Bible stories, and were quizzed on Bible lessons. Prizes were given for perfect attendance the past year and achievements. Parents were proud of their offspring who performed well. Often, visitors from other churches and communities attended and sometimes parents provided "dinner on the grounds," and made a full day of the event. Uncle Iredell was superintendent for a few years and was usually the song leader in the church as he knew the notes, pitch and timing and taught new songs. At one of the Children's Day programs he had taught me the song, *Love Lifted Me,* and he and I sang it as a duet.

When the new Baptist church was completed at lower Grassy Creek in 1927 and since attendance had fallen off at the Gap, that building was abandoned for a few years but was later used by the Lutheran denomination for a while.

Revivals

Each church held at least one and sometimes two revivals a year, which were well attended, especially those held at night. Revivals were for the purpose of saving sinners and the rededication of back-sliders. Christians and family members hoped that unsaved relatives, close friends and neighbors would escape eternal damnation, which was widely stressed by ministers at that time. Then, too, there were those who would get drunk, "cuss," gamble, neglect the family, hold grudges against neighbors and relatives, and sometimes disrupt church services and the quiet of the neighborhood and these sinners should be saved not only for their own good but for the peace of the community. After the sermon by the minister, an altar call was made. Some might respond to the invitation at once and go to the "mourners' bench." Then family members, church members and the minister would go to those who did not respond and urge them to go to the altar. At the altar, very often there would be loud sobbing and weeping — thus the name "mourners' bench." When someone became saved, he/she might shout and praise God! Too, at the same time or after an especially powerful sermon, there would be shouting Christians. I recall seeing Aunt Sarah Ann going up and down the aisles as if on air, clapping her hands and praising God and her little son holding on to the back of her skirt and following right with her.

My father told me of the time when a revival or church service was going on, all at once the front door opened and a drunk wandered in and started up the aisle staggering and mumbling loudly. When he had passed where my grandfather, John Spencer, was sitting, Grandfather Spencer got up from his seat and although he walked with a limp, he stepped up behind the drunk and took a tight hold on the back of the man's shirt collar. The man said, "Who's hold of me?" Grandpa responded, "A man, Sir!" With that another man got up from his seat and the two escorted the drunk to the door and tossed him out into the yard.

One time some church leaders and laymen in West Jefferson evidently got together and decided they should hold a nondenominational revival. They had heard of an evangelist who was highly regarded in holding great revivals. He was contacted and agreed to come. A large tent with chairs was set up on a spot between the car wash (of recent years) and the cheese factory. The minister and a song leader came. Services were held at 11 A.M. and at about eight o'clock in the evening after people had gotten off from work, had dinner and prepared for the services. The minister urged the people to pray for the revival. A group of men, church leaders, town leaders and business leaders organized a time to get together in the afternoons for prayer. So did the ladies and small groups who lived near each other. In one small group of ladies, each lady would pray about some particular person or need. A young girl in the group, about fourteen or fifteen years of age, prayed, "Lord, bless the people in Glendale Springs. You just don't know how mean they are."

I recall two Methodist ministers, the Rev. Vestal and the Rev. Blankenship, who held revivals at Upper Grassy Creek. Reverend Vestal held services in the morning at eleven o'clock, since the church had no lighting for night meetings. I do not know the year but it was while my mother was still living and she, my sister and I attended and so did my father and other men when they could get away from pressing farm work. The Rev. Blankenship came later and held night meetings.

When Preacher Vestal held a revival in the Upper Grassy Creek Methodist Church around 1910 or '11, he brought a harp to use with congregational singing and with his solos. One of the solos I remember was *The Wayfaring Stranger*. I can't be sure of all the verses the Rev. Vestal used, but recall some of it. In my research I found that there have been various words and arrangements since the first introduction of this song around 1800 when tremendous religious revivals broke out in Kentucky, Tennessee and the Carolinas. This period resulted in a number of folk hymns of personal religious experiences. A century later folk singers began to revive interest in some of the old hymns. The sad and personal quality of *The Wayfaring Stranger* began to be popular with folk musicians, especially after Burl Ives adopted it for his American native music for his radio show. Although only about four years old when I heard this song, I think the words, "I'm going there to meet my mother" and finally "my Savior," made a lasting impression on me.

The version used by Burl Ives differs somewhat from the one I've heard by Doc Watson and the one generously given me by David VanHoy along with some history accompanying each of the published songs, but the meaning is the same.

The Wayfaring Stranger

> I'm just a poor wayfaring stranger
> Traveling through this world of woe,
> And there's no sickness, no toil, no trouble
> In that fair land to which I go.
> I'm going there to see my mother,
> She said she'd meet me when I come:
> I'm just a-going over Jordan,
> I'm just a-going over home.

Our Baptist minister held a revival in this same little church. After my mother died, my father married a neighbor girl. They eloped and her father was very put out with them and the families stopped associating with each other for a few years. Some very petty and ugly incidents occurred like yelling taunting remarks when passing or when they could be heard. In this particular revival, one of the boys from my stepmother's family went to the altar several times and cried and sobbed. The minister asked my father to go to the altar and talk to the young man. The young man apologized to my father and asked to be forgiven and made a profession. The following day, the minister and Dad went to the home, talked to the parents, had a short service and friendship was restored.

In the late '20s or early '30s, a local Baptist minister was taken to the Baptist Hospital in Winston-Salem for surgery, perhaps for an appendectomy. This was probably the first time he had ever been out of Ashe County. All the Baptist churches in the Ashe Baptist Association knew of the Baptist hospital as all Baptist churches in North Carolina were expected to support this hospital financially as best they could. Ladies from surrounding Baptist churches visited patients in the hospital, carried flowers, and inquired of patient needs. One group of ladies gave this minister a pair of pajamas. After the minister was home and able to attend church, he wanted to tell the church of his impression of the Baptist Hospital. He told his fellow church members, "The hospital is wonderful. Everybody was so good to me. They fed me good, they waited on me and it's just a great hospital. And look at this summer suit I'm wearing. Some Baptist ladies gave it to me."

People attended different churches and were always welcomed and of course, a different denomination did not hinder intermingling. For after all, weren't we all headed for the same place? Mrs. Arnold, a shouting Christian lady, said, "If there are fences in heaven, I'll jump over them."

Some of the churches frequently visited were: Pleasant Home, New River, Healing Springs, Corinth, Landmark, Little Helton, Greenwood, Grassy Creek Baptist and Grassy Creek Methodist. (Greenwood was an ME Church.)

Local preachers I knew: the Rev. Oscar Spencer, Jesse Shumate, Estil Eller, Banks, Cousin Franklin Barker, David Blackburn, Henry Gaultney, Coy Blackburn, Carroll Burkett, Jeter Blevins, Edgar Denny.

I believe that none of these ministers attended Seminary, but felt the call to preach. They were examined by deacons of their church and it seemed that other ordained ministers took part in testimony given by the applicant and decided whether he should be ordained and then he was presented as an ordained minister.

We heard of a church denomination called Pentecostal. Some called them Holy Rollers. It was said that sometimes members were so imbued with the Holy Ghost that they would lie on the floor and "roll around." I have a feeling that these people were demonstrating such humility that not only "every knee shall bow" (Romans 14:11), but they prostrated the entire body.

Schools

My First School

There was no compulsory school attendance law, but it was generally known that children could start school at age six. Some of our neighbors did not enter Johnny or Susie in school when he/she reached his sixth birthday. They said the child was too little or too young to be on his own and face walking to school, or was not very well and might catch some disease at school. But when I was six years old, in 1913, I started to school in the Upper Grassy Creek Elementary School, a two teacher school. My teacher was Miss Fanny Godsey who taught the first three grades. The teaching principal taught the other four grades. A center aisle ran from the front of the building to the stage at the back. This stage served as the pulpit for the ministers, and also as the principal's "office." Halfway down the aisle was a door, in a wooden partition wall which split the building laterally into two halves. In the front hall, on both sides of the aisle, sat grades 1–3. This was the "Little Room." In the back half, where the stage was, sat grades 4–7. This was the "Big Room." A flat-topped, wood-burning cast-iron stove was centered in the aisle, in each of the two rooms.

The partition wall, on both sides of the aisle, had an interesting feature. This was a section of 6- or 8-inch wide boards, about 30 inches above the floor, and painted black, hinged at the bottom and held in place at the top by wood buttons. These were, indeed, the "blackboards" for grades 1–3. Whenever a school or church program was held on the stage, these "blackboards" were let down so everyone in the building could see what was going on. A similar blackboard was found in the "Big Room," but this one had no hinges or buttons, of course, as they were not needed. This "Big Room" blackboard occupied the entire back wall behind the stage.

The desks had been made by parents but patterned after the manufactured ones, with a shelf under the top to hold books, tablets, slates and other student articles. The desks were not painted or varnished. The tops had a slot to hold ink pens or pencils and a hole for ink wells. Some of the tops bore carvings by pocket knives of initials or just plain cuts by past years' students. There were a few little, single desks for the smallest students but most were double desks to be occupied by two students.

In my first year, there was a boy, taller and larger than anyone else, who could not seem to stay in his seat or do any school work. After many reminders, the exasperated teacher finally said to him, "Why can't you stay in your seat and be as quiet as that little girl?" and pointed to me. I was so pleased at being pointed out as being quiet, that I then tried not to move a muscle or even get a long breath until my muscles ached.

Each room had a water pail and dipper. Water was carried from a little spring on Mr. David Spencer's place which adjoined the school lot. The spring was just a hole dug out where water bubbled out of the ground. (Incidentally, that spring water is still bubbling up — 1997, but it's not used as a spring anymore but is simply a damp place covered over with turf.) Sometimes this spring would get very low in a dry spell or get too low to

My first school in a wooded area on the hill. The Upper Grassy Creek Elementary School and the Methodist church shared this building.

be dipped out. Then Mr. Spencer would let us get water from the cemented spring at his spring house as long as the carriers did not throw water around, mess up the surroundings and leave the cover off the spring. Only the most dependable boys or big girls were allowed to go to Mr. Spencer's spring. Of course the teachers told us never to drink from the dipper but bring a cup from home and use the dipper only to pour water into our cups. When I was too little to be trusted with a glass, I had a pint size tin cup for milk and water. Miss Godsey told my sister and her teacher that I said, "I can't bring my cup. My sister put it in the old sour buttermilk crock." We were to keep our water cups turned upside down in our desks. Later there were tin or aluminum folding cups.

There were two outside johns or toilets — one for the girls behind the building next to Mr. Spencer's fence. The one for the boys was on the other side of the building near the edge of the school ground. Catalogs and newspapers were brought from home to use in the johns.

Mr. David Spencer had a little store at the side of the road near the entrance to the school lot. He carried tablets, cedar pencils (called cedar since not only made of but the color of cedar), with a tiny eraser that never lasted as long as the pencil did. The cedar pencils cost a penny each and were not the pretty colors of pencils of today. My father would take my first pencils, cut them in half, and cut a little groove to hold a string to be worn around my neck to prevent losing my pencil. I always hated to see my pencil cut in half while my sister and brother had whole ones, but they needed them more than I did.

Sometimes we had slates and a marker for writing on the slates. A cloth might be brought from home to use to erase the slates, but it was not unusual to see someone spit on his slate and use the arm or sleeve to erase the writing.

My second year in school, attendance had fallen off and there was only one room and teacher for all seven grades. A consolidated school had opened in 1913 at lower Grassy Creek—the Virginia-Carolina High School and Elementary School and a number of elementary students enrolled there accompanied by older brothers and sisters. My brother, sister and I remained in the one room school until we completed seventh grade.

In our classroom, there were two long benches—one on each side of the aisle—used as each class was called up to recite or respond to each assignment. When church services were held, ministers sat on these benches up front, but when revivals were going on, these benches were called "mourners' benches."

Of course, there was no lunch room. We carried lunches of biscuits with apple butter, jelly, eggs, ham or streaked meat (bacon) and molasses sweet cakes (molasses cookies. We never heard them called cookies) carried in a basket or bucket—enough for the three of us. Sometimes we might have three slices of apple or some kind of pie. I remember the children of one family that once or twice brought "crumbly" (corn bread broken up in milk in a tin syrup bucket with lid). They had brought spoons and gathered around the pail and ate their crumbly. Perhaps the family may have been out of flour for biscuits or some food to go in biscuits. And, who knows? Crumbly may have been the very favorite food of these children. Many nights we had only corn bread and milk for supper and I still like corn bread in milk with salt and pepper and maybe a bit of chopped onion! When Mrs. Mattie Spencer was our teacher, she'd rake a few coals from the heating stove out on the front apron of the stove, put her ham or meat on the coals and back in the biscuits to have a hot sandwich.

We had an hour break for lunch and when the weather was good, we'd hurriedly eat our lunches so we could go outside and play. The boys had their own games they liked—some kind of ball, marbles, pitch pennies, mumbly peg, use pop guns or sling shots or go into the wooded area and play hide and seek among the trees. Girls played jump rope, chanting ditties such as *Old Dan Tucker*:

My class when I was in third grade. *Row 1 (left to right):* John Roberts, Tom Spencer, Presley McGrady, Clara Reedy, Celia Eller, Fanny Halsey, Ala Reedy, Cessie Reedy, Ruth Reedy, Ollie Osborne. *Row 2:* ----, Delila Spencer, Maude Reedy, Jessie Davis, Joe Spencer, Burl Osborne, ----, Gee Spencer, ----. *Row 3:* Mildred Spencer, Zetta Barker, Lessie Halsey, Mattie Osborne, Vernett Spencer, Branson Spencer, ----, Monroe Osborne, Gilbert Spencer, Willie Eller. *Row 4:* ----, Elmer Eller, Herbert Barker, Kate Spencer, Mayme Barker, Wayne Reedy, Deedie Anderson, Etta Eller, Dent Reedy, Alice Spencer, Teacher.

> Old Dan Tucker was a fine old man,
> Washed his face in the frying pan,
> Combed his hair with a wagon wheel
> And died of a toothache in his heel.

We girls sometimes made playhouses with walls or rhododendron (we called it laurel) which grew in abundance in the wooded area around the school, and gathered moss for doll beds and furniture, played funerals with the dead person covered with the many fallen leaves except for the face, and the others viewing the body and weeping loudly as people did at funerals. Often boys and girls played together, London bridge, hide and seek, drop the handkerchief, blind man's bluff and other ring games. When the weather was too inclement to go outside, we'd sit around the stove and sing: *The Lone Cowboy, Red Wing, Rosewood Casket, Bury Me Not on the Lone Prairie, Cripple Creek* and other songs. The boys didn't join in the singing much. It never seemed too cold for them to go outside.

The soldier that I corresponded with during World War I. I do not recall his name but his home was in Zanesville, Ohio.

World War I began and, it seemed, every man, woman and child was affected by the war as we knew several young men in our area and surrounding areas who had been drafted and it seemed that everyone had a cousin, uncle or friend in the service. Our teacher found out, I suppose from newspapers, the names of service men who needed to have someone send them letters. She gave each student who wanted to participate in the project the name and address of a soldier or sailor who needed a pen pal. Although I was only about eleven years old I drew the name of a soldier from Ohio. I cannot remember his name and we wrote to each other for the remainder of the war. He sent me his picture and must have been stationed in a warm country, when the picture was made. We were very patriotic and learned and sang war songs such as: *Tenting on the Camp Ground, Just Before the Battle, Mother, Tramp, Tramp, Tramp,* and *America (My Country, 'Tis of Thee).* Many of the songs were of the Civil War period but seemed to be appropriate at the time. Another song, *K-K-K Katy, Beautiful Katy, I'll Be Waiting at the K-K-K Kitchen Door,* was learned and sung.

In addition to desks and recitation benches, there was on one end of the stage a piece of furniture, a secretary, which someone had donated. It was on legs to accommodate the user's legs underneath. A wood door when raised revealed cubicles for holding inks, paper clips, pencils, stamps and other writing articles. Above the desk part were two glass doors in front of three shelves for books. This was our library. There were probably twenty books donated by school patrons or those who wanted to get rid of a few books. We might be allowed to check out a book for a bit during the school day if we had completed all our assignments, but we were supposed to be studying or doing expected work during the school hours. On Friday afternoons, we could check out a book to carry home for the weekend. Upper graders had first choice in selecting a book and on down through the grades. I had to wait for weeks, it seemed, before I had a chance to get the book I most wanted — *The Mother Goose Book,* a book I've always enjoyed and still own and enjoy.

I don't recall how or when I learned to read. Perhaps watching and looking on as my sister and brother read their lessons at night. Before I was old enough to start school, Mrs. Jincy Spencer, who was teaching in the one room school at Long Branch, would come by on horseback and I would go to the road, climb up on the fence to wait for her to ride by, as she always stopped to talk to me. One day she brought a "brand new book," a large ABC book for me. Letters of the alphabet were in large size with a picture beginning with the letter as "A is for apple." We had very few books in our home then other than discarded or used text books and the Bible.

Dad had kept a copy of *The Blue Backed Speller*. When I spent a day or night at Grandpa's, Uncle Luther would be reading the Bible and he'd read a verse and have me read the next one, helping me with words I didn't know. Our six month school ended in February and on days when weather kept us indoors, I'd wrap up and run to Grandpa's to borrow *American Heroes*, *Robinson Crusoe* and *Aesop's Fables* to read again and again.

When all is said and done, the one room schools were not bad at all. In fact, some of the much larger elite systems in the 1960s and '70s began what was called the Open School in which students were allowed to "progress at their own rate." We were allowed to do the same. When I was in fourth grade I was allowed to spell with a higher grade. Some of us might go ahead in arithmetic or reading, complete his/her book and move into another grade in that subject. As we listened to other classes in their subjects, we better understood what to expect when we moved into that grade. When I moved to high school where there was a teacher for each subject, I was never aware that I lagged behind my classmates in any subject.

I enjoyed geography. When we had completed a large part of the study of a group of states such as the New England states, there were map studies for that group to learn the names and location of the state capitals, other large cities, mountains, rivers and lakes. We drew maps of each group, thus learning the shape of a state and relation to adjoining states. We parsed sentences, learned parts of speech, memorized multiplication facts, learned how to do square and cube roots and did compound interest of loans (which took up the larger part of the chalk board).

Each class from fourth grade through seventh lined up at the front of the room for spelling each day. The first day of spelling, we randomly fell in line but after that we knew exactly where we belonged in the line unless we had been absent. When someone misspelled a word, it was passed to the next one in line and if that person spelled the word correctly, that person moved past the one who had missed the word. Sometimes several people might not spell the word right. When a person reached the head of the line, that person received a "head mark," kept daily by the teacher. The next day that person went to the foot of the line and started over again. Headmarks were recorded by the teacher the entire school session and the one in each grade with the most headmarks the whole session received a prize from the teacher.

Our books were bought if we did not inherit books from an older sibling, and we tried to buy books from last years' students if they were in good condition, and sell our old ones. But at times we had to buy new books. The teacher would make a list of books needed and collect the money. My father would go by the school, get the list and money and go to Volney on horseback with saddle pockets (and sometimes a sack) to pick up new books from Mr. Fields Young, Sr., who carried new books and school supplies in the little buildings that are still there.

Wood for heating was furnished by parents who had wood. Usually one parent would haul sled loads of wood to use for a month or a specified time. Some families did not have a wooded area or there would be a widow with children in school who was not expected to furnish wood. In some old records of my father's, I found that one year, he supplied wood for the entire six months and was paid $2.50 a month. Teachers or older boys built the fires and when there was only green or soggy wood, a couple of boys would be sent to pick up dry tree branches, chips, or anything dry to get the fire going.

I do not recall ever seeing a teacher use switches for punishment. In earlier times it seems that there was always a bundle of switches in a designated spot near the teacher's desk. Punishment in our elementary school was usually staying in at recess or after school, standing in the corner on the stage, doing extra work such as writing the student's name or "I won't throw paper wads" fifty times or more.

A friend, who had lived in England, told me of being caned — really caned — with a cane rather than a switch or belt. Our father always told us if we were punished in school, we'd also be punished at home.

Punishment was usually for fighting, talking back to the teacher, using bad language, throwing paper wads, being out of one's seat, stealing, disturbing while a class was going on. Sometimes the teacher would draw a circle on the chalkboard and have the culprit stand with the nose pressed in the circle. Mr. Theodore Spencer had Ollie standing at the blackboard for something and she fainted. Mr. Spencer was very upset and sent a boy running to notify the parents while other boys carried an unused door from the little room (the room no longer used for classes) to outside in the yard and Mr. Spencer carried Ollie and placed her on the door so she would have plenty of air. Her father came on horseback and did not seem too upset as he said, "Ollie has a record of fainting." He put her on the horse with him and took her home.

I don't know when the practice of "treating" (giving students candy, oranges, nuts or something at Christmas time) began, but Dad said when he was in school the students would try to get a promise from the teacher that he/she would "treat" them at Christmas. The teachers were reluctant to let it be known whether they planned to give treats or not. One time their teacher would not tell the students what his plan was. Every day after lunch, this teacher would stretch out on the long recitation bench at the front of the classroom and take a nap while the students were using the rest of the hour long lunch period at play. One day the boys gathered a bunch of long pliable willow branches, slipped inside and quickly tied him tightly to the bench so he could not get loose until he promised the treat.

My elementary teachers always gave treats — usually candy, sometimes peppermint or lemon sticks, mixed candy drops, nuts or oranges. When I became a teacher I, and I think other teachers, too, gave "treats" but at times it might be a box of pencils, crayons or a little note pad. But when we reached high school, we were "too grown up" to expect treats!

In the seven years in this elementary school the teachers were: Miss Fanny Godsey, Misses Alice and Virginia Spencer, Mr. Theodore Spencer, Mrs. Mattie Kirk Spencer, and Miss Fannie Rutherford.

Misses Alice and Virginia Spencer and Mr. Theodore Spencer were sisters and brother. I doubt that either had attended Teachers' College when they began teaching but had been "examined" by the Superintendent of Schools or recommended by a person who had higher scholastic experience and was given a teaching certificate. Later these teachers would attend summer classes at Radford Teachers' College or summer educational meetings to renew and extend their teaching careers. For many years since, teacher hopefuls in this area have gotten their certificates and renewals from Radford College.

Some of the qualifications for teachers at that time were, they must have completed the school they had attended, were 18 years of age or older, were known to be sedate, to dress modestly and had to be respected in their community. I read somewhere that a man and his son were going along in a wagon when a horseback rider rode up beside the wagon and asked the driver to question him so he could be admitted to Appalachian College. The driver handed the reins to his son to drive while he examined the rider. This rider happened to be B. B. Dougherty, who later became president of Appalachian Teachers' College. Despite the above mentioned qualifications, some of these early teachers never finished high school. My Aunt Vesta taught a one teacher school one year and she had not completed high school. She never spoke of "teaching" but would say, "I kept school" at Long Branch.

Virginia-Carolina High School

As young people in this area completed elementary school, parents were deeply aware of the need for further education for their offspring. There were a few distantly scattered academies. Academy is defined as a group of people to promote learning in a particular field, and in early American life in many areas was a name for a school similar to high school. There seem to have been at least four or five schools in Ashe County called academies, at Helton, Grassy Creek, North Fork and Beaver Creek, Konnarock, Virginia, and perhaps a few more. But travel was so difficult due to poor roads that only those who could afford boarding or lived nearby could send their children to the academies.

Through the interest, planning and efforts of a number of citizens and the leadership of Professor Robert E. Lee Plummer, a consolidated school was built and opened in 1913 at Grassy Creek, N.C. (At that time Grassy Creek was the mailing address of residents in both North Carolina and Virginia who lived near the stream, Grassy Creek.) Mr. Greer Parsons of Ashe County, N.C., and Mr. Catlett Pugh of Grayson County, Virginia, donated land for the school to be known as Virginia-Carolina High School, although it accommodated students from first through eleventh grades. The finances for the support of the school were agreeably worked out by the two counties with Grayson County to be responsible for maintaining the elementary grades and Ashe County to maintain the high school.

Evidently, Professor Plummer served as principal of the school for five years after its opening, followed by Professor Floyd Crouse for two terms. Then Professor A. B. Hurt became principal for two years. The terms of 20-21 and 21-22 found Professor John Snapp in the principal's chair.

I don't have any record of graduates the first year of the school's opening but the following year, Miss Sue Mae Senter is listed as a graduate, followed the next year by two graduates, Eugene Duvall and Ophelia Plummer, Professor Plummer's daughter.

In February 1920 I completed seventh grade in the little six month elementary school and enrolled in the eighth grade in the fall at Virginia-Carolina High School. This meant walking the two miles each way on dusty rough roads when the weather was good, and muddy, rutty roads when the weather was rainy and snowy. We took short cuts when we could by walking through fields, crossing meandering streams looking for narrow spots where we could jump over or rocks to step on, to keep from getting wet in the creeks or branches. Farmers were generous in allowing us to walk through the fields rather than over muddy roads. Of course, this meant crossing fences, depending on the type of fences. Rail fences we might just climb on the rails on both sides. Some had rails we could lay down and crawl under. Wire fences, farmers would place a rail or board on each side of the fence from the ground at an angle to the top of a post to use for crossing. Overshoes were hardly known then and we often arrived at school with wet and muddy shoes. We'd look for a little stick, chip or weed to clean mud from our shoes before going in the building.

Professor A. B. Hurt was principal the year I entered high school and Misses Eloise Young, Myrtle Pugh and Lena Dickson received diplomas at the end of the year. Eloise and Myrtle became teachers in the same school after receiving teaching certificates from Radford Teachers' College later.

Enrollment in the school continued to grow and at the end of the 1921–22 term with Professor John Snapp as principal, ten students graduated.

The year I was in the sophomore class, our homeroom was in the office of Professor Snapp. Space was badly needed, and a "cloak room" had been built in the hall foyer outside the two high school classrooms, with hooks on which to hang wraps, overshoes (if one had any) and a shelf for lunch baskets and bags. Students began complaining that lunches were disappearing. Professor Snapp assigned some students to take turns watching the cloak room in the mornings. A boy was caught and sent home or expelled with a note to his mother. The following day while Mr. Snapp was in a history class in our room, the door flew open and the mother of the expelled student entered in a very defiant manner, ran over to the principal, pointing her finger in his face, proceeded to loudly bawl him out without giving him a chance to say anything. I remember seeing tears running down his face as he tried to keep the class going on. I felt so sorry for him. Relatives of the boy managed to alleviate the situation, the boy was allowed to return to school, but no more lunches disappeared.

Mr. Lee Anderson owned a farm on both sides of the road which we had to travel to school. Mr. Anderson had a big white-faced Hereford bull in a field bordering the road. As we passed the field the bull would often be near the road fence, bellowing and pawing the ground, sending chills up and down our spines until we were out of hearing. One morning when my six-year-old brother, Kyle, had started to school, we were walking through Mr. Anderson's meadow. Just as we were passing a haystack, there was the big bull lying on the ground. He had been moved to the opposite side of the road. I quickly snatched my brother by the hand and pulled him back behind the haystack. Keeping the haystack between the sight of the bull and us, we made a hurried exit to the muddy road.

There were no school lunch programs at that time and lunches were brought from home. When there were three, four or more family members in school, lunches would be carried in baskets and the students gathered around the baskets to eat their lunches. I always thought Lee Reeves' children seemed to have the most attractive lunches with a whole pie heaped high with whipped cream on top of the sandwiches in the basket. The mother and older girls in that family were excellent cooks. Vergie, my friend and classmate, often invited me to visit their home and her mother would make us delicious snacks.

We had an hour long lunch break at school and Mr. Gordon Sturgill had bought the Wagg General Store and we had heard that he had "all day suckers." We were allowed to go down to the store if we were back in our rooms when the one o'clock bell rang. The suckers were one cent each, in flavors of strawberry, grape, orange and mint. My special friends and classmates, Hattie, Vergie, Eva and I would hurriedly eat our lunches and on good weather days walk down to the store to buy suckers. After a while, rather than each one bringing a penny every day, we'd take turns at buying four. If we couldn't wheedle four pennies when it was our turn, we'd bring two or three eggs (depending on the price of eggs). Then we'd walk leisurely back up the hill, hoping the suckers would last but be finished at the right time.

In the school term of 1922 and '23, my class was in its junior year and Professor Plummer was back as principal. He had been in on the opening of the school, experienced the pride of students and community, and thought there was ample opportunity for future growth before he turned over the helm to other principals, but he had not been idle. Always in the forefront of projects to meet the needs of citizens and young people, he had been involved and working with

the Association of Accreditation of Colleges and High Schools. He found out what was required and how the requirements might be met.

In order for our school to be accredited, the infant home economics department had to be moved out of the basement and a new outbuilding constructed for that purpose. A library, with approved reading list, had to be built also, as did a gym and a repair shop. The agricultural department now had to have qualified instructors, and the classrooms had to be revamped in order to meet the new qualifications of space and teacher-pupil ratio.

Professor Plummer worked not only with the accrediting association, but with the state board of education, the state legislature, the school community and the local school board. There were finances and other problems to be solved. In 1922 Virginia-Carolina High School was accredited, the first in both Ashe County and Grayson County.

Now parents who hoped to send their children to college began to enroll them in this school which had met the qualifications of the Southern Association.

A building across from the school opened for boarding students, and families who had extra bedrooms also took in boarders. Soon students from Crumpler, Helton, Lansing, Warrensville, N.C., and from Independence, Va., and other places entered Virginia-Carolina High School. Some of the Helton students rode horseback in the coldest wintry months. Some boys did farm work for host farmers to help pay board. Teachers found places in some of the larger homes and another building just off the school yard was available to house a principal or teacher with a family. The rooms at each end of the stage were very useful for drama productions and one served as the music room. Miss Blossom Showalter, the music teacher, used one room during the day to teach piano and voice.

Enrollment continued to grow and my class graduated in 1924 with 22 members — nine of whom were boarding students. Professor Plummer deserves a lot of credit for bringing this country school to meet the requirements of the Southern Association.

Opposite: Virginia-Carolina High School in 1922 after accreditation by the Southern Association of Accreditation for Colleges and High Schools.

To meet the requirements for accreditation some buildings had to be erected. The white building on the extreme left housed the home economics department with health, study of foods and cooking done on the first floor. Sewing was taught on the second floor. The next building was the newly equipped library. The building on the lower right was the shop building where students were taught to repair motors, other implements, and use saws to make needed wood cabinets and other household articles. A cannery was housed in the basement where students and area residents could bring and can beans and the many other home grown fruits and vegetables. Mr. Matthew Reynolds headed the agricultural department. Each of the newly added departments were headed by duly certified teachers in their fields of teaching.

The Odd Fellows Lodge building on the upper right became a dormitory for boarding students or teachers. The other building was a teacherage for the principal or a teacher with a family who needed a place to live.

A gymnasium was added later.

Walter Weaver lived just a bit off the road that went by the school and had a horse barn that was not being used. As mentioned earlier, my six-year-old brother, Kyle, had started school and the two mile walk was a bit much for one so young, so sometimes we rode Old Maud, and Cousin Walter let us put her in the barn during the day. The stable had a large opening over the feed box beside the door. One afternoon when we went to get Maud, she was not there. The door was fastened just as we had left it. Maud had jumped out through the window and gone home!

COMMENCEMENT TIME

At this point in time, the end of April 1924, we proudly looked forward to commencement when we would be honored along with other classes and the attendance of our proud parents, relatives, neighbors and prominent speakers. In those days high schools (grades 8–11) stayed in session only eight months.

Following is a newspaper account of our commencement that appeared in the *Grayson County Gazette*, April 30, 1924:

GRASSY CREEK NEWS
COMMENCEMENT AT VIRGINIA-CAROLINA HIGH SCHOOL

Even the weather man smiled on the commencement at this school. From two states, twice as many counties, from far and near, people came to this notable occasion. And a great occasion it was.

The exercises began on Friday evening with an entertainment by the grades. The material was well selected, perfectly drilled and each parent was proud of his and her offspring. Miss Arlene Blackburn carried off the honors in the girls' speaking contest with her recitation while Dean Colvard won the medal for the boys.

Saturday was replete with good things, things intellectual, things spiritual, and things physical. Misses Ruby Davis, Zola Porter, Myrtle Parsons, and Nannie Sturgill charmed the audience with well rendered recitations, the latter winning with *The Little Rebel*. Seldom does one hear boys speak as did James Perry, Jones Barker, Dean McMillan and Robert Kirby, and it is inspiring to know that there are boys in these hills on whom have descended some of the fire and oratory of Patrick Henry. Robert Kirby gave flawlessly Woodrow Wilson's speech on Robert E. Lee, thereby winning the medal.

Mrs. T. E. Johnson, of the North Carolina State Department of Education, pled for a standard Elementary School and showed how Virginia-Carolina can have both a standardized High and Elementary School. Hon. Ira T. Johnston of Jefferson spoke eloquently on Service. His manner was witty, winsome and purely Johnstonian. Judge R. L. Kirby of Independence discussed Tendencies and sounded a note of warning to every American citizen when he said that extravagance and camouflage [sic] in the home lead to extravagance and graft in government. He bewailed the lack of industry among our people and proved most logically that government is but the product of many homes. "Simplicity, purity and industry in home life will correct many national ills," he said.

The class exercises which were original and unique throughout, were the feature of the afternoon. President Glen Dixon welcomed the visitors. Miss Mollie Hudler called the roll and each member responded in original rhyme. Pictures of memory [sic] were given by Miss Vergie Reeves. Gems of Knowledge were given by Frank McMillan, while valuables of the class were cried off at auction by Robert Gambill. Fitzhugh Barker weighed each member in the Balance and Felix Barker gave a specimen of oratory in a beautiful oration. Miss Kate Spencer peeped behind Father Time's curtain and gave dreams of the future. Benefactions were bestowed by Robert Kirby. The class poem was recited by Miss Ruby Davis and Miss Zetta Barker captivated the audience with the valedictory. Twenty-one received diplomas from the hand of Supt. Plummer.

Music by the School Orchestra, and songs such as *America, Carry Me Back to Old Virginia* [sic], *The Carolina Hills* and *Perfect Day* were sang [sic]. Games on the lawn by the Training Class, and a ball game with Helton in the afternoon varied the program. A play was given Saturday night; and a baccaluarate [sic] sermon in the church on Sunday by Rev. Mr. Williams of North Wilkesboro completed a most excellent Commencement.

Valedictorian Zetta Barker in graduation dress, holding diploma — 1924.

Supt. Plummer has given his very best to the school and this most excellent commencement only bore evidence to the fact that he is a teacher among teachers.

Recently when a group of us elderly people at a luncheon were reminiscing about our commencements, a young girl who was our waitress couldn't believe what she was hearing, and said, "We didn't want any part of a commencement. We just wanted to get our diplomas and get away."

After finishing high school, when I was teaching in Ashe County, I learned that Uncle Luther had taken the farm wagon, put a cover over the bed, installed a wood bench on each side of the wagon bed, picked up the children on Long Branch and upper Grassy Creek who had to walk the farthest, delivered them to school in the mornings, and picked them up in the afternoons. I do not know how he was paid or how the distance for picking up the students was determined. The one teacher school at Long Branch and upper Grassy Creek had closed, which certainly meant long walks for the children in those areas.

Then, I was told later, someone prepared a truck for carrying these children to and from school.

Of all the teachers of Virginia-Carolina High School whom I especially remember, first, of course, is Professor Robert E. Lee Plummer, who usually taught our history class in his office. Many cold mornings, he'd have us read or reread our history assignment while he tried to get the green soggy wood burning in the big pot-bellied stove. Then he'd take off his unbuckled rubber boots, sit down in his office chair and proceed with our lesson.

Hopefully someone or a number of people have written complete biographies of Robert E. Lee Plummer. I could not begin to know of all his civic activities and efforts for the people in Ashe and Grayson counties, but these are some of the things I remember about this remarkable man.

He was the most inspirational person I have ever known. He had assembly every morning in the school auditorium. When weather permitted, we lined up on the outside of the building with first graders in the front of the line and seniors last to march in and up the stairs to the auditorium. His favorite scripture was I Corinthians, chapter 13. Favorite song, *Work for the Night Is Coming*. He lectured and assured us that we could be anything we wanted to be with work and commitment. Time and again he urged, "Hitch your wagon to a star, aim high and work hard to reach your goal!"

He told us of how his father wanted him to pick up apples to make apple brandy and he refused.

How he carried a lantern to light the way to high school since he had to leave before daylight, hung it on a tree limb to be picked up on his way home from, I suppose, Helton Academy.

He was accepted in a college in a midwest area and told his girlfriend that he would be away for three years and if she wanted to wait for him, well and good, but if not it would be all right. She waited.

Cousin Kate Spencer had not completed high school and had been away working in Washington, D.C., but was back home. He persuaded Kate and her mother that she come and finish high school. He surveyed the communities for those who had had to drop out to care for aged and sick parents and urged them to finish school, no matter how long they may have been out.

One morning as we were lining up outside to march into the building, a partial eclipse of the sun was occurring. He let us stand about an hour to watch the eclipse. Mrs. Mattie Spencer's roosters began to crow and the fowls were confused — not knowing what in the world was going on.

Another teacher I remember is Myrtle Senter DeVaught Jones. While in college, Mrs. DeVaught had met and married an instructor, a Frenchman, but he had since died. She was highly qualified to teach French language and was my

French teacher for two or more years. She had our class put on a program with all the speaking parts in French and sing the French National Anthem in French. She played the piano and along with Miss Blossom Showalter, the music teacher (who taught piano and voice), and other teachers, planned programs so we were provided with many opportunities for singing. We learned and sang Stephen Foster songs along with lots of others from *The Golden Book of Favorite Songs* (copyright in 1915), which the school had purchased to use in assemblies and choral groups and could be bought by individuals for 20 cents. I still have a copy.

Other remembered teachers are Miss Ruby Reeves (McMillan) and her sister, Miss Hazel Reeves (Gambill) who taught English and Latin and other subjects as needed.

Prof. Hatfield taught math. In my senior year, he taught geometry to our class and I can still see him as he'd get so excited in explaining a theorem that an arm and leg would be moving up and down in time with his explanation. He told the senior class that if any members made 100 on his final test at the end of the year, their names would be put in the *National Mathematics Magazine*. No one made a perfect score, but Robert Gambill and I both had a grade of 98!

The 1924 senior class of 22 members were: Felix Barker, Fitzhugh Barker, Zetta Barker, Glen Dickson, Kate Spencer, Vista Hartsoe, Robert Gambill, Ruby Davis, Jean Graybeal, Myrtle Spencer, Frank McMillan, Clara Alexander, Hildreth Tyne, Vergie Reeves, J. C. Senter, Montague Cox, Mollie Hudler, Lillie Hartsoe, Nancy Sturgill, Hattie Wood, Robert Kirby. Felix, Vergie and I were tied as class valedictorians. I was selected to give the speech.

Of this group of students from mostly farm families, two became doctors, two lawyers, and one a judge. Some became principals, teachers and civic leaders, and every one would be a highly respected citizen.

Teacher Training

Professor Robert E. Lee Plummer again appeared before the North Carolina Board of Education and state legislature in behalf of young high school graduates who wished to become teachers. There were few automobiles in this area then and he knew there were those, especially girls, who would not have the opportunity or finances to go to colleges or Normal Schools, as they were called. He outlined a program whereby high school graduates could get teacher training and still stay at home. In 1922 and 1923 his request was granted and a class was begun at Virginia-Carolina to train young people to begin a career in teaching. There were some restrictions in the program. There could not be more than twelve students in the class. The class must be taught by a college educated instructor with a major in teacher education. In 1923 the first class was taught by Miss Meta Lyles.

In a recent article I was reading, the question was asked, "Have you ever met someone you didn't like at your first meeting, but learned to like when you got to know the person?" Well, I thought of Miss Lyles. At first, I didn't like her because on days when the weather was nice and pleasant, she'd go around to the classrooms at break periods and if she found students lolling around inside, she'd shoo them out. A few of us just wanted to stay inside and talk rather than participate in exercises or games. Well, the following year when I enrolled in the Teacher Training Class, I found her to be one of the finest people and college teachers I have ever known.

Miss Lyles put us twelve students through the hoops! She made sure we were familiar with all the adopted text books for elementary grades in Ashe County from first through the seventh grades. She took us completely through the seventh grade arithmetic book. I think she felt that arithmetic might be our greatest weakness. We had to learn to teach writing from the Zaner-Bloser Writing Text — know how to teach correct arm use, to do push pulls, ovals, and correct formation of capital and small written letters, submit samples of our writing to the Writing Publisher for evaluation and grading. Two or three of us received certificates from the company to teach writing for them. We did practice teaching on all grade levels — were evaluated by the classroom teachers and Miss Lyles. We did the physical examinations of the upcoming beginners (which is done today by nurses and volunteer parents) for the following year. We even worked with them as kindergartners for two weeks, long before there were kindergartens in Ashe County.

She demonstrated to us how to teach reading — that saying words was not reading but to get the meaning and how to find out answers. Then she and Professor Plummer contacted the Ashe County Superintendent of Schools, Professor James Goodman, to find out which schools had teacher vacancies for the following year and placed us in what they considered appropriate positions. Each of us, if we had satisfactorily completed the year's work, was issued an Elementary teaching certificate, which we could build on through a B and then an A Certification, and then go on to a higher certification by attending accredited Teachers' Colleges or Normal Schools, until we earned our bachelor's degree. After we had taught for a year we could pay for summer sessions at Appalachian Teachers' College or some other college. My salary per month the first year was $75. It was increased $5 per month each succeeding year until it had reached $95. Then North Carolina went into a road building program and became heavily in debt. Our salaries were cut and then there were delays in receiving our checks. I don't know what we would have done had it not been for store merchants and our boarding lady who were so kind and sympathetic and understanding. I recall especially the Scott brothers who had a store where First Citizens Bank was later located in West Jefferson. They would let us charge needed items.

Back to the Teacher Training Program. After Miss Lyles had taught the program two years she moved to Appalachian Teachers' College and was replaced in the program by a Miss Gore. When any of her former students were attending classes at Appalachian, Miss Lyles seemed to take us "under her wing" and encouraged us in our efforts. She was a teacher among teachers!

My first school placement through Miss Lyles and Professor Plummer was principal of a three teacher school at Dog Creek. When the school opened in August, I was eighteen years of age.

Dog Creek School

I had finished high school in the spring of 1924 and teacher training in the spring of 1925, having reached the age of eighteen in January of that year. I received a contract to be teaching principal at Dog Creek. My father was certainly concerned about the responsibility for an eighteen year old country girl. He arranged for someone with a car to take him and me to check out the situation. We visited Mr. James Goodman, Ashe County Superintendent of Schools, in his office in the courthouse, where we were given the names of the three local committeemen for Dog Creek. Then we went to see Mr. Preston Dixon, chairman of that committee, Mr. Ben Little and Mr. John Dixon, each of whom gave us an overview of the community and the school population. We inquired about boarding and each suggested a home about 150 or 200 yards from the school. We looked through the school building and noted a lot of things needing to be done. Later we contacted the chairman of the committeemen to set a day and get word out that a cleanup would be held on Thursday before the opening of school. I arranged to move into the boarding home on Wednesday.

At one o'clock on the set day, parents — men and women — came with wash tubs, buckets, scrub brooms, cleaning rags, soaps, rakes, mattocks and scythes. Men collected rocks to hold the wash tubs over fires to heat water brought from the nearby school spring. Desks were carried outside to be cleaned, floors swept before being scrubbed by the men, windows cleaned, weeds cut, trash picked up, and rough places smoothed. Then windows and doors were opened to let in the August sun and to air out the rooms. I was so pleased with the response and friendliness of the parents. Of course, I'm sure they were anxious to meet and evaluate the "new principal."

The following day I again opened the doors and windows for further airing of the fresh smelling building. I arranged desks, placed a box of chalk, two new erasers, new brooms and teacher registers in each room. A few text books and story books left from the year before were examined, sorted and placed in the appropriate rooms.

Sunday afternoon, Kate Wagg Spencer arrived with her mother and a couple of family members and checked in to board in the room with me. Our room had windows at one side that started at the floor and slid to the side to open. Kate's mother asked me to sleep on the side of the one double bed next to the windows, as she sometimes tended to sleep walk. Once or twice they had found her out on their porch roof in the night.

"Know Your State" Tour Acclaimed on Every Road

Dog Creek School Children Who Cheered Twin City "Good Will" Men

These Children Can Go to School Only Six Months. The Journal is in Favor of Giving Them an Eight Month School. Fifty Percent of the Children of North Carolina Go to School Eight Months. Why Shouldn't These Bright Boys and Girls Have the Same Opportunity?

They are still in this picture because of the urgent pleadings of the photographer. Ten seconds before they were yelling madly as they danced and screamed for joy while the cars passed and the Twin City men leaned out to shout greetings. The "Good Will" candy truck scattered them like so many fairy dancers in a super-speeded motion picture. It took three teachers, two photographers and a newspaper man to keep them quiet long enough to capture their likeness. The teacher on the extreme right is one of the reasons that a young man in the party has bought a new roadster and is planning to make the trip all over again. That is so far as Ashe County is concerned. Teach-

ers on the left are: Miss Kate Wagg and Miss Ruth McNeil, and the teacher on the right is Miss Zetta Barker.

In an editorial Saturday morning entitled, "The Heart of North Carolina," the *Journal* described the scene enacted by the children in this picture as one of the most inspiring of the trip. The editorial follows.

In the swing around the circle this week scores of men of Winston Salem learned to love North Carolina as they had never loved her before. One of the incidents that stirred them most happened far out in the woods of Ashe County. Swinging around a graceful curve in the broad thoroughfare that now links

the county seats of Sparta and Jefferson, where not a house was in sight, they found waiting for them more than a hundred children lined up on the side of the road with three young ladies who were their teachers.

It was the most inspiring sight the representatives of Winston Salem saw in North Carolina and Virginia — the hundred beautiful children and their fair teachers out there in the rugged mountain side singing a welcome and clapping their little hands with glee.

It was Winston Salem's first greeting from the fine county of Ashe — the county that the great Aycock loved so much and the county that he served so well by Putting the State

behind the famous turnpike from Wilkesboro to Jefferson back in the days before it had become popular to build roads in North Carolina.

Out there in the woods the great heart of North Carolina beats strongest. Out there in the woods where faithful teachers toil for the love of toiling for humanity is the highest hope of the greater Commonwealth that is yet to be.

God speed the teachers in the woods, and heaven's richest blessing rest on the little hands that cheer for progress and the little feet that have started up the long, long climb.

Miss Wagg taught the first and second grades and Miss Ruth McNeil had the third, fourth and part of the fifth grade. I taught fifth grade history and health and grades six and seventh. Some of my students were as large as I was and almost as old. There were no school buses in that area then to carry students to high school. Mr. Wiley Dixon had brought a Model T Ford car to carry his daughters, Mazie and Blanch, to high school in West Jefferson, but most of the students who had taken seventh grade at Dog Creek did not have a way to get to the high school. So they just came back to the elementary school. A few of the oldest boys helped their fathers with the farm work in the early fall and then entered school again.

Dog Creek School was scheduled to open in late August to save wood for heating. Word passed around that the *Winston-Salem Journal* and other business leaders were planning a tour of North Carolina to get to better know the state. The schedule of the tour appeared in local newspapers and THEY WERE COMING TO ASHE COUNTY! Of course this created much interest to those living near the parade route. We teachers thought it would be a wonderful idea for the Dog Creek school children to witness this event. We knew the approximate time the tour would come through the area from Sparta on the way to Jefferson, the county seat. We lined the children up and marched up the road, about a quarter of a mile, to highway 21, found a good spot and seated the children on top of a bank where they would have an excellent view of all those automobiles passing by. The smallest children were seated in the front row, with the largest ones in the back. The two primary teachers were seated at one end of the group and I sat at the other end where we were able to keep an eye on all the children. The children were wonderful. Finally the cars began to appear around the curve. All was well until cars sighted us and began stopping. One car started throwing out candy while the leader of the group wanted to interview us. Bedlam began! Despite teachers' efforts, no child was going to sit still while others were scurrying to pick up candy and pencils! The following week Mr. Walter Worth, president of the Bank of Ashe, had a call from the *Winston-Salem Journal,* wanting the names and addresses of the three teachers of Dog Creek School. A few days later the following picture and article appeared in the *Journal* and pictures were sent to Miss Wagg, Miss McNeil and me, along with a copy of the article. The three of us were single, busy with being placed in teaching positions, summer school, dating, getting married. After I retired some fifty years later, I was telling Gayle about the *Winston-Salem Journal* incident and she asked about the picture and article. Neither of us still had either — for lack of care. One day I received a large envelope in the mail from Forsyth Public Library. She and John Stewart had contacted the *Journal* but they no longer had the 1925 newspaper and picture in their files, but suggested they try the Forsyth Public Library. Success. Of course, the picture did not reproduce plainly but this is a copy of the article which has, I think, history pertinent to Ashe County. Some of the students have died, some have moved away, some are still living, and I still remember the event and the editorial, which asked why these children could go to school only six months.

Top: Kate Wagg with first and second grade students. Middle: Ruth McNeil with third, fourth and part fifth grade students. Bottom: Zetta Barker, principal, with part fifth, sixth, and seventh grade students.

I have said that one thing I considered a problem was that my primary teachers sometimes dated my oldest boys. There were not the serious school problems at that time as of today with drugs, disrespect for teachers, guns in school and killings. Children obeyed their parents and teachers.

One Friday afternoon, my three oldest students asked for leave to attend a funeral of a friend at Senter Church and, of course, permission was granted. We were to oil the dusty floors that afternoon after the students were dismissed — oil provided by the school system but to be applied by teachers or older students. The three boys came back to the building to help with the oiling. On the way from the funeral they had found a mouse, caught it, brought it and would slip behind one of the primary teachers and drop the mouse down the back of her blouse and laugh and laugh at the squeals and threats made by the teachers.

One Saturday afternoon, Miss Wagg and I started to walk up to the local store at the highway, a distance of perhaps a half mile or less. We met someone who told us that Mr. So and So was at the store drunk. I said, "Why, that's one of our school parents. I can't believe he'd do such a thing." I thought that only single men got drunk! We were so distressed that we turned around and went back to the house.

Because of poor roads and few cars, we did not get home more than once or maybe twice a month. One weekend, we asked our landlady if we could use the parlor and have our boyfriends in for dates. These were boyfriends we had been dating for some time — nice young men a year of so older than we were. We sat up, talked, laughed and had an enjoyable evening until eleven-thirty or twelve o'clock. The following morning at breakfast, the landlady said, "You girls were up mighty late last night. I think the committeemen should know about that kind of conduct." Later we saw her go out and come back about an hour later. We decided we'd have to see the committeemen. We were rather sure she had gone to the one closest by. Sure enough. He said he had told her that he was glad that we were respected enough that young gentlemen wanted to see us. That he didn't think too much of young ladies who did not have enough spunk to have boyfriends. My date happened to be the son of the chairman of the school committeemen.

There were so many teaching aids we did not have — maps, story books, construction paper, paste, scissors, and the magazine, *Normal Instructor*, and other materials — just a bare minimum compared to aids in today's schools. Even back in the 1970s when I was in school work in Northern Virginia, I used to say that my teachers and classes wasted more supplies than some schools here had. When Dog Creek School opened in the fall of 1925, the school board supplied only chalk, erasers, brooms, a can of oil for dusty floors but little more.

So we decided to have a box supper to get a few things for the school. The word was spread throughout the community and the date set. Parents and single girls began preparing. There was much competition especially among the single girls for the most beautiful box and reputation for excellent food. Young ladies who had a steady boyfriend expected him to buy their boxes, but they knew that other young men often, for fun, would bid on boxes to make the fellow pay a goodly price for his girl's box. Too, sometimes a young man with a crush on a certain girl would try to impress her by bidding on her box. Of course wives expected their husbands to buy their boxes; again, boys would tease by running up the price of a box against the husband.

The ladies decorated the boxes with pretty colors of crepe paper, trimmed with big bows of fluted crepe paper, flowers, ribbons or beads. As the boxes were brought in they were taken to a table on the stage and a number put on them.

An auctioneer was selected, known for his experience, personality or gift of "gab." When it was assumed that everyone had arrived, the auctioneer would begin with something like this, "Well, folks, I'm getting hungry. I can just smell fried chicken and ham, can't you? Look at all those beautiful boxes with all that good food! Let's begin." Another person would hand him a box while someone else would accept the money and keep a record of the buyer and price. Of course, the purchaser got not only the box of food but the privilege of sharing it with the lady!

I had been told that a young man who had been away working but was home had said he was going to see that my date would really have to pay for my box. I told my friend not to pay too much for the box. Ten dollars was considered a very good price for a girl's box at that time. Sure enough, the young man began bidding against my date. When the price was up to $20, I said, "Let him have it." I heard later that the young man had to hurriedly borrow some money to help pay for the box. Young Mr. Colvard was a fine dinner companion.

Boxes were usually filled with fried chicken, fried ham or cheese sandwiches, potato salad, pickled cucumber or peach or pear, some special fruit, and delicious pie or cake.

After all had eaten, the auctioneer again went to the stage. "Now we've had all that good food. Umh, umh! Wasn't that the best supper you've ever had? But now comes a mighty important part of this evening's event. See this big beautiful cake here on the table? Doesn't it just make your mouth water? Well, someone's going to have a chance to enjoy it. This cake is for the 'prettiest girl.' Now I know all you guys know your girl is the prettiest girl in the state and you'll have a chance to prove it. We're going to vote to see who the lucky girl is. Ten cents a vote. Call out how many votes or how much you're voting. Now let's have some nominations for your favorite girl. Bring your money up here to Mr. Taylor. He'll keep a count of who gets the most votes and announce the winner." Guys began calling out the names of girls they thought had a chance to win. There were three or four names nominated. Then the competition began. Usually this was a lucrative event. Boyfriends, even parents and others kept bidding for a time. Then when the bidding stopped, the money was counted and the winner announced. Of course, the chosen girl cut the cake and especially shared with those who had voted for her.

Our landlady had asked if I'd like her to bake the cake for the prettiest girl contest and I had said, "Yes." I thought this was very thoughtful of her. After all, by this time the three teachers were boarding with her. And a girl who was staying with the family was a school student. After the box supper was over and I asked the cost of making the cake, she said, "Five dollars." I was flabbergasted. I thought that was a very high price for a cake at that time, but I paid it from the funds.

When the six month school term ended in February, Kate and I wondered if the school trustees would ask us to return the following year. Should we ask if we could return? They did not ask and we did not ask. We thought if they told us they did not want us back, it would be very embarrassing. We were very naive! In late spring or early summer, I received a contract from Superintendent Goodman to teach the following year at West Jefferson and when I met one of the Dog Creek trustees, he said, "We're sorry you and Miss Kate are not going to be with us this year." I said, "We thought you did not want us since you didn't ask us back." Miss Ruth asked to return to Dog Creek and did. Kate continued teaching for a number of years.

After I learned that I would be teaching at West Jefferson, I convinced my father that I should attend summer school. He agreed. I enrolled for a six-week session at Appalachian Teachers' College. Mrs. J. B. Hash and I roomed together in a private home on a street just above the administration building at that time—1926. (When I was back visiting Boone in 1975, that street and others had been taken over by the University.) But in 1926 some of my classes were held in the administration building. I was often late for lunch or another class, as we stood in the door waiting for a rain shower to end. It seemed a shower could occur at the drop of a hat — or a book!

During the following summers, Con Dixon, George Miller, Paul Bower and others would drive to Appalachian and would have no trouble finding four or five teachers to help with gas and driving expenses to attend summer sessions. Some instructors would admonish us to spend at least an hour each day on our text book assignment and we certainly did as we sat on our books in the crowded Model T! Of course we were conscientious and anxious to successfully complete our courses.

One summer a Hawaiian film, *Little Leilani* was appearing at the Boone theater and some of our group wanted to go to the afternoon matinee to see it. Should we cut classes or not? We had been hearing some of the songs which whetted our desire to see the film. The driver said he'd pick us up at either of both places if we decided to attend. Each was reluctant and hesitant unless Mrs. Graybeal, a most gracious and respected lady, said she would go. In the end, we all cut afternoon classes and saw the film.

West Jefferson School

It was April and the end of the 1926-27 eight month term of the consolidated West Jefferson school and commencement time. As was the practice, the primary grades gave a program on Friday night and the upper elementary classes and the high school students had all day performances and graduation exercises on Saturday with a play that evening, followed by the baccalaureate sermon Sunday morning.

The first grade teacher opened the Friday evening program with the little ones. Miss Hazel Phillips and I taught the second, third and fourth grades. While searching around and looking for something different this year for our students, Mrs. Irene Greer Scott, the music teacher, offered to look through some of her materials that might be appropriate. Mrs. Scott was highly qualified in her field of music in both piano and voice. She found a copy of an operetta (a name for a light opera consisting of song, dance and some speaking parts for young children, and calling for beautiful costumes). After much discussion and questioning, we decided we would do the operetta, quite an undertaking for small town and country children and two teachers who had never attended or heard an opera. I'm sure Mrs. Scott had had many experiences while in college that Hazel and I had not had. Mrs. Scott taught the songs and helped us with the dances, while Hazel and I saw that the children knew their speaking parts and reviewed the words of the songs when a student was absent for a practice.

There were costumes to be made. A few mothers were good seamstresses and volunteered to help with costumes while others wouldn't dare, so they said, to make anything as complicated as we had suggested. So Miss Hazel and I spent many evenings making costumes. Miss Phillips lived in Beaver Creek, a few miles out of town and I boarded in the dormitory operated by Mrs. Goss. (The dormitory was in the building that now houses Badgers funeral facility.) Some nights Hazel would spend with me making little girls' costumes of crepe paper in pastel shades of light blue, pink, violet, white and green with lots of rows of fluted paper ruffles sewed onto the skirts of bodiced petticoats the girls had brought from home with names clearly attached. The boys' white vests and dress jackets were mostly worked out by mothers after seeing how they should look.

When the curtain opened on the scheduled Friday evening, the children looked so beautiful in the pretty colors, and despite a few bobbles, performed so well that parents beamed proudly and everyone praised the performance. While listening to congratulations of people in the audience, the principal handed me three dollars, saying, "You three people have worked so hard. Take this and go to the drug store for a treat and relax." We were so tired and still faced with helping excited children take off the costumes, find their own clothes without getting them mixed up with someone else's, we were ready to fall in bed and go to the drug store tomorrow afternoon.

We three got together the next afternoon and went to enjoy our treat. Ray Drug Store had a soda fountain at that time with round ice cream parlor-type tables and chairs. After we sat down, Quincy Campbell came to take our orders. Three dollars was far too much for a soda or just a dish of ice cream so we ordered banana splits. Quincy made three beautiful splits with strawberry, chocolate and vanilla ice cream over split bananas, topped with two kinds of syrups, nuts and whipped cream. We ate the delicacies leisurely knowing that our school days for that term were over — all except for final reports. Quincy cleared the table and we sat and reminisced over the events of the past months. Ben Goss, a very eligible bachelor, whom I dated some, came in and stopped to talk with Quincy for a bit before joining us at the table. I noticed that Quincy wasn't looking our way and seemed to be hiding a smile that lurked around the mouth and eyes as he spoke to customers coming by. Soon he came to our table carrying a tray with three banana splits which Ben had ordered. Of course we looked at each other, and said, "You shouldn't have. But thank you."

We were so full, we staggered to supper that evening but fortunately, Miss Myrtle Williamson, a Presbyterian missionary to Ashe County, who also boarded in the dormitory, saved the day for us! She was a most gracious and likable lady whom we had come to respect highly and be very fond of. When we were all seated and grace said, Miss Williamson said, "You teachers, please don't eat too much! I've enjoyed living with you this winter and I'd like to take you out for a treat after our dinner has had time to settle — about nine o'clock, say. Around nine o'clock to the drug store we went again, hoping the treat might be listening to a new record the drug store had gotten in. But when Miss Williamson ordered banana splits, we were glad Quincy had finished his day and gone home. Of course we didn't tell Miss Williamson or Mr. Ray, the druggist, who made the concoctions that these were the third banana splits we had had since 4:30 that afternoon!

Burnt Hill School

In the school term of 1931-32, I was assigned to a one room school at Burnt Hill in Laurel Springs, Ashe County, N.C. The building had two classrooms but evidently attendance had dropped and it was now a one teacher school.

Opening day came and students poured in. All the double desks were filled with two pupils and a number of little ones squeezed in with larger siblings or friends. I had the little ones come up and sit on the front of the stage where their feet could touch the floor. What must I do? There were small desks in the other room but no space for them in the "big" room. Only one thing to do. Report the situation to the county superintendent. He or a representative came out to check the situation and in nothing flat another teacher, Miss Lola Baker, showed up to teach the first three grades.

The United States was grappling with the worst depression in its history. Ashe County was aware that there were many poor families having a hard time feeding and clothing themselves, especially widows with children. There had been "the Poor House" for the most unfortunate families. Mr. Thompson of Laurel Springs came to me to tell me of a widow with two girls in sixth and seventh grades who was having an extremely hard time and might have to take the girls out of school because she was unable to provide school lunches and school clothing for them.

While Ashe County had a history of helping its poor as best it could, more populated towns, cities and areas were setting up welfare programs. In Ashe County the superintendent of schools was designated to be welfare head. Miss Ruth Reeves was appointed to be in charge of distributing articles of food, clothing and other necessities to needy families. I had made a survey of the Burnt Hill families who needed assistance and I reported to Miss Reeves. She explained that if these families could pay five cents for lunch, fine, but if not, lunches could be provided free. She gave me two large aluminum kettles, several cans of tomato soup, and cocoa. Well, I guess I'm an old softy. I worked out a system that if other students could bring five cents daily and their own sandwiches, they, too, could have soup and cocoa. The two older girls of the above-mentioned widow could be in charge of making the soup and cocoa. They washed their hands, made soup one day and cocoa the next day and washed up the pots. Each child brought his bowl or cup. Parents were so glad to have something hot for their children's lunches that they began sending half gallon cans of milk, their own canned tomatoes and other vegetables for the soups. We had to make a schedule of when each family would donate to the lunch program to avoid having materials on hand ahead of time. Students would usually bring a sandwich or cookie but they were happy and helped with carrying water, washing up and anything that needed doing.

The following year, I was transferred to Obids School as principal of another two teacher school. Miss Vivian Parsons was the primary teacher. There we made a kitchen by parents bringing lumber, paneling off a corner of the upper classroom. Mr. Hamp Burgess had gotten a new stove and the old one was still sitting on his porch. Well, he let us have the old stove. Two young ladies in the community had qualified for work to be paid by the government (the WPA program, I believe) and they cooked. Children brought milk, canned and fresh vegetables, and other commodities from home and the Social Services provided flour, corn meal and other food items. Again all children had hot, substantial lunches. One day, two boys brought two half gallons of molasses to school. I thought "What in the world will we do with a gallon of molasses?" I needn't have worried. Those two ladies turned out the best gingerbread with a lemon sauce I ever ate. My daughter and I still wonder how they made that sauce, but they have passed away and we'll never know. There were always paper table mats passed out to the students to be on their desk tops and silverware, donated or brought from home. Two older students carried the filled plates of food — pinto beans, mashed potatoes, sweet potatoes, cabbage, slaw, turnips, apple sauce or whatever was on hand and placed the plates on the desk tops. Sometimes there was hot chocolate or hot tea to drink.

Save the Children's Fund from New York found our school and others in the county. In fact they had an office in West Jefferson where the McFarland Publishers warehouse is now located and a representative stayed there for a time and would let people come in and get needed clothing. If they wanted to work for what they were getting, the lady taught them how to set a table, serve a meal, line wastebaskets and how to do many things they had not known before. Save the Children's Corporation sent cod liver oil for poor children — not capsules but real cod liver *oil!* I thought all the children should take the food additive. I explained the situation and the benefits of the oil but stated that only those for whom the oil was intended had to take it. Some declared they would not swallow that stuff under any circumstances. I bought sacks of hard candy and passed it around for those who would be taking the cod liver oil. The waitress girls had already placed teaspoons on the desks. Result? Soon everyone was taking cod liver oil!

Activities

Winter Activities

While the six-months of elementary school pretty well kept children occupied with school attendance, doing assigned homework, and after school chores at home, they were sleepy and ready for bed by 8 or 8:30 in the evening. The "old people," as we called them, those forty years and older, often had a set time for bed, about 9 or 10 o'clock. Come 9 o'clock, my grandfather would say, "Nine o'clock. Time for bed!" And to bed he went. No matter if there were visitors, elite or pauper, preacher or president, it made no difference to Grandpa. He went to bed! But there was the group aged, I believe, from about 18 to 40 years, single and married, faced with long winter evenings in November, December and January, especially, from 7 o'clock to bed time at probably 10 to 11 P.M. and they would plan some activities which they did not have time for in the summer.

There were no televisions, radios and very few, if any, phonographs in the community for entertainment. Church was *the* main social gathering. Singing was an important part of worship and was enjoyed and appreciated by young and old. Our country churches had a pastor who held services only one weekend each month. Other weekends, some people would visit other churches and hear other groups sing and were motivated to improve their knowledge of and ability in the art of singing. So, a singing school was planned, taught by someone who could use a tuning fork for pitch, who could teach soprano, alto, tenor and bass, who knew the shaped notes. Our country churches did not have organs or pianos, and while a few people could pick a banjo or play a fiddle, those instruments were for dances and parties and not to use in churches. Rather than the round notes found in most music today, the shaped notes were used. Each shaped note had a name and sound: do, re, mi, fa, sol, la, ti, do.

The following example is taken from *The Modern Hymnal*, compiled and edited by Robert Coleman with copyright in 1926, printed in round and shaped notes.

These nightly classes were held in the local school/church building for a period of two weeks of two hour sessions from 7 to 9 o'clock in the evening and

109

255   *At the Cross.*

Isaac Watts.   R. E. Hudson.

COPYRIGHT, 1916, BY MRS. MARY HUDSON.
RENEWAL. USED BY PERMISSION.

1. A - las, and did my Sav - ior bleed? And did my Sov-'reign die?
2. Was it for crimes that I have done, He groaned up - on the tree?
3. Well might the sun in dark-ness hide, And shut his glo - ries in,
4. But drops of grief can ne'er re - pay The debt of love I owe:

Would He de - vote that sa - cred head For such a worm as I?
A - maz-ing pit - y! grace un-known! And love be - yond de - gree!
When Christ, the might-y Mak - er, died For man, the crea-ture's sin.
Here, Lord, I give my - self a - way, 'Tis all that I can do!

CHORUS.

At the cross, at the cross where I first saw the light, And the

bur - den of my heart rolled a - way, (rolled away,) It was there by faith

I re-ceived my sight, And now I am hap-py all the day! A-MEN.

those I knew of were just held one time a year and in winter. At the end of the course, a Saturday night or Sunday morning session was held for the instructor to demonstrate to the invited community and public, the progress made, and have one or two people practice as song leaders.

The singing school instructor was paid a modest amount of money, with the participating families taking turns keeping him in their homes while the teaching was going on.

The people who attended these classes took them very seriously and followed through on what they had learned. My father had two sisters and two brothers who were not married and they would come to our house at night after dinner to practice their singing. Aunt Minnie and Uncle Luther were the sopranos! Aunt Lona sang alto; Uncle Iredell was the tenor; and Dad sang bass.

I recall many times seeing the song leader looking over the announced hymn and toning "mi, mi, mi," or one of the other notes. He might ask the sopranos to hold the sound he had just given until he heard the right sound from the other three parts.

I was talking with someone recently about the use of the shaped notes and two people from Charlotte overheard some of our conversation and joined in. The lady said she thought some of the most beautiful singing she ever heard was from some groups singing without accompaniment of an instrument and several people singing the four different parts. In congregational singing when there are, scattered throughout the crowd, people singing the four parts, the sound just can't be beat!

Singing was very important to us. I suppose it has been important to people all down through the ages. Babies were sung to sleep. I've heard people say they sang when afraid as it seemed to allay their fears and tended to soothe or distract an animal or person whom they thought might be threatening them. People not only sang in church and in "get-togethers," but they sang when alone as they worked. I can still hear my Dad singing loudly while doing outside chores. Had anyone been listening, they could have heard him a half mile away on the chorus of *Blessed Assurance*. Before I was old enough to start to school, and Mama and I were alone, she'd get the hymnal and sing. Two of her favorite songs were: *We'll Understand It Better, Bye and Bye* and *Unclouded Day*. Aunt Lona, as she was carrying water from the spring, would be singing *Sweet Hour of Prayer*, her favorite song.

At times we'd walk across the hills to a nighttime revival meeting at Pleasant Home Church, a distance of two or more miles each way. On the way home, when we'd crossed the line fence between Mr. Sexton's and Mr. Kirk's farms, Uncle Iredell would start a song and we'd sing as it was down hill the rest of the way home. If we awakened sleeping families, they never complained to us.

When we finally had radios, movies, and later, televisions, we enjoyed listening to and seeing Jeanette McDonald and Nelson Eddy as they sang duets. Then there were the Monroe Brothers, the Andrews Sisters, the Lennon Sisters, Mitch Miller's Sing-a-Long, Lawrence Welk's band, Perry Como, Bing Crosby and many others whose songs we enjoyed listening to. We could hear and understand the words, the tunes were catchy and after performances or coming out of the movies, people would be humming or singing favorite parts of songs they had just heard. These and other famous performers of the forties, fifties and sixties held their audiences spellbound without bodily gyrations for emphasis. I'm glad that there are requests for these songs today and they are being made available on records and tapes.

I remember my father holding me on his knee and singing *New River Train*.

> You will know that I am gone,
> You can tell the train I'm on,
> You can hear the whistle blow
> A hundred miles.

My father and most of my uncles, aunts and neighbors did not go to high school as there was not one nearby. But most of them who had finished elementary school were quite good in reading, spelling and arithmetic; *McGuffey's Reader* was the most used reading book and together with *The Blueback Spelling Book*, helped students learn to pronounce and spell even very long words phonetically. In spelling, they would pronounce the word, then if the word was, say, "insulate," they would say "insulate," in (pronounce in) su (insu) late, insulate. Uncle Luther would say, "Let me hear you spell chinquapin, or antidisestablishmentarianism (!) or aurora borealis," and laugh and laugh at our stumbling efforts.

My parents told me that Mr. James (Jim) Goodman taught the school in this community when they were in school in the 1870s, and boarded "among" the students for the three month sessions. In order to have a school, households would take turns in keeping the teacher. When I knew Mr. Goodman, he was superintendent of schools in Ashe County in the 1920s and lived in the Beaver Creek community.

After we had a telephone, a community telephone system (which is discussed in another chapter), my father and a few other men, in winter months, would call each other sometimes and give out an arithmetic problem to solve. When someone thought he had solved it, he would call back to the person who had started this on that particular evening. The others would hear the ring, all get on the line and discuss the problem. Often they would have several conversations before they decided on the correct solution. Some of these problems were of the following sort:

1. If a man dug a rectangular hole, so many feet long, so many feet wide and so many feet deep, how many cubic feet of dirt was removed? They might use fractional measurements sometimes.

2. Mr. Smith hired three men to do some work. Each was to be paid $2.45 per hour. John worked 2¾ hours. Bob worked 3¾ hours but Jim only put in 2½ hours. How much did it cost Mr. Smith to get the work done?

3. Mr. Haley lent Jerry $550.00 for six months at 4¾% interest. How much did Jerry need to pay to Mr. Haley at the end of six months?

It seems that only the men worked on these challenges. I never knew of any ladies taking part. Young men and boys were urged to learn arithmetic for handling finances in buying, selling, trading and salaries. It was not so important for girls and women to be proficient in math. But they memorized the multiplication tables, could add, subtract and do short division. After all, they needed to know how much to expect from the sale of so many pounds of chickens and butter. When I was learning the multiplication tables, I would follow my Aunt Lona around as she worked in the house for her to help me with the multiplication facts. Then, too, ladies were beginning to teach the elementary grades.

There wasn't a river, lake or body of water near where we lived to provide a place for ice-skating in winter, and, in fact, I never saw a pair of ice skates, or a commercially-made snow sled (like the ones so popular today). However, my brother and other boys would make small sleds, patterned after the farm sleds, using 2 × 4s for the runners, rounded on the front ends and boards nailed on top of the runners and a crude guide attached to the front. There were plenty of hills on the farms and in the roads, and we looked for places that gave the longest and safest rides. A hill with a gradual slope and a distance of 200 or 300 feet was better than a steep hill where the sled would go faster but end up in a level spot where the sled would just gradually slow down and stop on its own. Then we'd get off, laugh and laugh, and despite cold, wet hands and feet, gloves and shoes, we'd drag the sled back to the starting place and do it all over again.

A boy brought a board to school after promising his father faithfully to bring it back home. The board was an inch and a half thick, and about eight feet long. One snowy day after school, he persuaded six or seven of us to go to a hill just outside the school yard and ride down the hill toward the road, a distance of about three or four hundred yards. We piled on and the boys using their feet started the board and off we went. The farther we went the faster we went with no apparent way of stopping, ran right into a barbed wire fence at the road. Fortunately, no one was badly hurt except for scratches, torn stockings and coats and the dread of telling our parents what happened.

There were five or six homes in our immediate area with two, three and four grown single boys and girls, a total of about fourteen, of ages around 18 to 24. Sometimes they would plan a hay ride when it snowed. The young men would take the farm sled and put the slatted "corn box" on it. The box was about six feet long and four feet wide with a floored bottom, but with slatted sides and ends to allow air to circulate through if the husked corn had been left in it overnight before hauling it to the granary, or if the unhusked corn had been hauled to the barn hallway for a corn husking. The three foot high box would be filled to the top with hay, but after six or seven people sat down on the hay it was considerably less high. The sled was pulled by two horses through the community back and forth for a distance of one or two miles, letting some riders off and others on.

While children were attending school from 8:45 to 4:00 in winter, there were always chores to be done after getting home. There was milking, putting away the milk, feeding the animals, getting in wood and water for the night and morning, and supper to be made. Our parents usually did the milking to make sure the cows were "stripped" (all the milk drawn from the udder) so they would keep giving milk and not fail or go dry in the cold wintry weather. (Cows were known to "fail" or give less milk in very cold weather.) My 12-year-old brother would carry corn fodder from the stack behind the barn and perhaps some corn nubbins (ears of corn that were not fully matured) for the cows, throw hay from the barn loft and carry some corn for the horses. Dad would check to make sure the animals were properly fed. My sister's job was to collect the eggs, feed and fasten the chickens in the chicken house, carry in pails of water for the night and start supper, as she was now fifteen. Then Dad and my brother would use the cross-cut saw to cut off blocks of wood and split them for the fireplace and the cook stove. My job was to carry the shorter and more finely split wood to fill the wood box for the kitchen stove, and pick up and carry a basket of wood splinters and chips to use in starting the morning fires. I would set the table for supper and help with the dish washing.

Then there was school homework to do. We had a "little" table, 30 × 30 inches square which usually was kept against the wall in the living room. After supper Dad would put the table in the center of the room, set a kerosene lamp on the table and three straight chairs around it and say, "Time for homework!"

On winter days and nights of cold rain and snow, it seemed there were always things to be done. Men mended harnesses, checked the farm implements and replaced mattock, pick, shovel and ax handles if necessary. My father would take a cracked or broken ax handle to use as a pattern, get a piece of oak, maple, hickory or other piece of hardwood, cut it to the right length, trim off the excess wood, then use a plane to shave off and begin to shape the piece into the right pattern. Finally, he would use his sharp pocket knife to do the delicate trimming until the handle fit into the ax firmly. We would watch intently as he shaved down the ribbon-like strips of wood and cheered when he made a long one without breaking. We kept the shavings for the fire the next morning.

The women in the household mended garments, darned socks, sweaters, knitted gloves, mittens and fascinators (a loosely knitted or crocheted woolen triangle to wear on the head and tie under the chin on cold days), and patched cotton things as needed. Favorite occupations of the ladies were piecing quilts, crocheting yokes for corsets and chemises (shimmies). See chapter on clothing. Also crocheting edgings for petticoats, gowns, panties and dresses. Ladies liked pretty things, things to wear and things for homes and so they embroidered dresser scarves, doilies, pillow cases, pillow shams and bedspreads (see section on homes). When neighbors visited and a family had a quilt or bedspread or item they admired, they were given the pattern or design to copy. We saved everything—

wrapping paper, cardboard, strings from packages, and paper bags as they might be needed some time. Wrapping paper and cardboard could be used in copying patterns.

My grandmother almost always sat in her own chair at her special place at one side of the fireplace and by a window at one end of the sitting room, knitting socks and gloves. She and her daughters had winter gloves and summer work gloves. The gardening gloves were to protect the hands from splinters in hoe handles, from prickly briars, from staining weeds and plants, and to keep the hands soft and nice looking. These gloves were knitted from cotton and the fingers only reached the finger knuckles on each hand, leaving the finger tips free for tedious weeding, handling fine seeds for planting and free for whatever they might be doing.

Our elementary school closed some time in February depending on whether measles or whooping cough had forced a week or so of closing. I don't recall school ever being closed because of weather. However, after the session had ended, we children would after supper want to play some sort of game.

When one is very young, say from five to ten years of age and small, to boot, people anywhere from eighteen to thirty or more, in age and size, appear to be much, much older and grown up. When my father was forty, I thought he was an old man. But these people who were forty and younger, liked to have fun in their way. They enjoyed funny stories, jokes and pranks and things to laugh about. To be able to laugh just made one feel better, I'm sure.

At Halloween, some would go out and overturn the outside toilets or privies of neighbors, and particularly those of someone who might be cranky or not very friendly. Even married men might go along with a group of young fellows after they thought the family had gone to bed, take the wheels off a wagon or buggy, put the vehicle on top of a barn, and put the wheels on again. When it was known that a young man had gone "courtin'" and would be walking home later, he might find himself falling over a rope or twine tied across the road.

Hobby horse

Sometimes on a dark night when answering a knock on the door, one might be confronted by a "hobby horse." After the shocked "OOH!" loud laughing from a hidden group outside could be heard. A hobby horse was made with a bed pillow in a white pillow case by tying two large ears at the closed end of the pillow and case, drawing big ugly eyes, nose, mouth and teeth with charcoal on a big face, putting this over the wearer's head and upper body and tying the huge face under the chin. Once after I was in bed, my uncle came to our house, along with my aunts. I knew who it was and yet I cried and huddled at the backside of the bed as far as I could get. Also if they knew someone was out walking after dark, they might plan to meet the walker in a dark, ghostly spot.

Another prank I was told of, and to me it seemed rather cruel, but I knew two families whose grown-up children participated in these pranks in their own homes. Some families with several girls to make dresses for, had gotten dress forms to use for fitting dresses and patterns. These forms were on a metal stand with an adjustable upper body shape from neck and shoulders to just below the waist. The entire form was about five feet tall.

A group of young single boys and girls were in the home of some friends whose mother had died quite some time earlier. The father was in the living room reading, and the group decided to play this prank on the father. While some got the dress form and slipped it under the covers of his bed, the girls in the kitchen made a thin flour dough round as if making a pie crust. They cut out eyes and made a nose and mouth and placed the pastry or "dough face" over an upside down rounded bowl. Then the finished product was taken to the bedroom, placed on the pillow at the head of the dress form. The other similar incident was told to me by one of the girls in the home where this took place. A young minister was holding a revival in the local church. His young wife was accompanying him, and they were spending the night with parishioners who had several teenage girls and boys. While the young preacher and the host and hostess were conversing in the parlor, the minister's wife helped do the dishes in the kitchen. The girls told her about the dough face prank which she thought was very funny. She suggested they play this on her husband which they did. Of course she could not go to bed until after her husband had.

Then there was the half-sheet thing, folding the bottom sheet in the middle of the sheet length so the sleepy occupant could not stretch out.

A young man I knew and a group of friends were partying in his home. The older brother was a teacher and quite sedate, and rather than spend the evening with the younger group, he stayed in the living room reading. The young people gathered some dried, very prickly and stinging chestnut burrs and put them in his bed, laughing all the while that George would forget his dignity when he got in bed. Since some of the guests were staying over night, my friend had to share the bed with his brother. He had forgotten what they had done and sleepily got in bed before his brother.

When the school had ended and there was no homework after supper, we three children would want something to do. Sis might want to read. My brother sometimes wanted to whittle something — maybe a ramrod for his pop gun (pea shooter). But sometimes we three would play "Authors" with cards. I don't know why they were called Authors because the cards had pictures of presidents on the face sides from George Washington to McKinley. Three or four people could play. Each player was dealt six cards with the rest of the deck upside down on the table. Each player would draw a card and discard one from his hand. Four cards of the same face or president made a "book" which was laid down and the one with the most books was the winner.

A game which didn't last long was called "Club Fist." Someone made a fist with the thumb sticking up. Another player made a fist around that one and three, four or five might do this until all hands were in the stack except the one of the bottom fist. Then that player would say "Take it off or knock it off." The owner of that thumb might say, "Knock it off." The leader could use three trials to knock if off. If he couldn't, that player became the leader, and the game started all over again.

We played checkers. If we did not have a checker board, we made one of cardboard and used small colored buttons or red and white grains of corn. Dad also made Chinese checker boards for us. Later we played Rook and when we moved back to Grassy Creek in 1975, I was surprised to learn that Rook was still being played by some locals and that there were Rook competitions.

A traveling salesman who came by in a buggy drawn by a horse would stop and spend the night at our house. I can't remember his name but he had white hair and was good-humored and pleasant. He and Dad would play games with us or rather play pranks on us. We youngsters would go out of the room and be called back in one at a time. One of them would hold up two saucers in front of their face and hand one over to the child and say, "Keep your eyes on me and do as I do." He would rub his saucer and then rub each cheek. We'd do the same and then they'd hand us a mirror to look at our face. Our saucer or little pie plate had lamp black on it and we had black cheeks. They would sometimes hang a sheet over the open doorway, they would stand on the other side of the sheet with a lamp back of them and a black image would appear on the sheet doing all kinds of contortions, kind of like a clown might do.

But when several friends of cousins visited, we'd play Rumor, Thimble, Guess or learn a new game from someone. Thimble, we'd sit in a row or half circle and put the palms of our hands together. The leader who had the thimble would hold the thimble between the palms of her/his hands and go from player to player as if placing something in their palms. After she had gone to all the players, she'd say, "Mary, who has the thimble?" Mary might say, "Timmy has it." Timmy opens his palms and if Mary has guessed right, she gets to drop the thimble. But the game continues until someone has guessed right.

Rumor: A leader whispers a sentence or expression into the ear of the person in line or circle next to her. That person whispers what she/he believes they have heard. After this has gone to the end of the line or circle, the last one is asked, "What was said to you?" She repeats what she heard and the leader tells what was started. Some very funny and different sentences or expressions made the rounds. Perhaps one way many rumors get started.

Guess: The leader says, "I'm thinking of a bird. We see this bird most every day. What bird am I thinking of?" Players may ask questions until the correct bird is named. Others may use flowers, or colors or states or cities or any group of objects.

Writing School

Writing schools were held, too. These courses were attended by middle-aged folk and older students who wanted to improve their writing. Staff-pens (old ink pens, wooden with metal nib) and ink were used. School desks, although made by people in the community, had an ink well to hold bottles of ink and a slot for the long staff pen. The one instructor or teacher that I remember seeing was either Mr. Delp or Mr. Sage (one taught the singing school and the other the writing school). Arm movement and the correct way to hold a pen were stressed, along with the formation of capital and small letters of the alphabet. Ovals, push-pulls and slants were taught. Whenever the teacher gave the students a break to rest their arms, he would make beautiful birds, flowers and objects using, first, colored chalk on the chalkboard and later on paper with blue, red and green inks. I was not allowed to attend these classes because I was too young. This teacher, too, was paid a modest sum and took turns at boarding in the students' homes for the ten day or two week sessions. Once when the writing teacher was spending the weekend at Uncle Charlie Shelton's home, our family went to visit early on Saturday night. The teacher was showing those not enrolled in the course how he used ovals, push-pulls and slants in writing and the pictures he could make using these methods. He made large bird pictures for my brother and sister and older cousins. I began to cry. My mother and other adults asked if I were sick. "No." "What's wrong?" I wouldn't tell them but kept crying. I'm sure the writing teacher didn't dream that that little "youngin" wanted an ink bird.

Handwriting was very important at that time since most business deals were recorded by hand. When someone in the community had clear flowing cursive penmanship that person was often asked to write deeds, contracts, wills, IOUs, and personal and business letters. Too, there were some residents who had never attended school and didn't read or write.

When I finished high school in 1924, Professor B. B. Daugherty, President of Appalachian State Teachers' College in Boone (now Appalachian State University), delivered the commencement address to our senior class. His theme was: "If a man can build a better mouse trap, or write a better letter than his neighbor, even though he lives in the woods, the world will make a beaten path to his door." As a class we heard, "Whatever you plan to be, be the best." We were from farm families and accustomed to work — hard work — and we knew our parents had made it possible for us to attend high school and wanted us to make the best of their efforts. We were, I guess, the most unlikely group one might find to amount to more than farmers and housewives. But parents and Professor Robert E. Lee Plummer, high school principal, had instilled ambition and determination in us, and from our class of 22 students as mentioned before, many became professional people. Even the one or two members who did not go to colleges, became along with the rest of us, community and civic leaders. Despite the fact that our parents could not afford to send some of us to college, many of us found a way to get started and then work our way through a bachelor's degree and some through post graduate degrees. I suppose that today we would be considered naive but we weren't. We believed that honest work was honorable and, I think, all of us tried to see that our children got a college education.

When someone sold a parcel of land or a portion of a farm, a deed was copied from the original or the section that was needed. A few people had land grants that were passed on to later owners and were rewritten. (Land grants were issued by governors in the early days to encourage settlement in this rugged mountain area. I have the grant issued by the governor of Virginia, James McDowell, in 1845, which was passed on as the land changed hands, ending up with my father about 1900.) Sometimes a family member was designated to inherit a part or a whole farm for caring for parents or some other person, and each party wanted a copy of the contract. Those who may not have had any "schooling" had to get someone to write deeds, transfers, personal and business letters. I recall my mother writing a letter dictated by my father to the Honorable Claude Swanson, governor of Virginia. Evidently, she had a better "handwriting" than my father did at that time. We children proudly looked and looked at the addressed envelope, "Our father is sending a letter to a very important person."

Some of the old deeds are interesting to read. They often began, "Beginning at a white oak tree at the road and running 32 poles to a stake on the wagon road near the top of a ridge near a barn." A pole was a rod length or 16½ feet used in measuring land.

An elderly man, who had been the recorder of deeds in Grayson County for a number of years told us of one deed that began, "From where I am now standing."

Entertainment

One day my father had walked down to the store at Grassy Creek, and when we saw him coming home, he was carrying a wooden box and another carton. He set the wooden box on a table, removed the 10 × 14 × 8 inch deep top and inside was a phonograph. From the other carton he took out a cylinder tube, slipped it over an arm that protruded out from the machine, lowered the diamond needle on the record and we heard the first recording we ever owned. There were two records of funny stories and jokes by "Uncle Josh," who evidently was a comedian. I never knew what Uncle Josh's real name was, but we laughed and laughed when we played those records. One record was the song *The Preacher and the Bear*, the other three recordings were hymns — one was *In the Sweet Bye and Bye*, and I don't remember what the other two were. We were always glad when Dad would play the phonograph. We children were not allowed to play the instrument lest we ruin a record or the needle. Uncle Luther would come to hear the Uncle Josh records and Grandpa liked the hymns.

Someone had taken the gramophone to the general store hoping someone like Dad would buy it. After the diamond needle needed to be replaced, and Jefferson was the only known source to get a replacement, Dad sold the machine to someone else.

Later we had a little record player that used the 78 rpm records and had to be rewound after each playing. When it was my turn to do the week's ironing which usually took a half day, I would hire my brother, Kyle, to play records. At times I would give him 10 or 15 cents or something he wanted. I was dating a young man who was a candy salesman. He had given me some boxes of Whitman's candy that came in an attractive metal box and which my younger brothers wanted to carry their school lunches in. Chocolate covered cherries were familiar but he gave me a box of chocolate covered strawberries, the first and maybe the last of those I ever had.

Herbert, five years older than I and being a boy and stronger, would be hired to do odd jobs for our uncles, Grandpa and neighbors at times and although he received little pay (I don't know how much since that was his secret), he would buy small things he wanted. He bought a "juice harp," as we called it. Research shows that this instrument, from the fourteenth century, has been around in many Asian and European countries with many different names such as, Jew's harp, Jews' harp, Jaw's harp, and Jew's trump. No doubt it is a primitive instrument, vibrated by plucking rather than by percussion. The brass frame is a small two-pronged, lyre or horseshoe-shaped frame with a little metal tongue or finger which is plucked when the frame is held between the teeth. The harp seems to have only one tone which may be varied by the mouth cavity. Again, my brother came home one day with a harmonica which we called a "French harp." The saying goes, "Music soothes the wildest animal." It seems that music is a language of all creatures, no matter how isolated, no matter how poor or rich, no matter how educated or illiterate, people find a way to have music even if they have to make their own by clapping two sticks together.

I think I was about six or seven years old when my father sold a cow and bought an organ. Another neighbor bought an organ for his family but had the cash to pay for his. A "sour grapes" neighbor said, "One family put a cow in the corner to 'Moo' for them. The other man let his money jingle for his family." I learned to play the organ a bit — strictly by ear but never had any musical instruction. Grandpa would come by and ask me to play something for him. Grandpa had served in the Confederate Army in the Civil War. I had learned to play *Marching Through Georgia*, and not knowing the history of the song, I thought it had a snappy tone. Grandpa would say, "Don't play that. Play *Dixie!*"

While in elementary school, some of the songs we would sing while sitting around the stove during the lunch hour were: *Red Wing, Little Mohee, The Lone Cowboy, Long Long Ago, Darling Nellie Gray, Carry Me Back to Old Virginny, Auld Lang Syne, Juanita, Comin' Through the Rye, The Old Oaken Bucket, Love's Old Sweet Song, When You and I Were Young Maggie, K-K-K-Katy, Rosewood Casket, Bury*

Me Not on the Lone Prairie, My Bonnie Lies Over the Ocean, Home Sweet Home and others.

There were war songs, of course: *Dixie, John Brown's Body, Tramp, Tramp, Tramp!, Tenting on the Old Camp Ground, Just Before the Battle, Mother, Keep the Home Fires Burning,* and *Over There*.

And there were the beautiful and inevitable Stephen C. Foster songs: *Oh, Susannah, My Old Kentucky Home, The Old Folks at Home, Mamma's in the Cold, Cold Ground, Old Black Joe, Uncle Ned, Old Dog Tray*.

Toys

Cornstalk Fiddles

In the fall when corn was almost ready to harvest, but before the stalks had dried out, two stalks about an inch in diameter were selected for a cornstalk fiddle. Matured corn stalks have joints every 10 or 12 inches apart and have grooves in the center of one side. After the best joints were selected to be used, two or three inches of a joint on the end of the picked joints were left to have ends for holding. A sharp pocket knife was used to make very straight slits under the sides of the grooves. A tiny piece of wood was cut into quarter-inch squares and one placed under each slit near the end of the joints. Now one finished piece was the fiddle, and the other was the bow which was rubbed over the fiddle to make sounds.

Pop Guns

An elder branch an inch or 1¼ inches in diameter and about a foot long was selected. Elders have a pith in the center of branches and trunks. With the point of a very sharp knife or awl, some of the pith was removed from each end of the selected length. Then a piece of strong straight wood pushed through the center of the elder would get the rest of the pith out. Another piece of hard wood was made into a ramrod. A branch of hickory or oak and about 3 inches longer than the gun made a good ramrod. In order to fire this weapon, you inserted a pea in the firing-end of the barrel, then you blew down the other end of the barrel, filling the chamber with air. Immediately you then put another pea at the end where you'd just blown down, creating a "vacuum" inside the barrel. Then, aiming the weapon, you shoved the ramrod down the barrel as fast as you could toward the pea lodged in the firing-end. This action pushed the second pea down the "vacuumized" barrel, and the original pea, wedged in the firing-end, would pop out at great velocity, hopefully hitting the desired target. In later years there were pea shooters. We also used spit balls. The ramrod, therefore, had to be three inches longer than the barrel. Most of the length of the ramrod was trimmed to fit inside the barrel, of course, but the top three inches, the ramrod handle, was left the size of the branch it was cut from, so the ramrod could be held. If we were hit by one of these spit balls, it really stung and we girls tried to avoid boys when we knew they had a pop gun.

Spool Tops or Whirligigs

We children watched anxiously for a spool of thread to be used and the spool empty. Certainly, no spool was to be thrown away. My father would shave the sides of the spool under one end which was left to be the top of the "top," sloped to almost a point at the lower end. Then a small round stick about five inches long and shaped to a point at one end was inserted into the hole in the center of the spool with the point protruding below the end of the spool. It might take a number of tries at first but we would find a level spot and see how long we could make our top whirl.

Willow Whistles

A willow branch with a diameter of about ¾ inch was selected. From it a piece seven or eight inches long was cut. This was done when the willow was in a green stage and there was sap in the branch. The next step was to get the bark surrounding the wood off in one piece, so it was massaged gently until the bark was loosened from the wood. Now we had a bark tube seven or eight inches long, as well as a piece of wood the same length. We cut a piece of this wood about ½ inch in length and inserted it in one end of the bark tube. We cut another piece of the same wood, about an inch long, or perhaps 1½ inches, shaped it like the mouthpiece of a reed instrument, and inserted it in the blowing end of the bark tube. Then we cut a tiny hole in the bark, just below the mouthpiece, so that the air could escape and a willow whistle was created.

Baseballs

We had no manufactured baseballs but we made our own. We unraveled any old socks or sweaters we could get our hands on. We always tried to have a marble or other round object to have in the center to start winding on. We would wind the yarn around and around and watch to make sure we had no lumps or spots thicker than others so the ball would be symmetrical. When the size felt comfortable in the hand, we used a darning needle and heavy thread and sewed and sewed over the yarn to keep the strands from raveling or getting out of place.

Balloons

We usually butchered two hogs in the late fall of the year. When the entrails were removed from the carcasses, my brother would be very sure to get the hog bladders. He would wash them repeatedly until they were really clean inside and out. Then he used a hollow weed or some other hollow gadget to blow the bladders as large as possible, tied the small ends and let them dry for a week or more. When they were dry and full of air, he sometimes inserted a small rod or round stick about 18 or 20 inches long in the neck of the bladders and tied them tightly. Dried beans or peas could be placed inside the bladders, if desired, to make them rattle and designs could be lightly painted on the outside. These bladders were very strong when dry and not as easily popped as balloons of today.

The described homemade toys were those that were for use any time. However, that does not mean that our parents never bought or gave us any other toys or gifts. At Christmas we each received one special gift. One year, my brother's gift was a wind-up monkey which climbed a string or cord. Each end of the cord had a small metal ring — one end was held on the floor with a foot and the other was held as high as one could reach and the monkey climbed the string. My gift that year was a toy replica of a kitchen wood burning stove, with four removable stove caps or eyes with a little gadget to lift the burners, and a little iron pot and fry pan. I could actually put a fire in the little fire box as long as the stove was over a rock or a surface that would not burn. My sister, who was seven years older than I, got a mirror in a wood frame on a wood stand, and a fancy comb. We hung our stockings from the mantel, real stockings, not flannel or red felt ones, as we had never seen those. In the morning there was an orange, some sticks of peppermint and lemon flavored candy and some nuts in each stocking. Sometimes, we might find a pencil, a one cent one, and a stick of Long Tom chewing gum. This gum was a round white stick about 8 inches long and wrapped in paper, and after being chewed a bit was very tough, perhaps had lots of paraffin in it. One year I received a locket with a hinged back in which a picture could be placed. My sister got a gold (plated, no doubt) bracelet. I was so elated with my locket that I do not remember what my brother got. Another year I got a doll which I named Josie. Josie was held in a box by two elastic cords and after I played with her for a time, she was placed back in the box and put into a dresser drawer.

Ice Cream

We were in bed and likely some of us were already asleep around 10:30. The phone rang. Dad got up and answered the call. He said, "Everybody get up. Luther called and is bringing ice cream." We all got up and slipped on our clothes. Mom got dishes and spoons.

When Uncle Luther arrived, he explained, "We had an ice cream supper at the school house and had some left over. I didn't want to throw it out and thought you might like it." One must remember refrigeration was not common then, so this was "urgent business." I was perhaps four years old and had never heard of ice cream and wondered what it was. I said, "It's awful good if it wasn't so cold."

Another time I went with Uncle Luther in a wagon to Troutdale. At that time, Troutdale had a drug store. Uncle Luther went inside and came back with a cone of ice cream for me. Of course, I had had ice cream but not like this. I ate the cream down to the cone. "Now what do I do with this? There's more ice cream there but how do I get it?" Finally, I bit into the cone and found it could be eaten.

An ice cream supper was a social affair, mostly thought up and planned by the young, single people of ages of about 16 to 25 and especially promoted by those who were dating, and those who were looking forward to finding a date. A couple of weeks or more might be needed for the planning of the event and time to contact a special person in another community which might lead to a date.

First, who had an ice cream freezer? Mr. Isham Thompson had one or more and also had an ice house! Ah, and who else? Someone knew of another one or two. Roscoe, Alma or Willie Thompson will surely get permission from their father to let us use his freezers. And maybe a block or two of ice from his ice house. Someone else had a few blocks of ice cut from frozen creeks or the New River and stored in sawdust or straw and other coverings in the root cellar. (Ice was prized for lemonade in the hot summer months.) Some root cellars were dug in banks with earth serving as insulation on the boarded two sides, back and top. The front door was of double wood thickness.

Other needs were cream, egg yolks, sugar, flavorings, coarse salt and cakes. Young ladies either volunteered to supply some of these things or would contact friends who were known to have lots of cream or other ingredients. The young men would buy the sugar and coarse salt. What flavors were wanted? If in season (summer), there would be wild strawberries, raspberries, peaches. Or maybe vanilla, chocolate or lemon. If in winter there were canned berries and fruits. Two or three ladies were responsible for providing cakes.

Then there was the matter of the making of the ice cream. A custard or mixtures of cream, egg yolks, sugar and flavor must be put together. Names were suggested of people known to be the best and most creative cooks in the community. It was a sure thing that flattery would easily persuade any woman to maintain her prestige as the best cook.

Young men were appointed to round up the freezers, the ice, coarse salt and have them at the homes of the ladies who were putting together the custard or mixture, and have them there four or five hours ahead of the time scheduled for the supper. A couple of batches should be made and ready and then more would be made at the meeting place.

Of course there was no electricity at this time and the ice cream freezers were turned by hand. The freezers had a metal can a half gallon or larger, in the center of a wooden pail or bucket. The can had a dasher, a paddle-like affair, which fit in the center of the can and which was turned by an attached handle. The can was filled no more than three-fourths full to allow for expansion as the mixture froze. Then ice and coarse salt were placed around the can in the bucket.

Top: Row 1 (left to right): Minnie Barker (Aunt Minnie), Bessie Spencer, Uncle Iredell Barker, Betty Spencer. Row 2: Estel Waddell, Aunt Lona Barker, Flora Waddell. *Bottom left:* Uncle Luther Barker, Albert Spencer, Fannie Spencer, Aunt Minnie Barker. *Bottom Right:* Aunt Minnie Barker, Uncle Iredell, Bonnie Sexton.

These were some of the young unmarried people of this era of time who planned "get-togethers," ice cream suppers, box suppers, hay rides, attended writing and singing schools, knew and sang the Stephen Foster songs, Negro spirituals, *The Old Oaken Bucket, Love's Old Sweet Song, Juanita, Maggie,* and many others.

To me they seemed old but ranged in age from around 20 to about 25 or more before marriage. Only one of the group, Aunt Lona, I believe, did not marry — but had two boyfriends — both of whom died. Muncay Handy was killed from a falling tree and Norman Peak died of an illness. Norman's mother was a cousin of my mother and I went with my mother to visit him a short time before he passed away.

Two or three fellows took turns in turning the handle. As the cream began freezing turning became more difficult. When the mixture became too stiff to turn, it was done. The can was removed, the dasher taken out and cream scraped off into the can. If the freezer was needed again the cream was put into a container and covered with lots of airproof materials and kept in a cool spot. If the freezer was not needed again, the whole thing was covered and let sit surrounded by more ice until the cream had mellowed and was ready to eat.

Lots of work but worth it when everyone gathered around 7 P.M. to enjoy this specialty which was not available otherwise. And then the fun with friends and neighbors and pranks of slipping some ice bits and dropping them down the backs of some unsuspecting person's shirt, the squeals and getting even made the evenings a special event.

From some pictures I have these were some of the single fellows and girls at that time. Some have only first names:

Bonnie, Etta, Curtis Sexton, Joe, Frank, Betty and Bessie Spencer, Estil and Flora Waddell, Luther, Iredell, Minnie and Lona Barker, Wiley Albert, Becky, Mary, Fannie Spencer, Verna Pugh, Roy and Bradley Davis, Callie Ballou, Theodore, Alice, Virginia, Bly and Hicks Spencer, Flossie Millard and Willie Robbins, Cleve and Lessie Reeves. There were Hayneses, Greers, Osbornes, Dicksons, Ellers, Richardsons, Reedys, Debords, Hudlers, Blackburns and others.

Not only single people attended ice cream suppers but some whole families came.

Ice was a rarity that people liked to have for lemonade which was the special drink of that time and made with real lemons, served in the homes and for special occasions and for take-out picnics and "dinner on the grounds."

Box Suppers

Box suppers were held to raise money for some community need. A church group might want to get new hymnals, a pulpit Bible, or to help with a medical bill for someone, or for a family whose house had been lost in a fire. Small country schools had very few supplies furnished other than some chalk, a few erasers, water pails and oil to help keep down dust on the school floors. Teachers would involve parents and community in holding a box supper to get a wall pencil sharpener, a school flag, construction paper, paste, some library books, a dictionary, more erasers, and other items to be ordered from school supply catalogs.

Again, one of these events might be planned just as a social event for pure enjoyment and fun. Box suppers are described more fully earlier on.

Playhouses

I believe that young children all over the world like to play, and play at things they know about. We, too, liked to play and we played things we knew about. We didn't have television, radio or Nintendo games to sit and look at.

Left: The author. *Right:* Guy and Kate Spencer, Gwyn Hamby "threatening" Ruth and Edgar Ashley.

As some of my close friends and I became "young married couples," and had old cars, we began to venture out a bit for varied activities. Guy and Kate Spencer, Edgar and Ruth Ashley, and my husband, Gwyn and I, began camping. We had a tent which we had bought from someone who no longer was interested in camping. We selected White Top Mountain, a mountain in the state of Virginia, for camping. We were camping there when White Top was hosting a music festival in 1933 in a large, locally built pavilion. Eleanor Roosevelt, wife of then president, Franklin D. Roosevelt, and Burl Ives, the singer, were there. We considered this event a special occurrence in our venturing out, which we never forgot. In fact, Ruth, Edgar, my husband and I dared to take a trip to Chicago to a World's Fair, using a tent for sleeping and shelter when we wanted to spend a day or two in a special location.

My closest playmate, until I was eight or nine years old, lived just across the hill from our house, probably one-eighth of a mile by way of the path over the hill. However, the road around the hill was perhaps a quarter of a mile for wagons and horseback riders. She was older than I. Her birthday was December 5th and I was born a month later on January 5th. Their mailbox was at the road near our house — 40 or 50 feet from our mailbox.

The hill between our homes was wooded and she and I would meet in the woods just above "their road" and in sight of our house and make "play houses." Lots of laurel (rhododendron) grew in the woods. We'd find a tall thickly branched laurel for one wall of the house and break limbs from other laurel bushes for the other walls, by sticking the broken stems in the ground. If there were bare spots in the walls, we'd gather branches from ivy (real name mountain laurel but was called ivy here) which grew abundantly in shorter clumps or bushes, to cover these spots. Then we'd make rooms, maybe not divided, but each corner was a room. We knew houses had beds, a kitchen and "setting room," so we gathered pretty green moss for beds and pillows for our dolls. Furniture, too, was of moss with white flint pebbles for marble tops. We hardly ever brought our best doll but one which we or our mother had made from rolled up white cloth of worn-out petticoats or sheets. The kitchen stove was a rock or tiny piece of thick board with a metal top if we could find a thrown-away piece from a farm tool. The kitchen table, a piece of wood, perhaps 3 or 4 inches square on a little flat rock. Dishes were from pieces of broken plates, saucers or bowls or whatever we could find, and likely to be changed every day or so. We'd scrounge at home for tiny things — teeny mirrors, big white buttons for plates. The rag bag or box was slipped into to make bedspreads, table cloths, and dresses for the babies (often just tied or pinned on). Of course, we'd each try to have some things the other did not have. We took our dolls and visited each other and talked about the illnesses the babies had had. When rain kept us inside or one could not come, the other was disappointed. But summer didn't last forever. I was allowed to sweep and clean one corner in our granary for a play house where I could plan and play alone or when a little friend visited. My friend, too, had her indoor playhouse.

We did not have a lot of bought toys but we'd find or make things. My brother would make sleds from discarded lumber, wagons with four wheels sawed from a green log, make a flutter wheel to use in a tiny dam in our little branch (fashioned after the dam and water wheel of flour mills). When my cousins or neighbor girls visited, we'd put saddles on large logs, hauled in for fire wood, and go places we'd heard of or read about. Uncle Tom Hash had a surry (a four wheeled carriage with two seats), my three cousins and I sat in it and traveled to far away places such as Maryland where we had relatives and, often we dipped brown sugar for snuff from a little tin snuff box using birch toothbrushes. Vivid imaginations might be rampant but served to help pass the time, even when doing chores and "day-dreaming." I doubt if our parents ever heard us say, "I don't have anything to do."

Clothing

Some of the clothing our people had was bought from the local store but mostly ordered from Sears Roebuck, Montgomery Ward in Baltimore, and Charles Williams Stores in New York, N.Y. Men and boys, ladies and girls had one Sunday outfit for summer and one for winter, ordered from the mail order stores. The few local stores carried bolts of cloth, a few shoes, men's and women's hose, men's work shirts and bib overalls, red, blue and green bandanna handkerchiefs, a few white ones, combs, hair pins and a few toiletries and that was about all in the clothing line. As more drummers (salesmen) came by, merchants were persuaded to add to their stock of clothing, especially items which were frequently asked for.

Most of the family clothing was made in the home, mostly from cloth available in the stores. There were a few spinning wheels in homes and some of the older ladies spun "linsey-woolsey"— a fabric spun from a mixture of home grown flax and home spun woolen thread, dyed to the desired color. This cloth was used for the most part for men's suits and jackets but sometimes for skirts and jackets for women. But the greater part of the family clothing was made by the women for themselves, husbands and children. A fabric, called domestic, which now is called bleached or unbleached muslin, was widely used for underwear for all the family members. It was also used for bed sheets, pillow cases, bed straw ticks, and bed spreads. I suppose that was the reason it was called "domestic." For Sunday underwear, especially for women and children, a white muslin cambric or nainsook was used. Petticoats, corset covers, gowns, chemises were often trimmed with crocheted lace and yokes. Those trimmings were crocheted with very fine thread and a fine hook — so fine that some of the work was done with what looks like sewing machine thread. Ladies were supposed to have very slender waist lines and to attain this look, corsets were a must. They extended from below the hips to above the waist line just under the bosom to give a buxom appearance, were laced either in front or back with long laces which could be drawn extremely tight at the waist while the wearer drew in and held her breath at this point until the corset was laced and hooked in front or back. Corsets which laced in the back were fastened in front with rustproof (as advertised)

Child's summer petticoat

Winter petticoat with long sleeves

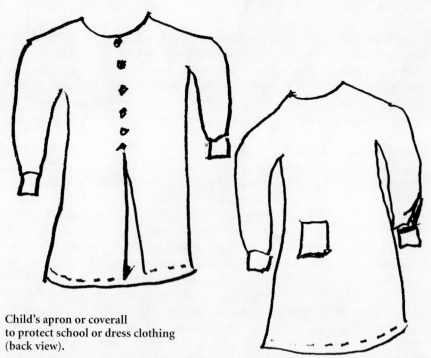

Child's apron or coverall
to protect school or dress clothing
(back view).

Front view of child's apron or coverall

hooks and eyes and all had staves of light aluminum boning from top to bottom to prevent the garment from drooping and showing body bulges. All these garments had four or more attached hose supporters, to hold up stockings two or three inches above the knees.

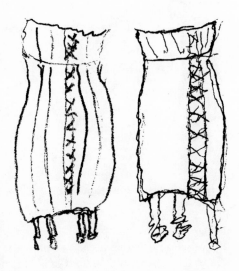

Dressy blouses, always called waists, were of lightweight sheer material of voile, organdy, georgette, crêpe de Chine, dimity or eyelet embroidery, so pretty corset covers were a must to cover the tops of the corsets and to look dainty and feminine. Brassieres, at that time, were usually boned and reached down to the waist line. For those who might have had large hips but did not need

Corsets

the long corsets there were boned hip slimmers that covered the hips and just reached to the waist line where the brassieres could be attached. Catalogs referred to these garments as "figure formers" or "hip reducers" and customers were advised to order the articles 2 to 3 inches smaller than the dress sizes at the waists. How hot and uncomfortable these garments must have been on hot summer days!

Dress shirts for men were always white and when laundered were stiffly starched, especially the front, the collar and cuffs. Ironing these shirts had to be done by the most expert ironer of the household.

Dress shoes for ladies were pumps, sandals, oxfords

Corset covers

Chemise
(often called "shimmy")

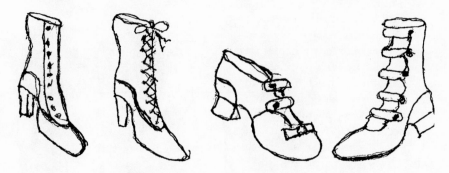

Ladies' high top buttoned and laced shoes   **Button slipper and button shoe for little girls**

or high tops. The pumps might have one or two straps that buttoned and have high, medium or low heels. (Although we do not think of pumps as having straps, that is what the catalogs called them.) The most fashionable ladies' shoes of the time were the high tops — laced or buttoned with tops which reached the calf of the leg. They came in solid black or white, but some had black patent leather bottoms which surrounded the foot part but with white tops. Of course there were slippers — buttoned, laced or slip-ons.

There was a limited selection for young girls, white leather or black patent Mary Janes with a one button strap. Then some which reached just above the ankle and had four buttoned straps. For men and boys there were the laced or buttoned low cut oxford types, but mostly the laced or buttoned kind that came above the ankle. For years and years my father wore, on Sundays, horse hide shoes in a soft black material that laced and came just above the ankle.

Sometimes stout ladies had to have someone lace or button their high tops. What a task to get ready for a fancy function — putting on the corsets, lots and lots of petticoats and high top shoes. Every household had to be equipped with shoe buttoners for each member to have his or her own. The buttoners were of metal about five inches long with an oval for easy hand hold and a curved hook at the opposite end to reach through the button hole and pull the button through.

Since much of the clothing was made in the home, ladies, especially, always observed what friends and neighbors were wearing. Patterns were exchanged or borrowed. Wrapping paper from the store and newspapers were saved for copying patterns and for cutting patterns by using garments on hand for shapes and fitting them to the person. There were those who seemed to have a "knack" for making clothes. Once my parents had gotten green wool cloth for winter dresses for my sister and me. My mother got our Aunt Lona to come and stay at our house to cut, fit and make the two dresses. She used an old dress for shape and size and began cutting and fitting paper patterns until she and our

Shoe button hook

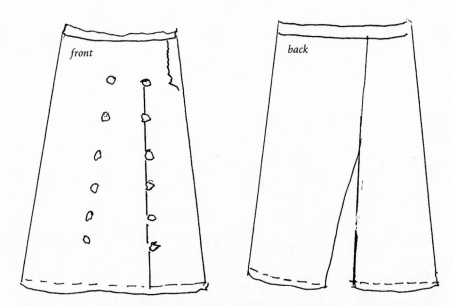

When ladies decided to ride horses on stride saddles, instead of the side saddles, they needed "riding skirts." The skirts were divided but could be buttoned on the front to look like a skirt when walking around. Molly Hudler made mine of tan khaki cloth.

mother were satisfied that she could cut the material. The dresses were trimmed in green velvet of the same shade as the wool, matched by Sears when ordered.

At one time middy suits were the fad. Ours had pleated skirts with tops that came below the waist line and had collars made like those on sailors' blues or white dress uniforms, square in the back and sloped to the center front and trimmed with braid. Mothers made most of the everyday or "knock about" clothing. Older women wore dresses that were almost ground length while younger ladies' dresses came to about shoe top or ankle length. Taffeta was a popular material for ladies' skirts, a stiff like silk material with a smooth glossy finish and when worn over several petticoats made a swishy sound when one was walking and may have been what Robert Louis Stevenson had in mind in his poem of the Wind when he wrote, "And all around I heard you pass like ladies' skirts across the grass." Sleeves were long and cut and gathered for fullness at the shoulder — some were called "mutton leg." Everyday dresses were of gingham, calico, chambray or inexpensive material and usually buttoned at the front closing. Button holes were handmade and some people were expert at making beautiful button holes — certainly those who did lots of embroidery and were in much demand for their work on fine and special garments. Country people made aprons to protect their dresses while cooking and doing the many household and gardening chores. It was necessary to have some clean aprons to put on if company were coming or if someone walked in unexpectedly. My grandmother even had a black, lace trimmed apron which she some-

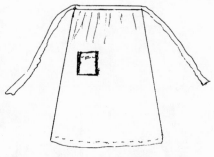

Waist apron, to be tied in the back, to protect the front of a dress or skirt.

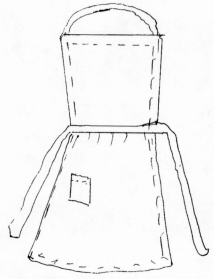

Bib apron to protect the entire front of a dress.

times wore over her black taffeta dress to church along with her lovely black bonnet that Aunt Lona had made. Children had what we called aprons but were really more coveralls, made of light weight materials with long sleeves, long as the dresses underneath them, practically straight, opened and buttoned in the back from the neck to the waist, and were truly to protect our school dresses or good clothing while eating or doing chores.

Newborn babies were at first dressed in long "outing" flannel gowns which were 16 or 18 inches longer than the babies' body to keep the feet warm. Then later the baby dresses and coats were long for the same reason, I suppose. Some of those dresses were beautifully made of embroidered lawn or fine white material, tucked, lace trimmed or with eyelet embroidery. Some can be seen today, used as christening gowns. There are old pictures of babies seated in a chair and the long dress reaching the floor. However, country people used whatever material they could for baby clothing. When the baby could walk, then he was dressed in rompers — a one piece garment, usually buttoned in the back from neck to waist and with drop seats in back for use while being toilet trained.

Little boys progressed to little suits made of chambray, poplin, corduroy or a lightweight fabric. The pants were mostly knee length with hemmed legs. The jackets usually had sewed on belts and pockets. Then came the eight to twelve year old period and the knickerbocker suits. The pants legs had elastic in the bottom and were worn just below the knees and the length and fullness of the material ballooned over the elastic. The jacket, too, had sewn on belt and pockets.

Although money was scarce, there were bargains to be had. I have a 1917 sales catalog from Charles Williams Stores in New York, the sale to cover the months of July and August of that year in almost every kind of clothing for the entire family from babies to adults, as well as furniture, cosmetics, tonics, sport-

Beautiful dresses and hats and brooches.

ing goods, auto and bicycle parts and many, many kinds of cloth. Below is a copy of an ad for three petticoats for ladies:

> Look at this bargain — Three well made durable cambric skirts for the special low price of $1.69. One skirt has a deep flounce of beautiful eyelet embroidery headed by ribbon-run insertion to match. Another has a deep flounce headed by insertion to correspond and the other has a deep flounce of embroidery. Front length, 36 to 44 inches. Delivered free. 3 for $1.69.

Uncle Luther Barker, Albert Spencer, Uncle Roscoe Barker. Albert was considered by some to be a "fancy dude." He wore a monocle, had stylish suits and showy ornate watch fobs. He was popular with both the young ladies and young men.

They and other summer underwear for ladies were beautifully decorative and in price from 52 cents to 92 cents each. One doesn't see such elaborate petticoats and lingerie today.

This store featured lots of shoes in that catalog but I was looking for overshoes and the catalog did not show any. We did not have overshoes for many years and the first ones I remember were low rubber ones and it seems just for men. When it was rainy, snowy and muddy, our shoes were muddy and we'd look for a little stick, splinter or chip to clean off as much mud as we could before going into the house and we were embarrassed to go into neighbors' houses with muddy shoes. There were leggings for men. There were a kind of heavy khaki cloth leggings with stays to keep them from drooping down and they were laced with long laces. Then there were leather leggings which had hooks and eyes. They were worn over the bottom of 18 or so inches of the pants legs and when removed left the pants legs very wrinkled.

We each had one pair of shoes which were called "Sunday shoes" as they were worn only when we went to church or on special occasions. We children were not allowed to run and play in our best shoes so we tried to keep on hand the old worn Sunday shoes to use for casual visiting or going to the store when we didn't want to go barefoot.

Left: Tena Debord whose fancy dress is topped with an "overskirt" and wide sash. *Right:* Cousin Effie Childress, her husband Ed and son Raymond in Lansing, N.C. Note little boy in his white dress. Little boys often wore dresses until 2½ or 3 years of age.

My brother, sister and I had shoes for winter but went barefoot on week days from the tenth of May (traditionally the first day of guaranteed warm weather) until it became cold in the fall. When there were some very warm days in early spring, we begged to take off our shoes, but Mother always said, "Not until the tenth of May." The shoes worn all winter in rain and snow had been wet and dried until they became somewhat out of shape, wrinkled and hurt the feet in spots. We thought "how good it would feel to have our feet free again." Two days before the special day, if the weather was warm, we were allowed to walk around outside without our shoes but with our stockings on. The stockings were almost worn out anyway and not fit to keep another year.

Our winter everyday shoes were made by Mr. Bob Peak. If Dad had a chance to go to Troutdale or Lansing he would buy leather for our shoes but Mr. Peak usually had leather on hand. Dad would have us place our feet on a piece of cardboard and he would draw around each foot with a pencil. The pattern he took to the cobbler was always a bit larger than our feet to allow for growth.

Ethlyn and Velma Barker, Uncle Ira's daughters, in matching organza dresses with tucks and lace and bows.

The tops of the shoes were two or three inches above the ankles and were laced with strings of dried groundhog pelts. When the shoes were picked up from Mr. Peak they looked quite nice, but to our dismay, Dad would melt beef tallow and rub all over them to make them waterproof and they never looked as nice any more.

Worn-out shoes were kept to repair those that needed new half soles, heel taps or had holes that needed patching. Families had on hand an iron "shoe stand" about twenty inches tall that stood on the floor and different size "lasts" (shaped like feet) that fitted on the top of the stand to use for half-soling shoes or putting on heel taps. Holes sometimes occurred in the sides of the shoes, requiring patching. A patch would be cut from the best part of a discarded shoe, holes punched through the patch with an awl and around the hole in the shoe and sewn with heavy thread drawn through a lump of tallow or beeswax. It was embarrassing to have to wear patched shoes to school or to any gathering, but parents had a hard time keeping shoes for a large family, and, I'm sure, did the best they could. Dad usually kept on hand a large piece of new leather for replacing worn-out half soles and heel taps of the best shoes.

Mr. Peak also made beautiful saddlebags for my father and others. Travel in the early years was often by horseback and saddlebags were mighty convenient for carrying groceries, books, clothing or anything bunglesome or that needed protection from the weather. Mr. Fields Davis in the Long Branch area was also a cobbler, but mostly in shoe repair.

Embroidered cambric, batiste, voile and a fabric called Swiss embroidery was available for camisoles, corset covers, slips and other underwear and also

Top: My half-brothers, sons of Etta Sexton and my father: Joe, Harry and Kyle, bare-foot but wearing knickerbockers. *Bottom:* Nathan and Ina Reedy in Sunday dress before they were married. On the back of the picture Nathan had written, "Will the news be good or bad? Can we be together tonight?"

for dresses. And there were fancy laces for these articles. Instead of panties for ladies, there were drawers with ruffles of embroidery, lace or of cloth at the bottom of each leg which reached, usually, just below the knee. Then when dresses and skirts became a bit shorter, up to the calf of the leg, there were bloomers with elastic at the waist and at the bottom of each leg which allowed

Joe and Jane Reedy, Nathan's parents, with Nathan and Ina in their everyday dress. Note the aprons, the bib overalls.

them to be pushed above the knee, if desired. Everyday bloomers were mostly of black sateen, but some were available in white fabrics.

Men's suits, especially their best or Sunday suits, had watch pockets. These were little pockets on the vest or on the top side of the pants just below the belt line. Most watches were on chains with a gadget on the end of the chain to go through a button hole to keep from dropping or losing the watch. There were openfaced watches with a glass over the face. The fancier and more costly gold watches had covers. Often the watch chain passed across the chest with a fancy ornament, called a fob, hanging from the chain.

Men's and boys' everyday shirts were made of rather heavy chambray and pants of denim or twill. Men's summer drawers might be made of domestic that reached from the waist to the ankles. For winter there were knitted one piece union suits or the knitted undershirt and long drawers called "long johns" with long sleeves and legs.

As everyday clothing became worn and had holes in it, it was patched. Ripped seams were resewn. Socks, stockings and sweaters were darned. There was always the "rag bag" with parts of worn-out clothing and scraps saved from leftover pieces of cloth used to make dresses and shirts and for patching. No respectable housewife would allow her husband or son to go off the farm with holes in the elbows or knees of his work clothes.

Some parts of old sweaters and socks could be salvaged to ravel yarn for darning holes in the heels and toes of socks and elbows of sweaters. Darning needles were a must and possibly a rubber ball to put under the hole to be darned to keep it the

Aunt Jennie Sheets. Note the bonnet, the print dress, the ample apron with the pocket on the left so her right hand is free for the cane.

right size. For cotton stockings and socks, they might be darned with cotton thread gotten from the store which came in little balls which cost two or three cents.

Women and girls wore wide brimmed, lightweight hats or homemade bonnets when working outside. Single girls used special care to keep the face, neck, arms and hands from getting tanned as it was fashionable to have a white, soft complexion. Frequently one could see young ladies hoeing corn, picking berries or working in the garden with the arms covered with the legs of long stockings, wearing gloves, a handkerchief or cloth tied around their neck, and wearing a broadbrimmed hat. No one ever heard today's compliment, "You've a nice tan!"

Today, people go to the beach, lie in the sun, even pay to lie under a tanning lamp to get as much tan as possible. When people in the earlier days went to the beach, the bathing suits of both women and men covered most of the body. What would people think if they suddenly appeared at beaches today?

Hats & Head Dress

Hats and head dress of some kind have been important down through the years, and still are in many countries today. Ladies always wore hats to church. Men removed their hats in church and tipped their hats when being introduced to a lady as a token of respect and also removed them in other situations expected of men.

Sun bonnet. The part covering the forehead was lined and cardboard staves sewed in to hold the bonnet shapely. A small apron piece protected the neck from sun.

Men's hats were usually made of felt from the fur or pelts of animals. Then there were and still are the caps with brims.

Panama hats for both men and women were considered to be fine head wear. They were of plain construction — rather narrow brims for the men's hats with a band of black or white around the bottom of the crown and an inside sweat band in the crown that fitted over the forehead and hair. Panama hats for ladies had wider brims with the black or white band the only decoration. The material for these hats had plaited strips from the tender young leaves of a plant called the "jipi-japa" which grew in Panama and was made into hats by the Panamanians. Sulfur from a volcano was ground into "milk of sulfur" and used to bleach these hats to a dazzling whiteness.

Other head dress for ladies were straw hats decorated with artificial fruits — grapes, cherries, crab apples and leaves — all very stiff. Some other decorations were feathers and artificial flowers. Then there were tam o'shanters in different colors. And for winter wear fascinators — a knitted or crocheted triangle to cover the head and ears and tie under the chin, decorated with ruffling of the same material or some bought shiny baubles. Everyday ones might not have any decorations. And, of course there were always the winter toboggans for children and adults. Some ladies made hats from dried corn shucks by folding them to have triangular points and in overlapping layers for the crown and brim separately and join them together and a band of grogain ribbon or other material to cover where they were joined together.

Most ladies had veils which they wore in winter to protect their faces from cold. These veils were not the decorator veils of later years but of material as thick and heavy as cheese cloth. I recall when I was very small — in fact when I was being carried, over my toboggan they put a veil over my face and tied in the back. It was a cold day and the veil became wet from breathing and was cold in front of my nose and mouth. Later on summer veils in different patterns and colors were attached to the hat brims and came down as far as the chin. Hats were also known as bonnets as in "Easter bonnets," but bonnets as we knew them were used and worn by elderly ladies and others for protection from the sun while working outside in summertime.

Clothing Material

Dresses, Blouses or Waists

Chambray, voile, pongee, silk, lawn, poplin, gingham, calico, madras, cambric, crêpe de chine, linen, georgette, taffeta, shantung, batiste, serge, gabardine, cashmere, satin

Suits

Suitings (cotton & wool), serge, corduroy, denim, cotton, khaki, shepherd's check, linsey-woolsey

Underwear

Cambric, nainsook, batiste, muslin, eyelet-embroidery, sateen, voile, domestic, crinkled crêpe, gray and brown outing flannel

Hose

Lisle, silk, cotton, wool — held up on ladies and children with elastic garters

Hair

Long hair with twist or bun in back. Plaited to hang down the back or pinned around the head. Parted in the middle and braid on each side with ribbon bow on each braid.

Hair rats — to place over ears and cover with hair to protrude at sides. Made from natural hair saved from combings. Fastened with metal or bone hairpins.

When babies were expected there were certain items that were absolutely essential. Of course, diapers were a must! The few local general stores carried bolts of white birdseye cloth for diapers in widths of 30 and 36 inches. The 30 inch width was fine for newly borns but many babies wore diapers until they were quite large and for economy, many parents would buy the 36 inch width. The birdseye cloth had a tiny design of thicker weave (hence the name of birdseye) but was soft and rather long-wearing material for the frequent washings and boilings necessary for diapers. The family tried to have no fewer than a dozen and half of diapers so this meant buying at least 19 or 20 yards of birds-eye to be cut into squares and hemmed on each end with the tiny shirt-tail type hem.

In addition to diapers, there were little shirts, gowns, belly bands and receiving blankets to be made. These garments were made of white outing flannel which was also carried in bolts by the merchants. If the family could afford them, they tried to have six gowns made with long sleeves and 12 or 15 inches longer than the infant's body to keep the feet warm. Little shirts had long sleeves, open fronts with ties at the neck. The "belly bands" of the white flannel were about 3½ inches wide and long enough to reach around the body. They were put on just after the baby was born to cover the navel where the umbilical cord had been cut to prevent navel hernia that may occur when the baby cried. The bands were hemmed all around to prevent raveling. They were pinned with three safety pins. Lots of safety pins were a necessity in every household and especially for pinning the triangularly folded diapers at the front waist and around each leg.

Then Johnson's baby powder was needed to prevent chafing irritation.

Of course, if the family could afford to buy dresses, petticoats, coats and dress items from the mail order houses, there were long dresses with eyelet embroidery or lace trim, petticoats and long coats with shoulder capes for babies. Some of those items have been carefully preserved through the years and used as christening garments for grand-, great-grandchildren and nieces and family kin. But there were not Pampers and the galaxies of bright colored garments in those days that are available today.

Not only farm families but most families had lots of children back then and any clothing and items that could be saved were saved for the next baby.

My father sometimes shaved only on Sunday mornings before going to church unless he was going somewhere or visiting. I remember when he was getting ready to shave, he'd get his razor with the long blade, take the razor strap hanging beside the mantel and with strokes, first on one side of the blade, then on the other, "flip-flap," "flip-flap," alternating back and forth to sharpen his razor. When he thought he had the blade sharp, he'd draw a hair from his head, hold it up and see if the razor would cut it without any pressure. Then he'd pour a bit of hot water over the Castile soap in his shaving mug, use the shaving brush and lather his face. I remember the Williams boxes of regular shaving soap and how nice it smelled, but if he were out of the Williams soap, my mother would find a cake of her carefully guarded Castile soap. I was always so glad when she used Castile soap to give me a bath. It smelled so pleasant it was almost a treat to have a bath.

After Dad had shaved his face someone had to shave his neck and be very careful to leave the back hairline even. Some dress shirts for men did not have attached collars but just bands around the neck part with a button hole in the center back and front. Store bought collars were attached with collar buttons and usually someone had to put the back collar in for the wearer and they fastened much like cuff links in special dress shirts.

Health and Remedies

After the first three decades in our area, people would laugh and smirk when they were told of many of our home remedies and medicines made from roots, barks, herbs and blooms. Also laugh and scoff and feel so sorry for those poor people when told of our gathering herbs, roots, barks and flowers to sell for necessities. These people are more than likely paying lots of money for and complaining of medical costs of drugs made from these same items today. After all, everything we eat, wear, live in, use and have, all comes from the good earth the Lord made for us.

Herman, my husband's nephew, was always saying funny things, even when serious. When Herman was in second grade and his teacher, Miss Vivian, had a sprained ankle, he said "Put a rotten apple on it." Miss Vivian was telling her mother what Herman had said that day. Her mother said, "He was right. You put a vinegar poultice on a sprain."

The first doctor I knew was Dr. Wagg, whose office was in the back room of the store which he and his son, Charlie Wagg, owned and operated at Grassy Creek. The building, now old and falling down, can still be seen at the intersection of old route 16 and 725. Dr. Wagg was somewhat elderly when I knew him, with white hair and white mustache.

One night we were awakened when our father let out a scream of pain. (Some years earlier, he had owned a team of mules which ran away with his wagon and him in it. Dad had been thrown out of the wagon and his shoulder dislocated.) Dr. Wagg was sent for and since Dad was in so much pain, he was given chloroform as an anesthetic. (I have known of people under the influence of chloroform, while feeling no pain, who would talk.) While the doctor was pulling Dad's arm to put it back in the socket, my father, not aware of what was going on, spat in Dr. Wagg's face. This made the doctor so angry, he picked up his bag and started to leave, and my mother had to follow him outside and plead with him to come back and finish the job.

After learning that throwing his arm in his sleep could dislocate the shoulder, Dad had a cloth strap made to fasten that arm to his side and used it at night as long as he lived.

145

Evidently this was before Dr. Fielden Osborne moved to our area and became our family doctor. He lived about three-quarters of a mile from where we lived. In those days doctors made house calls, traveling on horseback with saddle bags to hold bottles of medicine and pills.

In the meantime we heard of Dr. Pennington, Dr. Tom Jones, Dr. Lester Jones and another Dr. Jones. (I don't know if this was Dr. Dean Jones, Sr., or not. Of course not the present Dr. Dean Jones, Jr.) These doctors lived in the Helton and Lansing areas. My grandparents, who had moved from Silas Creek in Ashe County, always said that Dr. Manley Blevins had the reputation of being the best "pneumonia doctor" in the surrounding area.

Because of distance, dirt roads, and doctors' fees, a doctor was called only for serious and prolonged illnesses. Families had remedies passed down from parents, grandparents, relatives and neighbors who were always ready to share their knowledge of "remedies that never failed." Some home medications that people relied on were: sulfur, Epsom salts, castor oil, alum, camphor, calomel, honey, molasses, turpentine, lamp oil, Watkins and Raleigh liniments, baking soda, castoria (for babies), charcoal, burnt clay from rock chimneys, teas made from elder bloom, mint, sassafras bark and roots, boneset tea (ugh), penny royal (penny rile), burdock roots, salves from Balmgilead buds, and Rosebud and Cloverine salves bought from peddlers. Then there was asafetida (sometimes spelled asafoetida or assafetida), a gum resin that flows from certain plants and trees, especially from pine and fir trees. Because of the gummy character of the resin, it could be made into little balls. Sometimes a ball of asafetida was put into a little cloth bag, tied onto a string and hung around children's necks to ward off disease. Perhaps it did for no one wanted to get near a person wearing that yukky, foul garlicky smelling stuff. Sissy and Herbert would not wear the bags but I had to once.

I heard elderly people tell of doctors using maggots to heal sores that nothing else had seemed to help. A Mr. Shepherd told me that he had a wound in the bend of the elbow that wouldn't heal and the doctor used maggots which did the trick and the sore began to heal. Maggots look somewhat like worms, have no legs and move only by wriggling the body. During World War I, maggots were used extensively by doctors to heal seriously infected wounds of soldiers because of a chemical they produced.

Doctors, at one time, would bleed people. I recall that the doctor bled my Aunt Sarah Ann two or more times. When visiting the Hermitage near Nashville, the home of President Andrew Jackson, there were records showing bills to the doctor for "blood letting." In the days when doctors let people bleed to cure them, a worm, called a leech or a "blood sucker" was considered very important and was used so frequently in blood letting by making a wound with its three small white teeth and sucking the blood that some doctors themselves were often called "leeches."

I knew of no licensed midwives at the time and babies were born at home, assisted by women who were called midwives from their great deal of practice.

A midwife or older woman, especially older mothers, were called even when a doctor was present to deliver the baby. There was water to be boiled, the mother-to-be's hands to be held, receiving blankets and "belly bands" to be ready, small children to be cared for and other chores to be done.

Mrs. Cora Reeves was much sought out for her expertise in identifying and treating illnesses and delivering babies. I've heard her called a midwife but she was much more than a midwife. Her records show that people came to her from distances of ten or more miles for advice and counseling. Mrs. Reeves was not and never claimed to be a licensed doctor, but word of mouth brought people to ask what she thought their health problem might be and what to do about it. She taught people how to use herbs and household commodities for treatments of various illnesses, injuries and to care for their bodies. She also shared her knowledge of drying animal skins for floor rugs — sheep hides for floor rugs and chair pads, groundhog or woodchuck skins for strong shoestrings and other uses. She knew how to best keep eggs and other foods fresh longer. She had forceps and pulled aching teeth.

Many young nursing babies were taken to Mrs. Reeves to be treated for "thresh," a sore and whitish condition of the mouth and gums, causing the baby pain and difficulty in nursing. When my brother, Kyle, was a baby, his mother took him to Mrs. Reeves to be treated for the so-called thresh. Her treatment for this was secret as she never allowed the mothers to watch what she did, but she would take the baby and a clean white cloth to the barn. Whatever she did evidently worked, for mothers continued to take their babies to her.

Mrs. Reeves was indeed a blessing to her community and many people. She kept records of her patients and remedies which she had tried and recommended. A number of these remedies appear at the end of this chapter as written by Mrs. Reeves. (We need to remember that these records were written or jotted down in the midst of a busy schedule of this lady with her own home and family to care for — three daughters to be educated, Misses Ruby, Hazel and Myrtle. Misses Ruby and Hazel were college educated and became high school teachers of my class which graduated in 1924.)

Sometimes, during an extremely difficult childbirth of several days, the midwife might stay with the patient for some hours after the delivery to watch both the mother and baby.

There were a few people who were reputed to be able to stop severe nose bleeds. Mr. Roscoe Sexton, as a young man, was visiting Mr. Theodore Spencer and developed a nose bleed which they couldn't stop. Theodore's mother, Mrs. Dora, called Mr. Sexton, one of these nose-bleed stoppers, and coincidentally the father of young Roscoe to tell him that their efforts had failed to do any good. Mr. Sexton said, "Hold the phone while I get the Bible and find the right place." In a few minutes he told Mrs. Spencer to follow up with a few simple procedures. Evidently it worked. The nose-bleed stoppers did quite a business.

Colds

I doubt if anyone, especially in our area in the first thirty years of this century, escaped having a cold and most had several a year. The common cold was either allowed to "run its course" or was treated with teas or other home remedies. The most formidable and dreaded tea was "boneset tea," a bitter, bitter tea made from the dried leaves of the boneset plant which grew in fields. Other teas, much more palatable and even welcomed sometimes, were those made from sassafras bark, spicewood bark, dried elder bloom, catnip and mint leaves and even pennyroyal. A severe cold or croup was treated by placing a flannel (outing flannel) cloth saturated with melted lard and turpentine or lamp oil and fastened on the chest or back over the lungs. A few hidden sticks of horehound candy might appear to coax children to drink the teas or submit to other treatments. Colds were very infectious and spread by sneezing without a handkerchief over the nose and mouth. There were no facial tissues in those days and handkerchiefs were used several days without laundering. Kleenex, with its 1924 slogan "Don't put a cold in your pocket," had not reached our area yet.

Croup

Children, and especially, it seemed, young children would get croup. Severe attacks of croup could be very dangerous, even life threatening. I knew of one case when the doctor had to make an incision in a child's throat to remove the phlegm to save the person's life. Croup is inflammation of the throat and windpipe causing extreme hoarseness and difficulty in breathing.

Once I awakened in the night and felt I was choking and was breathing with difficulty and loudly. My mother had died, my father was away for the night and he had gotten Aunt Lona to spend the night with us children. My gasping for breath and loud hoarse cough awakened Aunt Lona and my sister. Aunt Lona, who usually had remedies for almost everything did not try any of them. She called Grandmother, who told her to give me a spoonful of lamp oil on sugar. "Lamp oil!" I had never heard of such a thing and would not take the conglomeration! Aunt Lona called Grandmother again. She said, "Try again and if she won't take it, call back and I'll come up there and she'll take it." I knew I might as well swallow the lamp oil for if my grandmother came, I'd take it. I can still remember I could just feel the choking going away and what a relief! I found the same remedy in Mrs. Reeves' list.

Sore throats were treated with salt water gargle, and at times with rubbing on the lard and turpentine mixture if no Vicks Vaporub was available. Sometimes the stockings we had worn that day were wrapped around the neck over night. Strep throat was treated by putting black pine tar between a few thicknesses of folded cheese cloth and wrapped around the neck.

Measles

Of what is called "childhood diseases," measles seemed to sweep through the community each winter catching those who had not gotten the disease the year before, and causing schools to be closed for a few weeks. The measles virus was spread by coughing, sneezing, handkerchiefs, and drinking from the same cups or glasses. Often the disease started with fever, redness and swelling of the face and red spots covering the face and body. If one were slow "breaking out," teas were given and the body kept warm to speed up the breaking out. Often ears and eyes were affected by measles and doctors advised parents to keep children warm and protected from bright light.

One year when our school was closed because of an outbreak of measles, my sister, brother and I did not get the disease. We begged our parents to let us visit a home where we could be in contact with measles but they would not let us. Then the three of us got measles as adults and I have never been sicker, from fever and coughs along with swollen face and itchy body.

Whooping Cough

Whooping cough was another infectious children's disease characterized by fits of coughing, losing breath, tears running down the face and soreness of chest and tiredness after coughing spells. This could be very hard on some people. In fact I had a little brother die of whooping cough at age three. Usually this disease was treated at home with home remedies, keeping the patient inside, warm and using whatever seemed to work best for each one's cough.

Scarlet Fever

Scarlet fever was another contagious disease which seemed to attack children more often than adults. However, I knew of adults who had scarlet fever and it seemed that the older one was, the more severe the infection, and it took longer for complete recovery. When scarlet fever was diagnosed in a home, the family or patient was immediately quarantined until the doctor felt there was no longer need for isolation. Aftereffects from scarlet fever might be damage to ears, eyes, heart and kidneys. The disease usually began with fever, headaches, sore throat and after a day or two a rash of red spots on the chest, throat and sometimes over most of the body. Doctors advised that the room of the patient be kept from bright lighting to protect the eyes.

Diphtheria

Diphtheria was a dangerous infectious disease that would occur in dreaded outbreaks, especially in rural communities at times. It is a disease of the throat resulting in the formation of membranes which hinder breathing, accompanied by high fever and weakness. It was not unusual for several members of a family to be extremely ill at the same time with diphtheria and sometimes several deaths occurred in the matter of two or three days. One lady told me her father had gone by wagon to Saltville, Virginia, and when he got back home, three of his children had died from diphtheria. So many children attending York Ridge school came down with the epidemic one year that the school remained closed for two or three years due to loss of students. Dottie Tucker Taylor was one of those students who got the disease and one or more of her siblings died and she was too sick to be able to attend the funerals. After one funeral, she decided she wanted some cornbread to eat but was told that cornbread was too, too hard on her blistered throat. She begged. The adults were afraid that she, too, might not live and they hated to deny her food she really wanted. The crusty cornbread broke blisters in her throat and she began to get well, and lived for many years.

Consumption or Tuberculosis

A dreaded disease in the teens and early twenties occurred in our area since we could not be sure how it was spread. It was called consumption here probably because consumption was easier to say than tuberculosis.

The disease could be spread by human contact, from milk from cows with the germ, from dust or the many ways the bacillus was carried in the air. One family in the area had five deaths from the disease. Sunshine and an even temperature were recommended by doctors and some patients went to Arizona hoping for cure. Some did improve but one local person died there.

Later, the son of a friend of mine, came from Poland and was found to have tuberculosis. He was sent to a sanitarium where air was pumped into the abdomen to alleviate pressure from the lungs and with a healthful environment and good food, he recovered.

Smallpox

The very word, smallpox, sent a chill through anyone here in the early part of this century for it portended death or at the very least bad scarring. Most of the stories we had heard of smallpox were either told by someone who had been in a city where there had been an outbreak of the disease or had read in a newspaper about the scourge.

A few men would go "down the country" (below the Blue Ridge) to buy horses to bring back to sell. Mr. Felix Davis had gone on such an errand and the family received word that he had smallpox. It might take two or three days for a message to reach the family in those days, and of course, he was in quarantine and none of the family went to visit or see about him. When it was safe for him to come home, his face was very pocked from the blisters accompanying smallpox. Then my Uncle Aris had been away and was exposed to the disease but quickly hurried home. The entire family was quarantined and he stayed in a room by himself, with only one person allowed in, wearing a heavy face mask and clothing that could be sterilized. No other member of the family got smallpox. Aunt Sarah Ann must have done a good job of protecting her family as the disease could be spread by tiny droplets that might shoot out of the mouth by sneezing, coughing, or even talking. After the patient was well all the bedding, clothing, utensils used had to be sterilized by boiling. Even the bed was carried out and washed with hot water with lye soap and rinsed with boiling water.

Chicken Pox

Most everyone got chicken pox while going to school. Chicken pox usually began with a red rash on the skin followed by a fever. Soon the rash turned into blisters which enlarged and filled with a liquid and itch. Parents might sprinkle cornstarch or baking powder on the patient to try to ease or prevent scratching which might result in scarring. Dresses and men's pants with waist bands rubbed the blisters making them larger and larger. I recall that my sister had blisters around the waist line an inch or more long.

Chicken pox appears much like smallpox but the diseases are far from the same. Inoculation for chicken pox does not protect against smallpox nor the other way around.

Flux

Another illness, called flux, occurred quite frequently in summer, sometimes in adults but mostly in children. Thorndike Webster's Dictionary defines flux as an "unnatural discharge of blood or liquid from the body." Children sometimes died from this illness.

My three year old sister, Marie, had flux and became very, very ill. The Yellow Transparent apples, an early variety, were not quite ripe but the children would get them, mash them in the peel until they were very soft and eat them. We believed eating those unripe apples caused the flux. After using a few home remedies, and Marie becoming sicker, the doctor was called. He gave her the child dosage of medicine for this illness, but she was getting even sicker. The doctor was stopping by every day and increased the medicine to adult dosage. As there was no improvement in her condition, he suggested that our father get some fat mutton. Dad found someone who had butchered a sheep and got some. We cooked the fat mutton until it was very tender. Marie had become so weak from the body discharge and lack of food that she could hardly talk. I was carrying her through the dining room where lunch was on the table. She reached her arm toward the table of food, she was so hungry. I cut some of the fat mutton into small bites and she ate it hungrily. Evidently the fat was healing to the intestines and she began to improve and got well after we had feared for her life.

In many cases of flux, people took mud which was being used as mortar in field rock chimneys, mixed it with water and had the patient drink the water. Others tried water with pulverized charcoal from the fireplace. I suppose flux may have been what we today call severe diarrhea but I have never known diarrhea to affect people as flux did back then, But, of course, there are medications now to check the problem early.

Influenza

In 1918, I believe, influenza hit our area as well as much of the country, resulting in many deaths. In our family, five of us were in bed with flu at the same time — all except baby Joe and our father. Those in the community who had not gotten flu were afraid to go into the afflicted homes as it was so very contagious. Dad set up three beds in one room so he could look after all of us without going through the cold hall and rooms. It was winter and very cold.

Dad tried to prepare some food for us but he had never done much cooking and we didn't have much appetite for food. Some of us wanted only canned tomatoes, very cold with salt and pepper on them. People would telephone to say they were sending a basket or box of food, would put it on the front porch and leave before Dad opened the door. Finally, a lady, Mrs. Lizzie Tolley, who had recovered from the flu, came and stayed with us until we were better. It seemed so good to have someone who could cook! Most of us were getting better and our appetites were improving. Also, Mrs. Tolley had a wonderful sense of humor and we enjoyed her jokes, stories and laughter.

Dad believed that smoking a pipe (which he ordinarily did not do) kept him from getting flu and when we were up and around, our place smelled of strong pipe smoke.

Infections

Due to the kind of work our people were faced with to eke out a living, building fences, splitting rails, repairing buildings, felling trees, splitting wood for fireplaces and cook stoves, dealing with animals and scores of other chores, they suffered scratches, abrasions, bruises and cuts. These injuries were viewed as part of life and not taken too seriously — often occurring in the woods or out on the farm, or while some distance from the house. Hand washing or cleansing a minor injury did not take top priority. People often said, "Aw that's nothing. Only a scratch." Sometimes those who chewed tobacco would take the tobacco out of the mouth and put it on the wound, or wipe the place with a handkerchief which had been used for several days. Of course we did not have nor had we ever heard of facial tissues, and "wash day" was always on Monday and people often wore the same clothes for the whole week.

Blood Poisoning

There were times when a wound was not treated properly or early enough and turned to blood poisoning. This could be detected in the early stages by a redness around the wound followed by red streaks running from the injury. Our neighbor was doing fencing and got a wood splinter in his hand. He pulled the splinter out and there was some bleeding, but not wanting to leave his work until it was finished, he held his handkerchief over the place for a bit and then put a chew of tobacco on it. Some time later he began having pain in the hand and arm, and tried turpentine and other home remedies. As the hand and arm became more painful, he was taken to a doctor, but blood poisoning had already taken its toll and the entire arm had to be amputated. He died a short time later.

Mr. Abe Reedy, who lived on Quillen's Ridge, had injured his leg and had to have it amputated. Doctors Osborne and Pennington did the amputation in the home on the kitchen table. They must have done an adequate job as Mr. Reedy recovered and had a wooden leg, called a "peg" leg to walk on. While the surgery was going on, people would call Mrs. Reedy (Frankie) to see how the surgery was going. The ten or twelve neighbors on the party line would hear the ring, pick up their phone and listen to the report.

Boils

A boil might start out as a red swelling on the skin and often under the arm, followed by pus around a hard core, was very painful and required opening to get rid of the pus and core.

Carbuncles

Carbuncles usually occurred on the back of the neck or on the buttock. It seemed that men had carbuncles more often than women and they were extremely painful. They were larger than boils, had several openings, filled with pus and had to be suffered until they came "to a head" when they could be lanced and the pus drawn out. Sometimes they might have to be lanced two or three times, some medication applied and a bandage put on.

Bone Felons

I never saw a bone felon, a very painful bone infection near the finger or toe nail, and caused by an injury, but have talked with people who had had them.

One of my aunts had a felon on a finger and after days of extreme pain day and night, went to a doctor who lanced the infected area and scraped the bone which had been damaged.

Stone Bruises

Stone bruises usually happened to children who went barefoot in summer. They were the result of a bruise on the sole of the foot caused by hitting a rock, a large stubble or some hard object. Much like a boil, the bruise would start as a red sore and after a few days would be yellow from pus that gathered at the point of injury. The foot would become so painful that we would hop around on one foot. My father would sharpen his pocket knife to be ready to lance the wound, but it was so sore we'd try to put off the opening as long as possible. Dad would suggest that "we take a nap and it would feel better." In the meanwhile, he'd disinfect his knife in hot water, lance the bruise, drain the pus. Then a piece of fat pork would be placed over the spot to continue drawing out all the infection, and the foot would be bandaged.

I've known a piece of fat bacon to draw splinters out of hands or anywhere tweezers failed to work and also to draw infection from ingrown finger- or toenails. A neighbor recently told me, "I had a very sore toenail that just didn't respond to anything I tried. I know that this is an old fashioned remedy, but I fastened a piece of fat meat on it one night and the next day, it was better."

Gum Boils

There were no dentists here and our toothbrushes were small stems from a birch tree, the bark removed and one end of the stem chewed into fine pieces. Men, mostly, chewed tobacco and women dipped snuff. My mother did not use snuff but Dad chewed tobacco. Those who dipped snuff would put the birch brush into the snuff box, let the brush pick up what would hold and put it in the mouth. No one I knew sniffed snuff as it was supposed to be used. Some people would pull out the lower lip and pour in some snuff. So, even children and grownups used birch toothbrushes until stores nearby began to carry the type of brushes we use today. Also, toothpicks were made from quills of the wings of chickens, turkeys and geese. A tiny piece of birch branch could be put in the quill when not in use to help keep its shape and keep it clean. Of course the birch brushes did not clean between the teeth or do anything like an adequate job. An infected tooth without dental care often resulted in a swelling around a tooth filled with pus. It was assumed that the tooth would either get better or have to be pulled. Medical doctors had forceps and so did some lay people and when the toothache became unbearable they went to these people to have the tooth pulled. Of course, no numbing was used and extractions were painful. But for gum boils, parents would hold a needle in boiling water, open the gum boil, try to press out as much infection as possible and have the patient rinse several times with warm salt water. Salt water is often recommended by dentists today after extractions. Gum boils were, I suppose, what we today call abscessed teeth.

Run Arounds

These usually happened around fingernails or toenails caused by an injury — a bruise or a nail torn loose from the skin, and treated as the above infections. A salve was made from the buds of Balm Gilead trees and this salve or Cloverine or Rosebud salve, if on hand, were put on some of these infections to complete the healing process.

The Itch

A contagious disease of the skin caused by a tiny mite found on chickens, and other poultry and birds. The mite would burrow into the skin, leaving a tiny red spot accompanied by a tickly, prickly feeling making one want to scratch. Scratching caused the red spots to spread and form sores. Parents and teachers were able to identify the disease early on as it seemed to appear between the fingers first, from handling or touching a person or property of someone with the itch. Treatment was by bathing with strong or antiseptic soap, clothing and bedding changed and washed daily until well.

It was not unusual for school children to get the itch from close contact sitting in seats with deskmates, handling books, and other materials nearby. Sissy, Herbert and I caught the itch in school when I was very young and we went through the process of lots of carrying and heating water, changing and laundering clothing and bedding, filling and emptying the zinc wash tub. I'm sure our parents were as tired and as glad as we were when the ordeal was over.

Head Lice

A louse (the singular of lice) is a small insect that infests the hair or skin of people or animals. It attaches the eggs or nits to hair with a gummy substance. The nits hatch in six days and the hatched lice are full grown in 18 days. It is easy for one person to catch lice from another. The best way to discourage lice is to keep the body clean. "Tincture of larkspur" is a good wash for head lice. It should be used about once a week until both lice and nits are killed.

My uncle and aunt took a little five year old girl from a Children's Home in Roanoke, Virginia, to live with them. I was young and glad to have a little playmate. One day it was discovered that I had head lice. Since no one else in the family had any, my parents wondered where I had gotten lice. After asking my uncle and aunt, it was revealed that the child from the Children's Home had lice. Families kept on hand "fine tooth combs," combs with small teeth on both sides of the center and perhaps just to use for checking for lice or fleas. Well, my Mom sat me down, ran the fine comb through my hair again to get any lice and drop them in very hot water. Then she proceeded to take hair by hair, use her thumb and forefinger to pull any nit attached to a strand of hair. Then my hair was thoroughly washed and watched daily.

In the rest of my years of going to school, of teaching and serving as principal, and hugging children, I never contracted the itch or head lice again. An educational supervisor in Fairfax County, Virginia, told me she had caught both from her experiences in schools. A barber contacted my school to let us know they had found lice on the heads of children of a school family.

We knew of two or three people nearby who constantly talked of their health. They were sure they were suffering from some illness. My mother asked the doctor what was wrong with her cousin Emma. He laughed and said, "Nothing's wrong with her. The pills I'm giving her won't hurt her or anybody, but she thinks she can't live without them. She's a hypochondriac."

"A what?" Mom asked.

"A hypochondriac. That's a person who has an imaginary health problem. Sometimes, like all of us, she doesn't feel good and thinks she has to have medicine or whatever she thinks she has will get worse and kill her," he explained.

"That big word you said, is that what 'hippode' people have?" she asked.

"That's right. That word is hard for some of you to say and you just call it hippode — with a long O," he said and laughed as he closed his medicine bag. "Hippode. Hippode." he repeated. "Use that ointment on the kids' fall sores. Keep them clean and they'll be well in no time."

Prescriptions by Mrs. Reeves

For consumption drink the strippings 1 quart morning and night.*

Remedy for burns: Fry poke root in lard and put the grease on burns.

For boils mix flour and molasses it eases the pain and draws it to a head. Wet tobacco in vinegar and put on for run around on the finger to take the soreness out.

Membranous croup: Give a little lamp oil every few minutes to cut the membrane loose for a few days. 3 drops of lamp oil on sugar every two hours and wring a cloth out of cold water and put to the throat removing when warm.

Lamp oil good to swab the throat in *diptheria*.

How many know that cider vinegar will stop the flow of blood when an *artery is cut*. Just put on bandage and pour vinegar on.

Bed wetting: Mix thoroughly 2 heaping tablespoons of light brown sugar & one teaspoon heaping of powdered resin. Give one level teaspoon on going to bed

---

*Strippings are the last milk in a cow's udder. Sometimes, that would be drawn separately to put in the cream jar to be used for churning butter.

until cured it may take some time but will cure obstinate cases.

A tea of elder blossoms to *break a fever*.

For blood poisoning: Soak in wood lye for 15 minutes then wash in warm water then make a thick paste of lard and bind on the wound alternating the soaking and poultising 3 times a day. Heal with a good salve and sulfur.

For rusty nail wounds bind a raw mashed onion on after soaking it in wood lye. To make the lye take two large handfuls of wood ashes mix enough warm water to cover the wound.

Whooping cough remedy: Simmer together equal parts of honey, sweet oil & vinegar bottle dose a teaspoonful as often as necessary.

For colic a few drops of peppermint.

For pain in bowels a few drops of wintergreen.

Rinse the mouth with vinegar to take the smell and taste of onion out.

For dreaded flux mix together one tablespoonful each sweet oil or mutton tallow and alcohol then stir in a tablespoonful each of pulverized charcoal and water give all the mixture at one time if severe every hour until better.

For bunions put alum in shoes.

A hot bath up to the neck will save the life of a child with *convulsions*.

Dropsy invaluable remedy take inner bark of elderberry stalk & cover with sour wine take a wine glass three times a day.

Cure for rheumatism: make a pill of asafetida take one for two nights miss two nights for three or four nights & so on until relieved.

For appendicitis take lard & salt spread on cloth and put to the bowels and when it is dry put on a new one until swelling and fever is gone;

Salt and lard is good in *pneumonia*.

> *for colds.*
>
> Take a cup of lard and put in a frying pan with 3 onions sliced a table spoonful of turpentine and as much quinine as will stay on the [blade] of a teaspoon handle let all fry together till the onions are brown pour the oil off and use to grease the chest and a cross the back between the sholders heat and rub in well and cover with a cloth and I am sure you will not need To call a Dr. for pneumonia If taken in time it will cure any cold.
>
> corns take vaseline & mix Borax an put on corns

Elder bark is good for *dropsy* make a tea.

Scrape raw beet and bind on the foot *when one has stept on a nail or for blood poison.* When it gets dry put on fresh.

Red corn cob tea for *poison for sheep* & give 1 pint every two hours.*

Bedbug use hot strong alum water to wash.

Lard and sulfur will cure *cows teats.* Never fails and take off warts on stock.†

For blight on cucumber & tomato vines spray with blue stone & lime.

To tan hides take alum & salt, soak the hide a day or so in clear water & warm the alum & salt water and dip the skin and tack it up 11 days & warm the alum and salt dip again and dry and keep it worked good to make it soft.

Give a sow a lump of salt as big as your thumb when she comes in§ and she will fatten as well as if spayed.

Put a pinch of salt in lamps when filling [with lamp oil] to make them burn bright.

Every spring the entire family took two or three doses of sulfur and molasses as a spring tonic.

Turpentine was a household commodity that every family tried to keep on hand and was thought to relieve any soreness on man or beast. Epsom salts and castor oil were kept for laxatives and both were hard to take. A bit later, someone would come around selling products for the Raleigh or Watkins Company. Whether the householder bought any of the brushes or cleaning items, they could not resist the sales pitch, "Surely you must have a bottle of Watkins liniment. It's good for aching bones, rheumatism and neuralgia. Then doesn't someone in the family get upset stomachs? Mix some of this liniment in water, add a bit of sugar and drink it and in no time the stomach problem is all gone. You have horses and animals, don't you? And they're always getting scratches, bruises, sore ankles and other injuries. No home can afford to be without this liniment." And usually this meant a sale. We kept some Watkins or Raleigh's on hand most of the time and used it as the salesman had said.

Then there were other salespeople who answered magazine ads to sell Rosebud or Cloverine salve. Each little round box of salve sold for 25 cents and the buyer received a premium of a rolled up picture. The pictures were about 12 × 16 or 18 inches, were not framed, and most had a Bible verse on a black background and were decorated with flowers.

*Sometimes sheep would nibble "ivy" (mountain laurel) and get very sick from it.
†Cows' teats would sometimes crack from dampness and cold weather just as people's hands do.
§"Comes in" is when she gives birth to a litter of pigs.

Food

In the period from 1900 to 1925 or later there were no grocery stores in this area as we know the big chain groceries today. In fact, there were very few stores and they were general stores carrying a variety of necessities, including some foods. To get to the few stores usually meant walking in muddy or dusty roads, or over hills and through fields, crossing streams and fences not knowing whether one might encounter an unfriendly bull, horse or sheep.

Families grew all of their food except sugar, coffee, salt, soda and rice and a few other commodities, and they prepared and preserved foods to last until another growing year.

Potatoes

White potatoes, which were called Irish potatoes, were grown in large amounts and always some were kept to plant the following spring. Most meals had potatoes as they could be prepared in various ways as boiled, baked, fried, creamed, mashed and roasted.

One way we roasted potatoes, they were washed and placed on the hearth in front of the fireplace and turned until done. We knew when they were done, because we pricked them with a fork. Of course, we did not have aluminum foil in which to wrap them and just put the potatoes on the hearth. Sometimes, a few coals were placed on some ashes beside the main fire, potatoes placed on the coals and covered with more ashes and coals and left until done. The peel was removed and they were delicious with salt and butter.

Sweet Potatoes

Sweet potatoes were favored when boiled or baked and eaten with lots of butter. And sweet potato pies were special with eggs, cream, sugar and spices mixed in the peeled and well mashed pulp.

Sweet potatoes were grown by setting out plants or slips as they were called. To grow the plants, a deep hole was made in the ground and a frame of boards placed around the sides. A layer of horse or chicken manure was put in the bottom of the bed and covered with five of six inches of fine soil. This was dampened with water and a cover put over the top and left a few days for the manure to heat the soil. When the soil had gotten warm, whole sweet potatoes were placed on the soil and covered with about six inches or more soil, dampened with water, the board cover put back over the bed, until the plants began to peek through. The bed was not allowed to dry out but kept damp by sprinkling with warm water. After the plants had a few leaves the cover might be left off on warm days but covered again at night. In the meantime ridges of 6 or 8 inches of soil had been made in the spot where the plants were to grow. When ready, the largest plants were pulled from the potatoes while the person held the bedded potato in its place to grow more plants. (This process was the reason the plants were called slips.)

Beans

Beans were a main staple of the family. They were planted, not only in the garden, but also in the fields with the corn. Bunch beans, which did not have runners, were usually grown in the garden, while those with runners were planted in the cornfield with the runners climbing the stalks of corn and producing more beans. Everyone hoped to have green beans to eat by the fourth of July from the first picking, snap beans were the main dish on the table for dinner (the mid-day meal) and for supper (the evening meal) the rest of the summer or as long as there were tender beans.

Sacks, baskets and buckets of beans were gathered from the cornfield while they were green and tender to be canned in half-gallon jars, others to be pickled in ten gallon crocks or jars or made into "leather britches." Picking, stringing and getting the beans ready for canning, pickling and drying large quantities, took many long hours of work and I would get so tired and sleepy but there was no getting out of the job until it was finished. To do the "leather britches" tender beans were picked, strings removed, and beans washed. Then heavy thread about two yards long was put in a large darning needle and the beans strung on the thread until the thread was filled and the two ends tied together. They were then hung over a rod and placed behind the kitchen cook stove to dry. They were then stored for winter use when they were cooked — dried hulls and all. Hence the term "leather britches." I did not particularly like the hulls but when they were on the table we were supposed to eat them.

Some of the varieties of beans: sulfur beans, kidney beans, cut shorts, Kentucky wonders, birds eye, butter beans. There were others whose names I do not remember. There were tender beans and tough beans — tender beans whose hull was tender for eating, canning, pickling and leather britches. Tough hull beans were not picked until dry on the vines and then shelled out by hand and stored for winter use. Sometimes there were so many of the dried beans to be shelled, they were poured onto a sheet or large spread and beaten with a stick or rod to open the pods. Then the hulls were removed and the beans winnowed to remove bits of crushed hulls.

One year we rented corn land from Mr. Arthur Graybeal. Dad would drive needed equipment, plow and harrow on the sled or wagon on the road to the field. We children walked through the fields across hills — a shorter distance. During planting, hoeing and gathering the crops, we carried a basket of lunch and spent the day in the field. Before corn cutting time, we children took large gunny sacks (made of a strong, coarse fabric) and picked the dried beans that had climbed the corn stalks. There were so many that Dad would bring the wagon in the late afternoon to bring the beans and us tired kids home.

Beans were easily grown and they did not need to be sprayed or dusted as they are today. It was much later that Japanese beetles appeared in the area. The first time we saw these beetles, we went along and picked them off into a can of kerosene and mashed the eggs underneath the leaves.

Cabbage

There are many legends and myths about cabbage and, of course, there are several varieties today, but the firm round green heads we know now were brought to our world by the English settlers. They thrived so well here that they soon became more popular, in some cases, than potatoes. Every family wanted to have a goodly supply of cabbage, not only because it required less work to grow but for the several ways it could be prepared for food. The leaves were often boiled with a piece of pork — sometimes pork tongue, with a big pod of red pepper. The broth from this method of cooking was delicious — called "pot likker." Then too chopped cabbage was fried in streaked middling drippings, made into slaw, or into sauerkraut in five or ten gallon crocks or jars. Children or adults vied for the core which grew in the center of the cabbage head.

If one did not have a root cellar or good place to keep cabbage through the winter, the cabbage was buried in the ground. A hole was dug out usually in the garden or near the house, and lined on the sides with boards and straw or leaves several inches thick put on the bottom. The cabbages were pulled out of the ground with the roots and stems left on which helped them keep better. After the cabbages were piled in the hole with straw or leaves over them, a top was placed over the whole lot, with dirt covering it. A spot was left to be opened to reach the cabbage when needed. Apples, and some other root foods were stored in the same way.

Apples

I cannot recall a year when we did not have lots of apples. We seemed to have severe winters which probably kept the fruit trees from blooming early only to be killed by late frosts. In early summer when the Early Harvests, Yellow Transparents or Red June apples were a bit more than half grown, people began to get some for fresh apple sauce or fried apples for breakfast. In the fall as a variety matured and ripened, gathering began for drying, making apple butter, cider, or some kind of jam or jelly. Before heavy frosts and winter set in all the apples had been gathered and put in the root cellar, apple house or buried.

Apples provided such an important variety for our people for food. I'm not sure that we realized what a blessing apples were for a bowl of apple sauce, a casserole of baked apples, apple pies, apple butter, dried apples for pies and filling for stack cakes, apple juice and cider to drink, apple jelly, and pectin to use in making other jellies and jams, vinegar, apples to eat raw or to roast in front of the fireplace. After supper and school homework was done, we'd have a pan of apples for snacks.

Vinegar was needed for cucumber and beet pickles, whole peach and pear pickles, chow-chow and other household uses. A large jar, keg or barrel was used to hold apple peelings, throwaway apples, some left-over cider with a bit of water added. My parents had a large barrel with a flat removable top and flat bottom with a hole in the side near the bottom. A tin spout or short pipe was inserted in this hole to draw out vinegar when needed and a whittled stopper or "bung" was inserted to keep the vinegar from running out or leaking. The apples had to ferment for weeks to turn to vinegar. The barrel was never filled to the top as air was necessary for fermentation. Sometimes a slimy scum would form in the barrel and would have to be removed to let air circulate or fermentation would be retarded. This scum was called "mother." When the vinegar was ready for use it was strained through a fine strainer or white cloth.

Cider made from Cotton Sweet apples was used at times in making apple butter to reduce the amount of sugar needed.

Varieties of apples were: York or Johnson Fine Winters (a long keeping apple), Grimes Golden, Winesap, Rambo, Early Harvest, Yellow Transparent, Red or Early June, Fallow Water, Cotton Sweet, Sheep Nose, Maiden Blush, Horse Apple, Virginia Beauty (a very tasty eating apple), Smoke House Apple.

At a later date, perhaps around 1916 or 1917, my father sold apple trees for Stark Brothers in Louisiana, Mo., who were promoting Red and Golden Delicious apples along with other varieties. The company would send 3 or 4 samples of the Delicious apples and after Dad had shown them to prospective customers, we were given slices to sample. The first linoleum rug in our kitchen was sent by Stark Brothers as a sales premium for my Dad.

To get a variety of apples one did not have, seeds were saved and planted, sprouts taken up and set out or grafting done. There were some who did successful grafting by taking a small branch with healthy buds, making a slit in the bark of an already growing apple tree, inserting part of the budding branch (about 5 or 6 inches) in the slit with some left outside, making sure there was sap to help in the process, and bandage the slit and buds with beeswax or a waterproof covering. Sometimes the grafted mother tree might bear two kinds of apples.

Apple Butter

Apple butter was made in large quantities in a copper or brass kettle outside the house. The day before apple butter was to be made lots of apples were gathered and brought into the house and peeling, slicing and removing the cores and seed beds began. Some of the apples might be cooked in large pots a bit the night before. Early the next morning the copper kettle was cleaned with salt and vinegar until it was bright and shiny. It was set onto an iron frame on legs and placed over a small wood fire. Some of the already cooked apples were poured into the kettle with a small bit of water and other raw sliced apples added until the kettle was about two-thirds full. The washed wooden stirrer was used constantly to keep them from sticking and burning. Someone had to be stirring all the time. As the apples cooked down, more were added until all were cooked. Stirring and cooking went on until the sauce became thicker and thicker and began to turn a dark red color. All along wood was added to keep the cooking going on. All too often a wind or breeze blew smoke from the fire causing the one stirring to move around and away from the smoke which changed often and sometimes brought tears to the eyes. Of course, one person could not do all the stirring but would be relieved after an hour or so.

When it was decided that the butter was near the desired stage, lots of sugar was added and thoroughly mixed and stirred. Then a bit was taken out to be tasted for sweetness. Just before removing the kettle from the fire, flavoring — cinnamon oil or peppermint oil was added and mixed through and through and again tasted for flavor. This process had taken 10 or more hours. The finished product was dipped into half gallon glass jars and sometimes put in crocks. The sugar and cooking produced a food that kept well without spoiling. Our twenty gallon copper kettle sometimes meant that we would get 18 gallons of apple butter, and some years we made two "runs." It was so good on hot buttered biscuits and was much used on biscuits for school lunches. The oil flavors came in small bottles which were bought in the drug store in Troutdale. These oils were so strong that it did not take much to flavor a batch of apple butter. Trips to Troutdale were infrequent but a list was always being made of needed things all along to be ready when someone was going.

Apple Peelers

Someone heard that there were apple peelers. The hardware stores in Troutdale and Lansing were carrying them and the little general store at Little Helton had gotten some. So, Grandpa and Dad bought one together. It could be fastened securely on a table or any work surface. An apple was pushed onto a three pronged fork or arm, a blade positioned to fit the size apple and a crank turned to take off the peel and remove the core. Some types sliced the apples in rings. Apples with deep seed beds had to have the beds cut out by hand. At that time most peelers just peeled and cored the apples, and slicing and checking for seed beds was done by hand. But usually the peeling was done by hand as bruised spots, worm holes, missed peels and seed beds proved the mechanical peelers were not as good as the human peelers.

Apple Cider

There were a few cider mills in the community and those who did not have one could use their neighbor's. Fresh apple cider was cooled in jugs or crocks in the milk run (or race) and was a delicious refreshing summer drink. Sometimes it was left to become hard cider, and I suppose had a "kick" to it. Mulled or heated cider with a stick of cinnamon and a bit of orange juice added (if an orange was on hand) was a tasty favorite drink.

Dried Apples

Apples were dried, not only for family food but to sell. The local stores would always buy dried apples to be shipped away to towns and cities. Of course the apples had to be peeled and cored and cut into thin slices which would dry quickly or more quickly than apple quarters. Some people dried them by placing them thinly spread on a cloth and laying them outside in the sun. This method might take three days of sunshine before they were completely dry as they must be carried inside at night. Others strung the slices on heavy string and hung them behind the kitchen stove. Some made a rack of lightweight wood, about 30 inches wide and probably 48 inches tall, with ten-penny nails driven into the end pieces about 6 or 8 inches apart to hold small rods. For this method, the apples were peeled, cored and sliced into rounds and placed on the rods and dried back of the kitchen stove or leaned against the sunny side of a building during the day. My grandparents built a field stone furnace about 4 feet wide and six feet long. Over this was a little houselike building with a roof. On the inside were 2 × 2 slats nailed to the two side walls about 8 inches apart to hold slatted shelves which could be pulled in and out. The floor was dirt and a fire was made on the floor and let burn into coals and fed with just a bit of wood to keep coals and heat going. The apple slices were rather evenly spread on the shelves and placed inside to dry in about 24 hours. Grandmother sprinkled a bit of sulfur on the slices, "so they will be whiter when dry," she said. The lighter colored dried apples brought a higher price when sold. A few pounds of dried apples were often sent to the store to pay for needed items.

Dried apples were often just cooked with some sugar added and a bit of spice — allspice or cinnamon, and eaten in this way. But dried apple pies are delicious, especially fried, dried apple pies. Then stack cakes were made with about 5 or 6 half inch thick layers of molasses cake with sweetened, spiced dried apples between each layer. Of course the stack cake was not to be cut for a couple of days until it had had a chance to "meller," as my neighbor said.

Wheat

We and most of our neighbors grew wheat for bread, biscuits, cakes, pies and the many, many uses of wheat flour. We could not go to the store and buy loaves of bread or bags of flour.

Of course the land had to be plowed and harrowed thoroughly to break up clods for the small grains of wheat. The plows and harrows were pulled by teams of horses or oxen, making the preparation for planting much harder and slower than today with tractors. When the ground was ready, the wheat was sowed or planted with a wheat drill. The wheat grains were put into a wood box-like container about four or five feet long, wider at the top and sloped to the bottom which let the seed feed toward the bottom and dropping through tubes to the ground, followed by metal prongs which covered the seed with soil. The drill box was covered with lids or covers to be raised for filling the sections.

There was fall planting or spring planting. My father usually planted wheat in the fall in time for the grains to germinate before a hard winter freeze. When we might have a three or four inch snow with moderate temperature, Dad would say, "That is a good blanket for the wheat." The first warm spring day would see the grass-like blades of wheat starting to grow. It should be mentioned that there were varieties of seed wheat — kinds for fall or spring planting depending on the climate of the area. With our rather temperate climate, either variety was used.

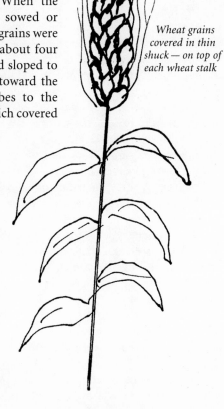

Prickly beards growing out of wheat grains

Wheat grains covered in thin shuck — on top of each wheat stalk

Stalk of wheat

At times we had a flock of geese and they dearly loved the young tender grass-like blades of wheat just coming up or a few inches high. It was my job to keep the geese out of the wheat field, as they could destroy a field of wheat if left alone before the wheat became too tall or too tough.

When the wheat was about eighteen inches high and there was a breeze blowing over the field, my brother would say, "Look at the sheep running," as the breeze bent the tops of the green wheat in alternating swaths and looked like a flock of sheep galloping up and down through a field.

Near the end of July or early August the wheat had grown to a height of 2½ or 3 feet, had turned a golden yellow in color and was ready for harvesting. This was the warmest part of the summer and cutting wheat was a hot and tiresome job. Usually on a small farm such as ours there would be two or three men with "cradles" cutting the grain, followed by the same number of men or grown-up boys who gathered up the cut wheat and tied it in bundles.

A wheat cradle was a sharp metal scythe, slightly rounded and three wood fingers shaped like the scythe, all on a handle like a grass scythe. The scythe cut off five or six rows of wheat with each swing which would fall onto the wood fingers. The cradler would quickly pick the wheat from the wood fingers, lay it or drop it on the ground for the men to gather up two or three bunches and tie them into sheaves, using about three wheat stalks to tie them. The main cradler would be cutting two or three feet ahead of the other cradler to be out of the way of the following cutter. Today, I'm amazed at how quickly those men swung the cradles and picked up and dropped the cut wheat, and started another swing in, I feel less than a second. It surely required strength and perseverance!

Toward the end of the day, the sheaves were gathered and about eight stood on the cut ends, making teepee-like shocks to be covered with two sheaves bent in the middle and used to protect from rain, birds or wind. If there was a goodly amount of rain, we'd have to take the shocks apart, spread them out in the sun and put them together again at the end of the day.

The wheat grains were surrounded with long prickly "beards" which tended to stick to hot sweaty bodies and workers were glad to get a bath after the day's work.

In the hot days of hard work, someone was kept busy carrying water for the thirsty men to drink. In mid-afternoon, ladies and girls would take large soup bowls and open top berry, peach or apple pies stacked three deep, along with milk, sugar and spoons out to the workers for a snack and a little rest period. The days were long and they might work ten or more hours.

When the wheat had reached maturity in growth but was still green in color before ripening to a golden yellow, there was a weed whose seed had evidently been accidentally planted along with the wheat seed, and grew with and looked somewhat like the wheat plant. I cannot be sure what Dad called the plant, but it seems to me, he called it "cockle." As I think of this weed, I'm reminded of Jesus' teaching of the tares in one of His parables. *Nelson's Illustrated Bible Dictionary* describes tares (Matthew 13: 25–30, 36–40) as "a poisonous grass resem-

Sharp metal scythe blade which cut 10 or 12 stalks of wheat close to the ground

Three wood fingers into which the cut stalks would fall. Cradler would pick up the cut stalks and drop them on the ground to be picked up and tied into sheaves.

Hand hold to help cradler swing the cradle

Wheat or grain cradle used to cut wheat, rye, oats and buckwheat

bling wheat, but with smaller seeds. The tares were usually left in the fields until harvest time, then separated from the wheat during winnowing." But Dad had us children go through the field and pull out the easily recognized green tares, before they were harvested with ripe wheat and the seeds mixed with wheat seeds saved for the next year's planting.

After the shocks of wheat were dry, they were hauled to a spot to be stacked around the poles already in place to await the threshing machine. Of course, consideration must be given in selecting a site with space for the thresher and not too far from the granary where the grain would be stored. In the meantime, bins which might hold 20 or more bushels of wheat each, must be cleaned out, and aired thoroughly for the new wheat.

When the threshing machine came to the community, it would move from farm to farm in an organized manner rather than retracing some routes, which meant that each farm must be ready when the adjoining farm was finished. One man was in charge of the threshing operation, but had two or three men who went along with the machine until the entire job was completed. In fact, my father was the manager of one outfit one summer. From about 1910 to 1915 or later, the thresher machine was driven by a large belt from a steam engine. The steam engine was pulled from farm to farm by a team of horses or oxen and the thresher box by another team. In doing research, most stated that that belt was driven by a tractor, but there were no tractors in our area until years later. Other than the manager, the other three men were in charge of their teams, the engine, the thresher box and of general repairs. But a large number of other people were needed in each threshing. Close neighbors helped each other so that in return they had help. Two men would feed the bundles of grain into the thresher part of the equipment, while at least two or more were kept busy stacking the straw on one side, while two others were caring for the kernels of wheat falling out on the opposite side — emptying the grain into sacks to be hauled to the granary so the sacks could be used again and again. Of course, these men had to be relieved by others for rest periods on those hot days and the machines running smoothly didn't stop for rest periods or a drink of cold water.

Men were not the only busy people at threshing time. Kitchens were abuzz with women preparing food for the workers. Big pots of green beans seasoned with a piece of fat or striped pork, mashed potatoes, chicken and dumplings, or meat of some kind, fresh garden corn in "rosen ears" or cut off the cob, peas, cabbage, coleslaw, sliced cucumbers and tomatoes, lettuce with chopped scallions wilted with hot bacon drippings, big pans of cornbread and biscuits, pies of berry, apple or custard, coffee, milk, buttermilk all ready for two seatings of tired hungry men.

Children who were big enough did not escape chores. There were buckets and buckets and more buckets of water to be carried to the back porch for the men to wash their hands, arms and faces, and dippers of cold water to drink, tea kettles and stove water tank to be kept filled for dishwashing, wet towels to be replaced on the nails over the wash bench, soap dish replenished with home-made or yellow octagon soap, more butter and milk to be carried from the spring house trough and on and on.

Some families had to have the threshers for supper and overnight. Women dreaded to have this happen, which not only meant feeding one meal but breakfast as well, and extra bedding and laundry. Of course, neighbors who were helping went home for the night. And some families did not have room for more than their own family. Neighbors were considerate and tried to steer the threshers to large homes when possible. We could always send some to Grandpa's. They always had extra beds.

After the threshing was over, the wheat kernels were stirred in the bins with a shovel or hoe to make sure that all the grains were completely dry before closing the covers over the bins.

After the threshing was completed in the community and things were getting back to normal, thoughts turned to taking wheat to be ground into fresh flour. The white heavy sacks (ours were mostly sacks from T. W. Wood, Richmond, Va., that came with ordered grass seed) had been washed thoroughly and were so closely woven they were excellent as flour would not sift through. They held about two bushels of wheat and because of distance, Dad would take enough to have flour for about three months. He usually went to the roller mill on Big Helton Creek and the trip by wagon was an all day one and might take into night, depending on how busy the mill was on that particular day. This mill, according to Arthur L. Fletcher's *Ashe County: A History*, was built and operated by

Win and Will Perkins. There was also a small woolen mill a little distance from the roller mill. Mother would give Dad an order for wool yarn to be used to knit our winter stockings and socks. Black was the usual color for everyday stockings but if that color was not available that day, white yarn was purchased and Mom would dye it black with Diamond dye gotten from the store.

There was another roller mill, the Blevins Mill, located near the mouth of Grassy Creek before it empties into New River and was a shorter distance from our home. The miller always took out his toll from each bushel before grinding the rest. With the toll, he could have flour to sell to people who did not grow wheat.

In most kitchens there would be a meal chest and some had a "meal room." Our "meal chest" was made of wood with legs that held the chest about six inches above the floor, had three sections — one for flour, one for corn meal and a smaller one for bran from sifting meal. The section for flour would hold perhaps 30 pounds, had a one piece cover that was kept closed except when open long enough to get what was needed at the time.

In later years when more railroads became prevalent and connected up with other lines in the East and smaller towns and roads allowed more travel, stores began getting flour shipped from wheat growing states in central and western sections. Flour came in twenty-five pound cloth bags. At one time flour sacks with flowered designs began appearing in the local stores and became very popular with our residents. These bags were laundered and it was common to see dresses, blouses, aprons, and pillow cases made from the flowered sacks. Then smaller cloth bags of five or ten pounds of flour and sugar came on the market and these bags were often made into table napkins, tea towels and dish cloths. When I was teaching at Burnt Hill School in Laurel Springs and boarding with Mrs. Scarborough, she had hemmed and made table napkins from small flour sacks. She would remind us to fold our napkins and keep them at our designated place at the table as they must be used for a week.

Once when living at Obids, my husband worked in West Jefferson and "winter quitting time" was after dark. One evening on the way home, his car stopped and had to be left beside the road. He walked the 2½ or 3 miles the rest of the way, carrying a twenty-five pound sack of flour on one shoulder and a two gallon can of kerosene in the other hand.

Sometimes when the wheat was ripe and ready to be harvested, we children would break off a head of wheat, rub it between our hands to remove the beards and husks, and eat the raw kernels. We rather think that was what Jesus' apostles were doing when accused of working on the Sabbath.

Once when my father took the family with him to Mr. Jim Blevins' roller mill located near where Grassy Creek empties into New River, he took us inside the building to see the operation of the mill. He showed us the water wheel operated from a dam and which turned the two big round stones that ground the flour. I recall the 6 or 8 inch belt that ran from the back of the building to the front end. I was only about five years old and I cannot relate the whole process operation, but later we heard of a young boy, eight or nine years old being killed at the mill. Years after, Mr. Blevins' niece told me about the incident. The boy would place his hand on the belt and run along beside it until it turned down over the stones. Then he'd run back to the other end and do the same again. He did not remove his hand from the belt in time once and it caught his shirt sleeve, hand and arm and threw him against everything in the path of the belt until someone could go up and stop the water wheel. Of course the poor boy was killed. How sad.

A nephew of Mr. Blevins told us that it was generally known that there was a "moonshine still" not far from the mill. He and some other young boys around age twelve, found the spot. The still was not in operation, no one there, no bottles or jugs filled with the "recipe," but a goodly amount of "leavings" or mash lying around. A bit of liquid was oozing out but they had no way to catch it, but they would put some of the mash in their mouth, kind of suck some juice out of it before spitting it out. He said he had never been so sick in his whole life.

Corn

All families had a garden spot even if they did not have enough land for the usual farm crops. In the gardens would be found several rows of "sweet corn," along with other vegetables. Everyone looked forward to the time when corn was ready to be used for creamed corn or "rosen ears" (roasting ears), as it was called. Those who did not have a kitchen stove did their cooking in the fireplace. The corn ears were opened a bit to remove the silks and check to see if worms might have gotten inside. Then the husks were closed back around the ears and were roasted in hot ashes mixed with a few fire coals. One always hoped they would have enough corn for lots of meals. Those who had a good deal of sweet or garden corn canned it for winter or later use. But most people boiled the corn on the cob and ate it well buttered and salted. Sometimes the corn was cut off the cob and added to beans that were being pickled. After the garden sweet corn had all been used, I have known some people to go into the field of corn, look for ears with silks which had not dried and collect ears for boiled "rosen ears."

When the field corn had been gathered and was ready for use, it provided a most valuable staple for cornbread. Most families baked a "pone" or cake of cornbread for dinner and supper, and if flour were not on hand cornbread was baked for breakfast and eaten with cream gravy.

Some cold evenings when we wanted to stay close to the fireplace rather than heat up the kitchen or eat in the cold dining room, we'd have mush for supper. The cast iron teakettle was set on a log in the fireplace to heat water to boiling. Then in a large bowl, sifted corn meal was stirred into the hot water, a bit of salt and butter added to the mixture and poured into the cast iron Dutch oven which was set on the hearth. Hot coals were then placed under the oven and on the iron cover with its turned up edge made purposely to hold coals on top. When the mush was cooked or baked, it was dipped into bowls and each one added his/her favorite spread of more butter, milk, chopped onion or even sugar. Along with the mush we'd usually have homemade tomato soup on those cold nights. By morning, the leftover mush was cold and easily sliced to be fried for breakfast with hot cream gravy.

Another use of corn was hominy made of dried grains of corn which had been soaked in a weak lye solution. The solution of lye and water caused the kernels to swell and the outside skins to come off and float on top so they were easily removed. Then the kernels were thoroughly washed in several waters to be ready to be fried or boiled.

By fall, the corn for meal and cornbread might be depleted and we could not afford to be without corn meal. Dad would gather and shuck ears of corn from the new summer crop before the ears were dry, or all the moisture was gone out of the grains. He would bring them into the "sitting room" and at night all the family was enlisted in shelling corn to be taken to the mill. This corn was hard to shell as we'd have to almost push off grain by grain. We tried to get one row off and then it was a bit easier. Of course we looked forward to the time when the corn would be dry enough to be shelled by the corn sheller in the granary. The sheller was attached to a sturdy table, the ears put in a hopper, a crank turned and the grains dropped into a container. When Dad and my brother had other farm work to do, he would put a bushel of corn in a sack and on a horse for me to take to the mill. Usually the miller had one day each week to operate the mill — like Friday or Saturday. The first mill I recall was at Long Branch, near the road in front of where Basil Kilby's house was located later on. There was a little porch where one could ride up to so the sack of corn could easily be taken off. The miller took out his toll before the rest of the corn was ground. The meal must be sifted to remove the bran. The bran was saved to make food for the chickens and hogs.

Later, Mr. Lida Robbins and Mr. Wiley (Little Wiley) Spencer had a mill, which was closer to where we lived.

Corn cobs were always saved to be used for starting fires in the fireplace and the cook stove. Dad also used a corn cob fastened on the end of a pole and saturated with lamp oil to burn caterpillar nests in fruit trees and other trees nearby.

Pork

Every family in the country tried to have hogs to butcher. A couple might have only one hog to butcher but a larger family would have at least two or three.

Someone in the community would have a sow (a female hog) who usually had two litters of pigs a year. A good breed sow might have from eight to thirteen pigs in each litter which the owner would sell to neighbors or people who did not raise their own pigs. The pigs were ready to be sold when about eight weeks old. Most people bought pigs in the fall to have large hogs of about 300 or more pounds to kill the following year around Thanksgiving when the weather was cold enough to keep the pork from spoiling since no one had refrigeration. Those who bought spring pigs might not need too much pork and did not want to feed porkers through the winter.

Hogs were fed table scraps, corn, vegetables, milk and bran, and slop. Slop was left over table scraps, dish water with food bits from washing a lot of dishes and perhaps some bran from sifting meal. Almost everyone had a slop bucket into which the peelings of vegetables and fruits and leftover foods were placed and some dish water added. Corn nubbins (short, poorly developed ears of corn) were fed to the growing shoats (those too large to be pigs, but not yet large enough to be called hogs).

In winter the hogs were kept in a "hog pen," with four walls and wooden floor and a partially covered roof and a wooden trough for the slop. In summer they might be turned out in a fenced hog lot with grass but hogs would soon dispose of the grass by eating and rooting the ground with their snout or nose. A summer job for us children was pulling weeds to feed the hogs. Purslane, a weed which grows abundantly in gardens or cultivated fields, and which we called pussley, or "hog weed," we were urged to pull lots of, not only to rid the garden and cornfields of, but my father would say, "It makes the hogs' tails curl." In late summer and early fall, feeding was increased toward fattening for butchering.

Of course, it should be mentioned that those farmers who raised pigs to sell — this was one way to make money. However, they usually kept a boar (a male hog for breeding purposes) and there was cost to keep a sow and male hog. Sometimes the pigs were born with tusks that protruded outside the mouth so they could not nurse and these tusks had to be removed. Sometimes the sow might lie down and crush some of the pigs, which was a loss to the owner. But everyone would ask the farmer to save them a pig, as sometimes they might have to go quite a long distance to find pigs for sale.

Hog Killing

If there were no large stout boys in the family, the head of the house would hire a worker to help with the killing. Sometimes two families might exchange work or prepare to do the work for both at one location. The hogs might be killed by hitting on a particular spot on the head with the back of a single blade ax and while the hog was out, his throat was cut, being sure to get an artery, to bleed. Or someone was ready with a rifle to put a shot in the brain, hopefully. After bleeding, the hog was taken to a spot to have the stiff bristly hair removed. Already a fire had been built outside near a branch or stream. After the wood fire had made lots of red hot coals, field stones were placed on the coals and heated until very hot. A wood trough had been made of heavy boards or a large metal barrel was filled with water, the hot stones shoveled into the water to make it almost boiling hot and the hog shoved into the hot water. The carcass was pulled and pushed back and forth to make sure that all parts of the body were thoroughly saturated by the hot water. Then the hog was pulled out onto a prepared surface where three or four people were waiting to begin scraping off the hair with knives, broken glass pieces or a piece of some sharp metal. Sometimes more hot stones had to be thrown into the water and the hog put through the process again before all the hair could be removed. A scaffold had been erected, a round stout stick sharpened on both ends was inserted into the ankles of the back legs of the hog and it was hung by this stick on the scaffold. There was almost always an elderly man or a man expertly experienced in cutting up the porker. First the head was carefully removed. A wash tub or large container was placed under the hog, and with a very sharp knife a straight incision was made in the belly from the rear end down to where the head was taken off. Extreme care had to be taken that the knife just went through the flesh and did not touch the intestines. Next the liver, heart and lungs were cut out and put in a clean container. The "entrails" or intestines were pulled loose and let fall into a tub below. Lots of cold water was thrown into the carcass until the inside was clean. After the water had completed draining, the hog was taken down and placed on a table (usually made of boards on saw horses, and the backbone and ribs were cut out. Then the hams, shoulders, side meat and fat pork belly were carefully cut apart, the four feet cut off and the parts allowed to cool to let all the body heat escape.

In the meantime, the wife or someone had a rather unpleasant job — going over the entrails and removing any fat clumps or pieces attached to the intestines and keeping them for lard. Too, when the hams, shoulders and other parts were cut apart, bits of fat were trimmed off to leave the pieces in proper shape and the fatty pieces used in making lard.

At our house, some back bones and ribs were started cooking that night to be ready for breakfast the next morning — cooked with a bit of home grown sage and oh! how good it smelled and we could hardly wait to have some. But with tired backs, arms and legs, we went to bed to dream of that delicious broth on biscuits and fresh lean meat to be plucked from ribs and back bones.

All the other meat was salted and spread on a table inside a building to let the salt soak in. Later the hams, shoulders and other pieces were put in clean cloth bags and hung from rafters to allow air to circulate around each side of the pieces. My grandparents and some others had smoke houses for drying meat. They were usually made of logs with a roof and dirt floor. At the right time a slow fire was made on the floor and kept going until the meat was completely dry.

Some shoulders were often cut in chunks and along with lean scraps ground with a sausage mill, seasoned with salt, pepper and sage and made into patties to be canned. Sausage could be placed in a gallon crock, covered with fat on top, kept in a cool place and as long as the fat on top did not melt, the sausages were as fresh as newly made. When the back bones were cut out there was lean meat attached. This could be cut into pork chops but was usually cut from the bones, chunked and canned as tenderloin. Canned tenderloin was prized for its flavorful taste and the good gravy from the lean and bits of fat, but was so convenient to have when company came. All one had to do was open a jar, add a bit of water, and warm it and there was the meat dish for a meal, with gravy on biscuits. None of the hog was wasted — the head was made into souse meat, and scrapple, the feet pickled, the liver sliced and fried with onions, the tongues boiled with cabbage, potatoes or greens. Even the skins were kept and rendered for the grease to use in making lye soap. When the fat pork belly meat was fried for the fat to put in certain vegetables or make "cream gravy," the fried meat pieces were saved to make crackling bread.

Hams and shoulders were conservatively used to have for special meals or lunches. Slices were taken out and fried slowly so they would be tender but not burned or tough but would leave browned bits in the fry pan in which cream gravy would be made to have a tasty delightful ham flavor. Or, if preferred, most of the fat removed, brown the ham bits sticking to the bottom of the pan until the pan is hot, pour some hot water or coffee into the pan, let it boil a minute or so, pour it over the fat in the bowl and there is "red-eye gravy" to serve on grits or biscuits.

After the hams, shoulders, sausage and tenderloin had been taken care of, it was lard making time. Lard was made from the fat bits from the intestines, fat cut from shaping the major cuts as well as from the pork organs. There was hardly any part of the hog which did not have some fat to be removed. The big oval shaped cast iron boiler at our home was filled with the fats, just a tiny bit of water added to keep the pieces from scorching or burning until melting began. After all the fat was melted, or "rendered," it was strained to remove any tissue or bits of flesh, and poured into five gallon tin "lard cans" which had been gotten from the hardware store. I always dreaded the day for lard making as the odor was so unpleasant!

Of course, today the lard we buy has a mild flavor and pleasant odor from modern developments which does not become rancid or sour at ordinary temperatures. Many cooks now want old time lard for making pastries especially pie crusts, while some elderly ladies may be heard to say "I haven't made good biscuits since the days when I had good homemade hog lard!"

Beef

Beef was not commonly a family food. Cows were kept for milk for the family and to produce calves to be sold for money. It would have been considered absolute waste to butcher a calf for meat. A heifer calf (a female calf) might be kept to become a milk cow in two or three years. At times someone would butcher a cow or steer and peddle the meat hoping to make a higher profit than selling the animal alive. This person would go around the community in a wagon and knock on doors of neighbors to sell beef. He carried a scale for weighing the meat and had differing prices for the types of beef — highest price for steak, lower price for "boiling" portions, a price for whole hind leg and another for a front leg.

Once when I was buying a few pounds, I complained of too much bone in the purchase, and the reply was, "When you buy land, you buy stones, when you buy beef, you buy bones."

However, when there was a special occasion in the area, as an all-day function with dinner on the grounds, two of three people might butcher a beef and others would buy portions to have meat for the affair. Usually the beef was boiled and sliced for sandwiches on homemade "light bread," as the loaves of sourdough or yeast bread was called.

Chicken

Today most families buy packaged chicken for a meal anytime they want. But in the early part of this century, chicken was served mostly when "company" was expected on Sunday. Chickens were raised mainly for eggs and were taken to the store to exchange for sugar, coffee or other needed commodities. Hardly ever was a fryer size chicken killed by a family but grown and fattened to sell by the pound.

When a chicken was to be killed, we were told, "Catch that old Dominecker hen as she isn't laying any more — just eating her head off." The chickens were usually boiled some to make them somewhat tender, then taken out of the broth, rolled in flour and fried. The broth was then mixed with milk and made into gravy or for dumplings. Chicken pot pie was a very special dish — usually made in a black cast iron Dutch oven.

There were no factories or public works in the area in this period and householders were faced with the problem of money for things they could not grow or make, such as clothing, certain foods, equipment, and many other needed items, for their families and to keep the farm going. Those who had large farms might sell some acreage, a few went away for periods of time to work in coal mines or in some other available works, while most stayed home and tried ways to make some money. What could they sell? There were demands for chickens, turkeys, geese, beef, pork, butter, herbs and dried apples.

Every family tried to have chickens for eggs and to eat but mostly to sell. It was reassuring to have eggs and chickens to barter at the local store for sudden, urgent needs. Raising chickens was not as easy as it might appear. There were diseases, predators, and weather which created problems. Gapes (a disease of the breathing organs) and cold and rainy weather killed many young chicks, while worm parasites, lice and other health problems attacked both young and older chickens.

Then there were predators — hawks, owls, weasels, rats and snakes to be protected from. Hawks circled around watching for baby chicks to swoop down on, pick up with their claws, carry away to eat or feed to baby hawks. Housewives and children tried to keep watch for these birds, sometimes alerted by the angry, cackling noise of the mother hen, when all would run, yell, clap hands, or beat on a pan or wave an apron or cloth to try to scare the hawk away. Sometimes a loaded rifle or shotgun was kept handy to fire at the hawk. If the bird were not seen to fall, the remark might be heard, "Well, maybe it scared him away."

Most families had a chicken house which could be closed at night to protect the chickens. These houses were usually made of rough lumber, with foundation boards of heavy 2 × 6s or 2 × 8s set a bit into the ground and the upright boards nailed to them to keep out enemies. Inside the house would be a trough for feed, a bank of nests fastened to the wall about three feet above the dirt floor for easy access for the laying hens, lined with straw, hay or dried grass to protect the eggs and to be more comfortable. An interesting feature were slanted pole or slat roosts, staggered so the chickens would not roost directly over each other at night.

Despite best efforts, weasels and black snakes would burrow under the foundations and get into the house, kill and eat chickens and eggs. Weasels were small, quick, sly animals covered with soft, sleek brown fur, and were about ten or twelve inches long without the tail. Some weasels change color in winter and summer seasons and provide ermine fur for expensive coats, capes, muffs and hats.

The only weasel I saw was a sleek brown one running from the chicken house when I started to open the door to let the chickens out. They seemed too cunning to get caught in a trap and too fast to get shot.

Black snakes, too, ate eggs and small birds. One usually peeked into the nests when collecting eggs to make sure a snake was not coiled up there. One year three coops of hens and chicks were placed in a spot away from the large chickens near the house hoping the babies might not catch some disease from older fowls or from the soil used by the older ones. I was sent to check on them. I saw the three mothers and the baby chicks. I also saw a black snake coiled up but with head up as if looking at things. I did not report seeing the snake (I don't know why!) and when my parents went to feed the three groups that evening, they found several dead chicks and some others missing. Some people said that black snakes could "charm" chicks, birds, other fowls and even people, by staring at them and swinging their heads back and forth as a hypnotist might do with a watch!

The chickens of those people who did not have a chicken house would roost in trees, make their own nests under a bush, in a fence corner or some hidden spot. Sometimes, the nests were not found until a missing hen showed up with her brood of little, fuzzy chicks. But a hen usually cackles after laying an egg and this alerts the householder to where the nest might be.

After a hen had laid eggs for some time, she might be found on the nest and refusing to leave. She was said to be "setting." A dozen or more eggs were placed in the nest and the hen would sit on them, turn them with her feet, keep them warm, leaving them only long enough to get food and water. This went on for 21 days, when the eggs began to hatch. When all the eggs were hatched (sometimes one or more might not hatch) the mother and babes were taken off and put in a coop—a triangular coop, slatted on one side and on both ends to allow for air to circulate. One long side might be completely covered to protect from sun and rain.

Food and water were put inside the coop—finely broken up cornbread or corn meal mixed with water for food for the little chicks while the mother could be given grain or eat the bread the chicks were eating. The baby chicks could run outside the coop but when cold or frightened and at night ran to the mother and hid under her wings.

When country people were planning to have a chicken to eat, it was caught—perhaps by children chasing it or throwing food to it and grabbing it unexpectedly. The head was put on the wood chopping block, and cut off with the ax or hatchet. The chicken was then quickly tossed off a little distance as it would flop around for a minute or two and throw blood about. Hence the saying, "So and so runs around like a chicken with its head cut off." Then the chicken was doused thoroughly in a pail of very hot water so the feathers could be easily plucked.

The body was moved over a flame to singe the hairs that remained after the feathers were plucked. The feet were cut off with a sharp knife, the entrails removed, liver and gizzard saved, wings and legs cut off the body and separated at the leg joints. Then the breast was cut into two or more pieces, the neck and two pieces of the back separated and all washed and made ready to cook.

Geese

We kept a flock of ten or twelve geese to have feather pillows and feather ticks to put on top of the wheat straw mattresses. The female geese laid only a few eggs each year and did not tend to "set" as often as chicken hens did. Goose eggs were much larger than chicken eggs, perhaps three times larger. They were even larger than turkey eggs. Sometimes goose eggs were put under a chicken hen for hatching but a chicken hen could not cover more than three goose eggs.

Geese made nests in a rounded place on the ground and lined them with dried grasses, straws and down which they plucked from their bodies. When the eggs hatched, and the goslings dried off, they were golden yellow masses of fluffy down with broad, flat backs, and legs spread apart with webbed feet. They were delightful to watch as they waddled about with their mother looking for worms or scattered bits of grain or wheat, then lining up behind the mother and following her to a pond or branch. We would dam up the small branch, deep enough for the mother to swim in. The goslings looked in amazement at what the mother was doing and if they hesitated to venture into this strange situation, we'd give each one a gentle push. One push was all that was needed, when they found that moving their webbed feet kept them above the water and allowed them to move in a delightfully easy way, they were as addicted as "like a duck takes to water."

We have already seen how geese loved to eat an acre or two of young wheat. They did not eat grass or plants as many other birds or animals by taking a bit and chewing it before swallowing it. They took fast nibbles of several blades of wheat before raising their heads. It was my job to watch the geese and keep them from the wheat field. I would drive them from the field back to the barnyard thinking they would stay nearby, but hardly was my back turned when they would head back to their favorite meal.

My father sometimes sent a note to school that I was to be excused at lunch time to go home to hold the necks of the geese as they were being plucked to keep them from nibbling the arms of the person doing the plucking. Instead of biting, and letting go, they would seize the hand or arm and with quick, rapid movements move along the limb, leaving red welts. This annoyed pluckers.

After the goslings were several weeks old and growing, a larger space was needed for all the geese at night. Dad underpinned the granary with boards to provide adequate space to accommodate the growing flock, and keep them safe from predators. But one morning we found the partly eaten bodies of three goslings. "Hoot owls!" Dad said. That night he set a steel trap and baited it with the leftover part of a dead gosling. Sure enough, when we looked out the next morning, there was a big hoot owl in the trap!

He (or she) was a big one, perhaps 14 or 15 inches tall with gray feathers edged with black and big, big deep yellow eyes with black centers. He watched us intently and followed our movements with his head which seemed to turn almost from front to back. He was the most beautiful bird I think I had ever seen close up. Now that we never hear the, "Hoot, hoot, hoot," just after dark or see a big, dark looking bird or two headed toward the woods at dusk, it seems sad that he was killed — but he was our enemy at that time. His wings were removed and spread out, a rock put on top of the portion that controlled the natural spreading of the feathers for flying, and let dry to be used to fan the fire coals to a flame and catch the fire logs.

Too, there were screech owls. They were much smaller than the hoot owls and were found in barns, small trees and bushes. They hunted mice and rodents. Their call was different, not at all like that of the hoot owl, but kind of like the sound of a screech and that may have been why they were called screech owls. One night after dark, I was going to the spring in the yard to get a bucket of water and one of these little owls hit my head as he was flying toward a shrub in the yard. It was hard to say who was more frightened, me or the owl.

Turkeys

Many families raised turkeys as a money crop. Usually a family in our community would have five, six or more turkey hens and a gobbler (the male, also called a "tom"), which were kept through the winter. In early spring the turkey hens would begin to hunt for good nesting places. They did not make nests or lay their eggs in the barn or chicken house as chicken hens did, but would "steal their nests out" in hard to find places, seemingly determined they would not be found. Often one of us children was assigned to watch a hen's every movement until we discovered where she was nesting. Eggs were gathered daily to be kept in a cool place so they would be fresh for eating, selling or to be hatched. Of course, one egg was always left in a nest for a "nest egg" or the fowl would move to another place if all her eggs were gone every day. Stores kept artificial eggs, a white hard egg-shaped nonbreakable gadget to replace "real nest eggs" which could be used over and over.

Turkeys often made nests rather far from the house, and likely under a bush along a fence row, on the side of a hay stack, on the ground in a thick blackberry patch, or under a rhododendron bush in the woods. Sometimes a nest might not be found and the mother turkey would show up one day, followed by a brood of babies. Turkeys were prone to wander far and near over the farm and even over a neighbor's farm. So, as soon as the twelve or fourteen large brown speckled eggs had hatched, the mother and babies were put in a coop to be fed and where the mother would more likely keep the babies under her wings at night and when the weather was cold and rainy. Cold rains and predators were hard on baby turkeys. It has been said that when there is a hard rain, turkeys have been known to stick their heads up, open their mouths and drown themselves. As soon as the little turkeys had grown too large for the coops, they were turned outside and children assigned to keep an eye on them and drive them back to the barnyard at night. To lose a turkey meant losing money, so they were fed well and cared for until about the end of October when they received special feeding and care for Thanksgiving was on the way!

Word was passed around that a buyer would be by on a certain day to buy turkeys. Good turkey hens and gobblers might be kept for two or three years or new ones selected from the current flock to keep for the next season and the older ones sold. Several days before the buyer was due to come, the flock was herded into stables or buildings to be given extra feed to gain as much weight as possible. The buyer had engaged several men to help with the turkeys, and they moved from one farm to the next driving and herding the turkeys along. At each place, one, two or three turkeys were tied by the legs, hung on the "stillards" (steelyards) or weighing gadgets, the weight written down, those turned loose with the already assembled herd until all had been weighed. After all the contracted turkeys in the community had been gathered, they were driven, i.e. walked, by the men to Troutdale, Virginia, and sold to a dealer to be shipped to cities for Thanksgiving. Mr. Paul Plummer, a close neighbor, helped with the drive one year. They drove through fields as much as they could to make "short cuts in distance" and avoid meeting any traffic which might frighten the flock more than it already was. At streams, the birds were allowed to drink water. Paul said they got as far as Grant the first day. A spot was selected with just three or four trees close together in a field to stop for the night. A wagon had gone along the road carrying feed for the flock and for the men, along with a coop for an injured or sick fowl. Some men kept watch over the flock at night to make sure that wild animals did not catch or frighten the turkeys roosting in the trees.

There are several varieties of turkeys but the Bronze variety was preferred in our area since it was heavier than the White Holland. Full grown Bronze gobblers might weigh up to thirty-five pounds and the young hens fifteen or sixteen pounds. The Bronze turkeys, especially the gobblers have beautiful feathers of bronze, copper, green and black and often the big gobblers would spread and lower their wings, raise the wide tail feathers and strut around as if saying, "Look at me! Am I not the most beautiful thing you've ever seen?"

Some gobblers, as well as roosters would attack people. One of our gobblers would follow us along until we stopped to open a gate or a door, then if we weren't very careful, he'd jump and partially fly and hit one of us in the upper back.

When my husband and I had a summer cottage on the Shenandoah River at Front Royal, Virginia, the road from the town to the river was about two miles through farms. Someone had flocks of around five thousand White Holland turkeys. Once my husband stopped to take pictures of the turkeys and evidently they thought he was going to feed them and when big flocks of turkeys started toward the car, he decided he had better get back in the car and out of the way.

Frosty

After a female fowl, chicken, turkey, goose or bird, has laid a certain number of eggs they decide it is time to raise a family, just as people and animals propagate. We had more chicken hens than other fowls and were accustomed to hens "setting." When a hen wanted to "set," she'd stay on the nest and when we'd try to look in her nest to collect eggs, she'd spread her wings as if to flog that "enemy" and scold in a voice as if to say, "Get away, Get away! Don't you see I'm settin'." We'd wait a couple of days to see if she was really in earnest about setting. If she continued to stay on the nest, then we'd put twelve or thirteen eggs selected for size and perfection under the hen, who'd stay over them almost all the time, day and night to keep them warm until they hatched in about three weeks.

One year an old hen began setting and hatched out her chicks before all the cold weather was over. One cold night as she spread her wings to protect the growing chicks from the cold, there was not enough room and one chick was pushed out too long in the cold and was frost bitten. The next day we found the young chick stiff and almost dead from the cold. But he was brought into the house, wrapped in a warm rag and placed in a box near the fireplace. He slowly began to move and recover, but the fuzz he was born with fell off and his body was almost bare. Of course, we fed him and kept him in a warm place and he decided we were his parents. When he was able to go outside he wouldn't stay with the mother hen and his growing, feathering out siblings, but instead would follow us to the house. He never grew feathers like the other chicks except a few scattered wing feathers and a toe that was almost falling off one foot. Well he stayed around the house and yard where we fed him, talked to him, made a real pet of him and named him Frosty.

Several weeks into summer, Dad had workmen helping on the farm and one day when eating mid-day lunch in the dining room, the kitchen door was left open. Frosty slipped in and the smell of warm food led him into the dining room where everyone was eating before he was noticed. All at once he spread his scantily feathered wings and jumped up on the table. Everyone screamed in unison and tried to grab Frosty, but Frosty proceeded to hurry the full length of the long table, snatching bites of food here and there as he went, before finally caught. When clearing off the table after the meal we found Frosty's toe which fell off in the mad scramble.

I don't remember what finally became of Frosty. No one wanted to eat him. We didn't dare to try to sell him at the store. I suppose he finally died.

Rabbits and Squirrels

In winter time the men and boys hunted rabbits and squirrels — mostly rabbits. When these animals were shot with a shotgun or rifle the meat was damaged some, so boys used to make "rabbit" gums. A rabbit gum was a box with four sides and a door that could be propped up with a small stick. An apple or carrot was placed inside the box and when the rabbit went after the bait, he bumped the little stick, the door dropped down and the animal was trapped. Sometimes an animal other than a rabbit had smelled the food and was caught. No one wanted to catch a skunk which meant the trap had to be thoroughly washed and allowed to dry and air out until the scent was gone. Squirrels were usually shot while in a tree. Of course either of these animals had to be skinned, washed, and fried. The back legs had the most meat, the front legs — not much, but the backs were meaty.

Mutton

Lots of families kept sheep, not only for the wool and lambs to sell, but to have mutton. At our home, we had sheep for several years but never butchered one or bought mutton for food. I don't know if my father shared the same attitude that Grandma and my two aunts had about mutton or not. At least I never heard him mention his like or dislike of mutton, but they were very adamant about their dislike of mutton. "That old fat stuff. I can't stand to smell it, much less eat it," they would say. After I was married, Dad asked my husband and me to drive him to Independence on some business. Although it didn't take as long as going on horseback, the Model T didn't make 55 miles an hour either. In addition to taking care of the business, Dad found many people he wanted to talk to. At lunch time, he said, "There's a boarding house down the street a little ways. We'll go there for lunch." A number of people sat around a large table loaded with platters and bowls of food which was passed from person to person to take out while they discussed matters of the day. Of course, my husband and I just ate and listened. Directly my husband said, "That was good meat, wasn't it? What was it?" About that time someone said, "Pass the mutton, please." We had second helpings!

Those who butchered sheep, very carefully removed the hide to dry for a floor rug or a cushion for a rocker or other chair.

Milk

Milk was so essential that almost everyone had at least one cow. We usually had three cows and sometimes four. That sounds as if we would have plenty of milk at all times but cows were bred every year and about two months before calving they were "turned dry"—that is were not milked. Having calves to sell meant some money to buy needed necessities, or a heifer calf to keep to replace an old cow which was failing in milk, or two male calves might be kept to make a yoke of oxen for work. A well built healthy male calf might be kept and not castrated, so it could become a bull for breeding purposes. Other male calves were castrated when a few months old and if they were growing horns they were dehorned — that is the horns were cut off close to the head, this to prevent them injuring other animals — or humans. After these processes were done by an experienced person (there were no veterinarians nearby) the calves were carefully watched to make sure infection did not develop. My father would sometimes put soot from the chimney on dehorned wounds — maybe to stop bleeding and soot should be free from germs from heat of the fireplace. At times a cow with horns was dehorned if she tended to use her horns on people or animals.

Two of three people in the community kept a bull and farmers took their cows to that farm to be bred. It was a familiar sight to see someone driving a cow with a rope halter on or going in front of her and leading her along. I recall one incident of a cow on the way to be bred and she refused to go across the bridge near our house. The neighbor pulled, pushed and tried a switch but the cow steadfastly refused to go over that bridge and he had to take her back home until he could get someone to help him get her across. Each cow owner had a preference of the breed he preferred — Hereford, Jersey, Longhorn, Guernsey, or mixed breed.

After the calves were born they were allowed to stay with the mother for a few days and if they did not use all the milk the mother had, the cow was milked and that milk given to the hogs, as people did not use the milk produced by a cow for several days after calving. Then the calves were separated from the mothers but allowed to nurse at morning and evening milkings before the owners finished the milking. The last milk drawn from the udder was richer. As the calves grew and became stronger it was often hard to separate them from the mother when we decided the calves had enough to drink. If they were a bit hungry they would tend to nibble grass.

In cold winter weather the cows tended not to give as much milk as in summer. They usually stayed outside unless there was a shed or free stable in the barn. Their food was corn fodder and some corn nubbins (corn that had not fully matured), as the best corn was saved for corn meal for the family. Hay was stacked on the farm and if there was no covered shelter for the cattle they would huddle on the side of the stack and, perhaps, nibble on some hay.

Of course, the main use of milk was for the family to drink, but also to use in making bread, creaming vegetables, making butter, cottage cheese or curds, (as called), to use on fruit desserts, in custards, in pies and in coffee and for babies when they were weaned.

As explained earlier, there was not always plenty of milk for supper with cornbread. I recall one time when we were allotted one glass of milk each, my father happened to overturn his glass and spill his before he had eaten much and I felt so sorry for him.

Churning

After the cows were milked each time the milk was strained through a clean white cloth or a metal strainer with very fine wire mesh attached to round tin sides. We fitted a cloth in the strainer to assure removal of any cow hair or any tiny object in the milk. The milk was strained into clean, aired and hopefully sunned crocks, and placed in the spring house in the "milk race" (a trough with cold spring water running through it constantly). The cooled morning milk was used for supper that night after some of the cream was skimmed off the top and put in the large crock used to keep cream for churning. Some of the cream was left in the milk for drinking. If all the cream was taken off the milk it was called "blue John" and had a bluish color and was never as good as milk with some cream left in — not completely whole milk but almost.

The milk pails, strainer and cloth were washed and pails turned upside down and the strainer and cloth hung on nails to dry and be ready for the next milking.

After about two or three gallons of cream had been saved, it was time to churn. Churns were of hard close-grained wood strips that were tapered so that the churn was large at the bottom and smaller at the top and the strips were held together with two or three wood, copper, or brass bands. At the top was a round

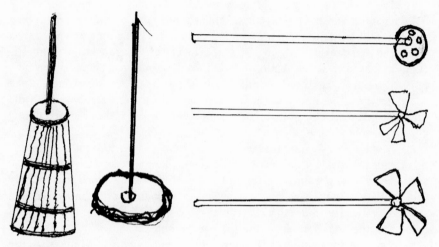

Churn with lid and dasher   **Churn dashers**

removable cover with a hole in the center for the handle of the dasher which
had four wood blades at the bottom end to beat the cream to separate the fat
particles from the liquid and gather them into butter. (When whipping pure or
heavy cream for whipped cream, one has to watch carefully to stop the whipping at the right stage or the cream will turn into butter.)

To get ready to churn the cream crock or jar was taken from the cold water
to allow the cream to warm a bit. In winter it was poured into the churn and
the churn placed in a warm room overnight or placed in front of the fireplace
when the fire had cooled down, perhaps, just before the family went to bed at
night. At other times when the cream was not at the right temperature some hot
water was added to the cream. As the dasher moved up and down it carried bits
of cream up on the cover and when bits of butter appeared the churning was
almost done, but movement of the dasher was checked to be sure the butter collected together at the top. Then the cover was removed and the lumps of butter collected in a clean container and washed in cold water several times to
remove all the milk particles. The butter was salted and made into balls or
molded in a wooden mold with a flower or star to show on top of the butter
which was in turn molded to fit in the round butter dish with a cover. The butter, ball or mold, was kept in a crock in the cold water until used.

Butter was sold to the community stores, who in turn kept it in a wooden
barrel and shipped to a city, perhaps Baltimore, Md., or Philadelphia. Burgesses
and Vannoys in West Jefferson, N.C., bought chickens and butter and hauled
them by truck to Baltimore or some city. Someone who accompanied a trucker
to Baltimore said the wholesaler ran a rod down into a barrel of butter all the
way to the bottom, took it out and tasted it before buying it. I presume it was
later sold to a creamery where it may have been reworked and packaged to be
sold in retail stores.

Families needed and used crocks and jars. We called the one gallon size ones used to hold the fresh milk for drinking each day "crocks." But two gallon, five and ten gallon sizes were called "jars." All these clay-baked crocks and jars, glazed in white on the outside and brown on the inside were round with a round-like thick lip at the top to help with lifting but slippery and sometimes easily dropped and broken. The larger jars were for buttermilk, cream for churning for butter, to hold sauerkraut, pickled beans, and grapeleaf cucumbers. Once when I went with Uncle Luther in the wagon to Troutdale when it was a booming town, we parked in front of a hardware store. On the sidewalk were two tall stacks of crocks! Instead of having straight sides and almost impossible to stack without danger of falling and breaking, those new crocks were wider at the top and sloped a bit to the narrower bottom and with a rim about an inch and a half all way around the top to help with lifting, and there they were easily stacked one over the other with about 10 or 12 in each stack. And there were not just the white ones, but light blue and brown ones! After that, when Dad went to Troutdale and we needed to replace some broken crocks, or add to those on hand, we firmly urged him to be sure and get "some of those pretty ones."

Beets

We always grew beets but used them only for pickling. We never made buttered or Harvard beets but used the tops for cooked greens and used the roots for pickling. The tops were cut off an inch or so above the beet itself and the roots left on until the beets were thoroughly washed and cooked to keep the color from bleeding and leave them a deep, rich red. Then they were peeled and chunked or quartered and put in glass jars. A mixture of vinegar, water and pickling spices were boiled and poured over the beets, sealed, and kept to eat with cooked dried beans or potatoes or other vegetables. A few jars were kept for pickled eggs at Easter time. The beet vinegar was drained into a large glass jar or crock, along with a few of the beets. A bit of sugar and salt to taste and more spices were added. Hard boiled eggs were peeled and dropped into the vinegar and left for a couple of days to absorb the vinegar and red color and be ready to eat on Easter Sunday along with rich egg custard pies. Eggs seemed to be a traditional food at Easter.

Cucumbers

Cucumbers were always welcomed to have with potatoes and green beans in the summer and to make cucumber sandwiches on buttered biscuits or homemade "light bread." But, hopefully, enough for making various kinds of pickles to perk up boiled dried beans, fried potatoes and other winter vegetables. There were sweet pickles, sour pickles, grape leaf pickles made in large crocks or jars.

If someone had a new recipe for cucumber pickles, they shared it with friends and neighbors.

Garlic

In spring and early summer wild onions or garlic or ramps would come up in some of the pasture fields and would be eaten by cattle as they ate the new grass after a winter of dry feed. We children were sent out to pull or dig these plants so the cows wouldn't eat them and make the milk taste garlicky. We hated it when the milk had the wild onion taste and however much we wanted our milk for supper, the pigs and chickens ended up with it.

Dairy

A number of farmers who had large farms with good soil, hills but not steep, and with wide almost level meadows, saw the possibility of financial success with cattle. Relatives and friends who visited or wrote from Maryland and Pennsylvania told of people there who were making money in the dairy business. There were Shorthorn, Shorthorn Hereford (mixed), Jersey, Guernsey and Holstein breeds in the area. Some farmers thought in terms of beef to market while others wanted to promote sale of milk and cream. A small cheese plant was built near the old route 16 in Grassy Creek between the Doctor Waddell place and the New River Road, and operated for a few years. Those who had several milk cows, bought cream separators, which separated the cream from the milk to be used for making butter to sell and provide milk for the cheese plants. Jersey and Guernsey cows provided milk with the highest butter-fat content, Holsteins led in milk production, but Shorthorns were heaviest for beef, and satisfactory for milk, especially in the warm months and appeared to provide the best calves for work oxen.

The first cheese I recall eating, Mr. Spencer had a round of daisy cheddar cheese in his little store. He must have had requests for cheese or a salesman had persuaded him to stock it. One afternoon after school Herbert had stopped in the store and had bought a few slices of the cheese and a bit of brown sugar. Since he and I were the only ones going our way, he gave me a slice with brown sugar on it, if I would not tell he had gotten it. He said, "There isn't enough for everybody so don't tell we had it." It seems that Herbert often had a bit of money to spend since neighbors were always in need of a 12-year-old boy to do little chores and his money was his little secret unless there was something he needed in the line of clothing — in which case he might have our parents keep his money until he had enough for the special item.

As I was writing this, I thought, "That's the only time I ever had brown sugar on cheese." So I tried it and it isn't bad!

Sometimes when we had more milk than we needed for the usual uses, our mother would put some in a kettle, set it on the back of the cook stove to stay warm, and make cottage cheese. One time she had gotten some rennet from the store or the little cheese plant and made a round firm cheese. The whey which was left was fed to hogs and chickens.

In the meantime, since the little cheese plant at Grassy Creek and others in Ashe County had closed, several farmers, not willing to give up their interest in the dairying program, sold their farms and moved to Maryland, in and around Bel Air, Churchville, Havre de Grace and surrounding areas. We knew several of these families, especially the Greers, Thompsons and Joneses.

Berries

Blackberries

Blackberries grew in abundance almost everywhere, it seemed. Their name evidently came from their black or dark purplish color. The berries grew on a thorny bramble or briar as they were called. Many a scratch on hands, arms and legs of the persistent gatherer were usually evident as well as picked and torn clothes at times. They grew on fence rows, along roadsides, along streams and in shady swampy places. An entire field, if not heavily grazed by animals or mowed by the owner might be covered with blackberry briars. The biggest and sweetest berries could be found in the damp, swampy shady places on the tallest and longest brambles surrounded by bushes, tall grasses and low lying briars. But it took lots of nerve and courage to venture into those places which looked like perfect haunts for black snakes or water moccasins. I had heard such horrendous snake stories, but would think of quickly filling the berry pail and dare to go in! They were gathered and canned for winter use, made into pies, jams, jellies and maybe into wine by some, and served as a dessert with sugar and cream. Our family, at times, made quantities of blackberry jam in the copper kettle outside by adding some apples for pectin to thicken the juicy berries.

Dewberries

Dewberries grew on briars close to the ground rather than on upright briars like blackberries. They were usually larger and sweeter than blackberries and made better flavored jellies. They, too, were canned and made into pies. One can hardly find a dewberry today.

Strawberries

Wild strawberries grew in clusters on a small plant six or seven inches tall in fields, orchards and along roadsides. They were much smaller than the cultivated ones but were sweeter and had a real strawberry flavor. One might find a spot on the side of a steep hill where one could sit down and break off stems from the plant and each stem have six or eight berries. A pint of berries might be gleaned from around where one was sitting. The plants were so short that lots of bending and stooping were required. The caps were usually taken off before putting the berries into the pail as they were small and it took quite a spell to pick a gallon and they tended to get juicy during the picking and were harder and messier to cap later. Of course, strawberry preserves were the favorite use of wild strawberries, but I can remember having gotten so many that we canned some in quart jars for pies or desserts for winter. I also recall one year we had a two gallon white enamel bucket full of capped wild strawberries on hand for preserves and while waiting for someone to go to Porter's Store on Little Helton to get sugar, the berries molded and were thrown away. Heart breaking.

Raspberries

There were black raspberries that grew in the wild just as they do today if the farmer doesn't keep his field and fence rows manicured or the highway department doesn't cut those beside the roads. People could find a good many of these berries and found them so delicious they began to set out some raspberry canes and cultivate them. The briars bore quite prolifically and provided the family with plenty of berries. They are a favorite berry, costly today, but are so tasty eaten raw, in pies, in jelly and as a dessert with sugar and cream.

There were also red raspberries which, I believe, were grown in gardens only. I never saw them in the wild. My father had three raspberry plants from some mail order fruit catalog. There were a black, a red and a yellow raspberry growing at the upper side of our garden, a part that was never plowed. They did not last long. I suppose he did not keep the old canes cut out each year which is necessary to keep raspberries producing year after year.

Wineberries

A few wineberries were found growing in spots. The berries when ripe are red and the shape of raspberries but grow in a kind of shell much like a chinquapin shell which opens as the berry ripens. The cane resembles that of a raspberry but doesn't have the sharp thorns and is covered with a kind of downy-like coat. Wineberries are good to eat raw, can be made into preserves by adding some type of pectin, and, I suppose were used to make wine — hence the name.

Mulberries

Mulberries, the type that grew in our area, grew on trees and produced a berry that hung down from the branch, was about an inch or inch and a half long and was of a dark purplish color when ripe. We used to look for the trees as they were very good eaten raw and I never knew of any other use for them.

Service Berries

In early spring a tree could be seen in full bloom with dainty white flowers. After the bloom was gone, tiny green berries could be seen where the flowers had been. About August the fruit had grown to the size of a pepper corn and turned a deep red. They, too, were sweet and tasty to eat raw after someone had climbed the tree and gathered them. They were so tiny they could hardly be picked up from the grass underneath the tree. My brother would climb a tree, break off a few branches and hand them down for us to eat while he picked some to take to the house. Sometimes we would stir up cake batter and put the service berries in, just as we use nuts or some fruit in cakes today.

Huckleberries

Huckleberries grew on hillsides along with bushes or in wooded areas. They grew on small bushes, looked much like a blueberry but were much smaller, but despite the work to gather a goodly amount they were hunted and picked for their special flavor for pies, jelly, preserves and desserts with sugar and cream.

Cherries

June and early July were cherry time. In April or the first of May cherry trees were snowy white with bloom, followed weeks later with full-grown but small-ish green leaves but competing for color with deep red or black or yellow well-ripe fruit. Red cherries, Honey-heart and Red Heart, and Bing were the most common, followed by Black Heart and fewer May cherries, a large yellow cherry with a firm fruit, and sour cherries.

Not everyone had cherry trees while some families had a good many. Sprouts from existing trees were taken up and set out in order to have cherries when older trees gave out or nature took its toll of them. Seeds were planted to see if they would germinate and sometimes young healthy-looking branches, about two feet long, were cut from a tree and buried in a damp spot, and more than half of the branch was covered with soil. The buried part might develop roots and the exposed part begin to develop leaves. These extra young bushes were shared with those who had no cherry trees or those who wanted different varieties.

When cherries were ripe, picking and canning kept households busy. Older boys and girls might climb the trees and men were often enlisted in the picking. An aunt, who was in her seventies, would find a spot on a low limb for this niece, then she (the aunt!) would sprightly climb almost to the top of the tree where the cherries grew more thickly and had not been gotten by "fraidy" climbers (like me).

Pails and pails of cherries were carried to the house and now the seeding began — removing the stones. A back porch or the shade of a nearby tree was selected for this job as the juice of cherries quickly turned brownish and stained hands and anything it touched. The cherries were put in a large bowl or pan, held on the lap and both hands used to push out the pits. The seeds and juice remained in the bowl or pan while the cherries were dropped in a clean container, ready to be cooked and canned in half-gallon glass jars. A large family might fill a hundred jars to be opened for pies or desserts.

Later, a gadget was found in some stores in Troutdale and Lansing called a cherry seeder. It sounded like a great labor saver and some families bought one. It could be fastened on a sturdy table or flat surface, cherries put in a small metal bowl or hopper on top of the seeder, a handle turned to let the fruit drop through, the stone pushed out and into a container on one side, and the cherry on the other side. Uncle Luther brought one home one day and set it up. Everyone watched anxiously thinking of the buckets and buckets of cherries sitting there waiting to be seeded. He and Aunt Lona were working the machine. After an hour and only one pail of cherries seeded, Aunt Lona said, "Shucks, I can do better than that. I'll go back to my seeding by hand!" Grandma said, "Look how it mashes the cherries. I don't think much of that thing. We better get to work and get these cherries worked up."

Those who had plenty of cherries for their family use, invited those who had none to get cherries. Grandpa had four or five very large trees that were getting old and the fruit bearing branches were so far from the tree trunk that it was not safe to climb out to pick the cherries. He would have someone climb the tree, tie a rope around a large branch near the trunk, saw the limb off and with the rope, gently let it to the ground where the fruit could be safely picked. It's sad to think that this abundance was completely wiped out by Japanese beetles in the late forties and fifties.

Cherries tasted best when picked and eaten right at the tree, and it was not unusual to see people standing under a tree or sitting on a limb taking their fill.

Cherries were sometimes made into preserves, pickles with stems and pits left in, made into vinegar and even wine.

Canning of blackberries, dewberries, apples and other fruits and vegetables was done almost always in half gallon glass fruit jars. For a family of five or more people, it would have been foolish to use quart or smaller jars which cost very nearly the same as the half gallons and the larger ones were far more useful for the family and company.

The jars were mostly blue glass rather than clear glass and most lids were of corrugated zinc and required rubber jar rings placed under the lids to make them air tight. There were some jars that had glass tops or lids, with a groove through the middle of the top of the lid with a wire which was pulled up from a wire ring at the base of the jar neck and placed in the groove to hold the lid firmly on the rubber ring. At the store we asked for "can rubbers."

Coffee

Many mornings I awoke to the sound of my father grinding coffee. In summer when the weather was warm and the room doors were left open, the odor of freshly ground coffee was so compelling that I didn't have to be urged to get out of bed and everyone seemed to be in good humor. The coffee grinder or mill would probably hold a quarter pound of coffee beans which was the only way we could buy coffee.

Salesmen did not get to the few stores in our area often because of road conditions and weather. Sometimes, all the merchant had on hand was green coffee beans. Then we had to put them in a large biscuit pan and roast them in the oven. Of course, I wanted coffee to drink along with the rest of the family and my mother would pour a bit of coffee in a cup and finish filling the cup with milk and a bit of sugar. I can still see the milk swirling around in the cup as she poured it in.

Later, the school teacher had told the students they should not drink coffee, and so my sister and brother stopped drinking it and that was the end of coffee drinking for me until after I was married. Then I used sugar and cream for a time but now I take it black, and only drink it for breakfast, as a rule, but enough to last all day.

The early coffee pots were a one piece affair. Ours was of light blue and white mixed enamel, larger at the bottom and sloped to the top, holding about two quarts of water. The pot was filled with water and set on the stove to heat and the coffee grounds were poured into the water. After it came to a boil it was set aside to let the grounds settle to the bottom. Someone suggested dropping some crushed egg shells in

Our first type of coffee pot

the pot to help the grounds to settle. I don't know if this worked or not. The pot was not always emptied and washed after every use.

A teacher friend who liked his coffee told me of an experience he had once when boarding in a home. One night the family was going to church and he begged to be excused from church attendance. While the family was away, he decided to make himself some good coffee. He emptied the coffee pot and washed it and when he poured out the old coffee grounds, there was a hole in the bottom of the pot!

Several years later there was the percolator with a basket to keep the grounds out of the water. The basket was at the top of a tube which rested on the bottom of the pot and allowed the water to go up the tube and over the coffee and back to the water.

Herbs and Greens

Sage — A grayish green herb — the leaves of which can be used when fresh but gathered and dried to use in sausage, cooked pork and in stuffing.

Horse radish — The roots gathered, grated, or ground to flavor dried beans, ham, various sandwich meats. The long broad tops were used for boiled greens, called "sallit."

Salad greens — In spring people were anxious for some fresh green foods. They would go out hunting wild mustard, cresses, dandelion leaves, water cress, branch lettuce to cook. This was called "sallit," I suppose from the word salad. Some gathered poke weed leaves but we never did. The leaves were first cooked a bit in water, then this water poured off and the leaves rinsed with cool water to remove some of the bitter flavor. This was called parboiling. The greens then were cooked until tender and some "middling" drippings added. (Middling meat was the side meat from a hog and sometimes had streaks of lean running through as the bacon we have today has.)

Teas

Spicewood

Spicewood was a small tree whose bark on small branches was good to chew and the bark was gathered and dried for teas. The bark was put in a pan with water and allowed to simmer for an hour or so. Then the bark was removed and the fragrant spicy tea used for drinks.

Peppermint

A plant with deep green leaves about 1½ inches long and that grew in abundance along streams and in damp places like spring run-offs. In summer the leaves were gathered, crushed and put in cold water for an hour or so and drunk for nausea. The leaves were gathered and dried to be used especially for tea for young babies with colic or upset stomach.

Peppermint was gathered, dried and sold to merchants who bought herbs. It was evidently then sold to a manufacturer to be made into oil for medicine, candy and flavorings.

Spearmint

Spearmint grew much like peppermint but with a kind of grayish green leaf. It, too, was fragrant but not as much used in this area as peppermint but dried and sold for oil and flavors.

Catnip

Catnip is a member of the mint family and grows to about two or three feet tall. The downy leaves are green on top and whitish underneath. Catnip was widely gathered in the community, especially by families who had or were expecting a new baby. Older people gathered catnip lest the younger couples had none and older ladies were often called on for help with babies of young mothers. The catnip stems were cut off near the ground and hung up to dry before the leaves were stripped off. The leaves were then saved to make a tea for colic and was used by some as a seasoning in cooking. Too, cats loved the catnip plants and leaves to roll around in and also to eat. Neighbors shared plants with those who had none by taking up some roots with the stems.

Elder Bloom Tea

Elders grow as a small tree or shrub in this area. Years ago they were found in abundance along streams, fence rows and on road sides, but are not nearly as plentiful since farmers keep fence rows cleared and the highway department cuts bushes along the roads. In summer elder bushes are easily identified by their clusters of small white flowers that spread out like a saucer or Queen Anne's lace. The flowers are gathered and dried and kept for teas for babies, children or family members with a cold or upset stomach. The tea with a bit of sugar added has a very pleasant flavor and there was never a problem getting children to drink it. After the blooms disappear, small green berries come out on the flower stems and later grow and turn purplish or almost black. The berries were gathered to make delicious jellies and perhaps wine. The elderberry juice was sometimes used as a dye. Also elder flowers were gathered, dried and sold. However, it took a lot of bloom to weigh a pound.

Sassafras

Sassafras could be found growing in the edges of wooded areas, in fields and along roadsides. It was easily identified by its leaves as well as the bark and tree or bush shape. The leaves on the same twig might each be different. I used to look at them and decide that one looked like the shape of a hand with the thumb standing out.

The bark on a youngish tree or shrub seemed to have a bright goldish brown color. The bark and roots were gathered and scraped off to make sassafras tea which was at times used as a tonic but was widely used for tea because of its fragrant smell and delightfully refreshing flavor. The bark and roots were gathered and sold to herb buyers. My grandfather would look for a sassafras tree or shrub, scrape away some of the soil around the roots to find a root that was straight out along the ground below a straight upright stem, get about six inches of the root and about thirty inches of the shrub, remove the bark of both, dry them and make them into a cane for himself. Dad made many canes and gave them

to friends and neighbors. I have one that must be 70 years old which he or someone had made and it is sturdy and useful as can be. The handle or hand hold of
the cane is the straight root part he always looked for.

Chestnuts and Chestnut Trees

Chestnut trees were considered to be very ordinary in the early part of this
century, certainly for lumber compared to oak, beech, maple and locust and
some of the other hardwoods used for hardwood floors and most furniture. Outside buildings, barns, woodsheds, granaries, chicken houses, fence rails and posts
might be made of chestnut lumber, possibly because there were lots of these
trees here in Appalachia. The trees sometimes grew to be 100 feet tall with dark,
green and glossy leaves which were narrow with large hair-tipped teeth making
them easy to recognize. The flowers were in long, yellow tassel-like clusters
around a central stem or axis. The fruit or nuts were in prickly burrs, green until
after a few frosts when they turned to tan and finally to dark brown. The burrs
then began to open, letting the nuts fall to the ground and finally whole burrs
dropped off. On a very windy night, we'd fall asleep dreaming of the ground
covered with chestnuts which wind-shakened trees had let go. The next morning, breakfast was gulped down as we hurriedly put on old coats, caps and everyday shoes, grabbed buckets or baskets and headed for the closest big chestnut
trees, calling back to remind our father to be sure to write an excuse for tardi-
ness at school. Many of the nuts had already fallen out of open burrs and were
hiding under masses of brown frost-bitten leaves. Some were still inside of very
prickly outside burrs but partly open revealing the velvet inside lining. Sometimes we had to use a foot to squash a burr to give up its fruit. Newly gathered
chestnuts were rather easily opened by biting the brown covering of the inside
meat, but as the nuts aged a bit the covering became harder. When we may have
gathered a lot, more than we planned to eat right off, we'd put some in a clean
cloth bag with some salt (to keep out worms) and bury them in the bins of wheat
in the granary. We often boiled chestnuts to soften the meats and sometimes
made a split in the hull and baked them in a breadpan in the stove oven.

Uncle Joe and Aunt Lucy Waddell at Little Helton had four or five big chestnut trees in an open field just outside their yard and they would kindly invite
us to gather some there. Picking up was much easier and faster since there were
not all the leaves, twigs and debris from other trees in the woods.

Later, a fungus tree disease hit the chestnut trees, killing them. Worms then
attacked the dying trees and many fell while others were cut down and sawed
into lumber. Years later the wormy lumber became very popular and costly. My
father had a sawmill installed near the wooded area and had a lot of chestnut
lumber sawed. In fact he had a barn and a few other outside buildings built with
the wormy chestnut lumber. I am now living in the house he once owned and
my kitchen cabinets are of some of the wormy lumber from that barn. Some of
those boards are 16 inches wide and others 10 and 12 inches wide.

Chinquapins

In the wooded area surrounding my elementary school, were scads of chinquapin bushes, small trees or shrubs and common to the Appalachian area. The bushes grew to only about 8 to 12 feet tall which made gathering the nuts easy as the branches would bend. The nuts were good to eat raw with the outside covering much less hard than that of the chestnut, and could be easily opened with the teeth. But we'd often boil the chinquapins, take a darning needle with a strong thread about 24 or 30 inches long and string the nuts into necklaces to wear. Of course we'd eat them from the necklaces from time to time. Grownups gathered the chinquapins and chestnuts and sold them in the local stores. But now the chinquapin bushes along with the chestnut trees are gone. A few chestnut trees are appearing in some places — whether they are the same variety or a different kind, I don't know.

Crops and Farm Animals

Clearing a "New Ground"

In the winter of 1912 or 1913, Christmas was over, my sister, brother and I were back in school. Dad and Mom began to take stock of what was needed for the new year. What had been accumulated or changed in the past year in the family, livestock and poultry? "Well, the children are growing and eating more," Mom said, "and we ought to get another cow."

Dad said, "I guess we should keep two hogs instead of one for more meat."

"We'll keep more pullets for eggs. They should start laying in early winter and they'll need corn to keep them laying," Mom added.

Our 55 acre farm didn't seem to have more tillable land for additional crops or for grazing land. Dad decided that the wooded areas were ample for firewood and any foreseeable needs and the answer was to clear a new ground.

"Now where?" he asked.

Both parents were 35 or 36 years of age, both having been born in the year of 1877 — Dad in February and Mom in December, and felt they had many years ahead of them. After suggesting and discarding certain spots, the site selected was an acre and a half below an old forested area which had new growth from seeds blown by wind from older trees, or nuts carried by squirrels or seeds dropped by birds, and fast becoming a new young forest. Too, this particular patch lay between two grass fields and above another and would be a natural connection of these fields one day.

While doing chores outside, Dad would look up the hill at the selected area and note that there were several trees of about five or six inches in diameter that could be used for firewood for the next winter. With no school on Saturdays, he and Herbert, my eleven year old brother, sometimes caught a few hours of weather that allowed them to take the cross-cut saw and ax and cut down a couple of trees, cut off the limbs so that on other days, Dad could take the farm sled and horses and haul the logs out to the adjoining field where they would be in the sun and begin to dry to be ready to use in the fireplace and cook stove, come winter.

196

The cross-cut saw was about six feet long with upright handles at both ends and teeth set so as to cut with both forward and backward motions. The weight of the saw let it cut through hard woods as well as soft woods and through both large and small logs. My brother had learned when about age 8 to help Dad saw. It was essential to keep the saw going in a straight, quick motion back and forth. When I was older, I tried to help but could not hold the saw in a straight line and jiggled it so that Dad disgustedly sent me to the house. The saw had to be sharpened often. Dad made a rack for the sharpening by nailing a six inch wide board and longer than the saw to the top plank of the yard fence with a thin shingle to hold the boards apart just enough to let the saw fit in snugly while filing the saw teeth in one direction, then turning it around to file the other side of the teeth.

Our six month school closed around the end of February. There were still cold windy and sometimes snowy days, but if there was a break in the weather for a day of so, we'd likely go to the "new ground." After the trees were felled, the branches sawed off, the trunks and largest limbs hauled to the log pile, the brush and little branches were piled together to be burned later. Each of us had our assigned tasks. Herbert helped Dad with the sawing, grubbing roots and prying out stumps, and hauling them out of the way. Sissy and I were to drag the smaller limbs and little saplings out. We complained of the bark and splinters hurting our hands. Dad made "bull nooses" from willow branches for us to use. At that time willows grew in abundance along creeks, branches and in swampy places. Fronds of young willows were long, slender and graceful, but tough and bent easily. After the leaves were stripped off, Dad would make a slit with his sharp pocket knife about eight inches from the large end of the frond. The small end of the branch was slipped through the slit making a circle. The circle was then slipped over the large end of a sapling or limb, pulled tight and the limb easily dragged to the log pile. Each "noose" might last four or five pulls and then was replaced with a new one.

As Dad and Herbert grubbed the small bushes and stumps, we asked, "Do you want Sissy and me to drag the brush out to the burn pile?"

"No," Dad answered, "We'll burn the brush on the ground here. That will burn the old leaves, kill weed growth and the ashes will be good for the soil, like fertilizer."

Days were getting longer and we'd leave the new ground about 4:30 in the afternoon, go to the house, rest a bit, do the evening chores and eat supper. Some evenings when the weather was dampish but the wind not blowing, we'd go back to set fire to one or two brush piles, use a rake or fork to keep the outside pieces pushed into the flames and coals. We kids would sometimes carry a few potatoes and roast them at the edge of the bonfires. (We never had marshmallows at that time.) The outsides of the potatoes would be black and burned, of course, but the inside was tender and had a special flavor with a bit of salt we'd carried along.

Some days, backs, arms and legs were dead tired and those who worked hardest felt like falling in bed by 9 o'clock and when 5:30 A.M. came it seemed as if we'd only just gotten in bed. However, the project might have been finished earlier had we not spent time exploring, examining and looking at discoveries. Dragging brush and branches, moving dried and wet leaves which had accumulated over several years, we found ourselves stopping and looking at things we had never really seen or noticed. We found little seedlings of various kinds starting to grow. "Look at this acorn," Herbert said. "A plant is growing in it!"

"See that big tree up yonder?" Dad asked. "That is an oak tree and it came from an acorn just like that."

"Mighty oaks from little acorns grow," Sis recited. We all looked at her. "Well, I read that somewhere," she answered, somewhat embarrassed at our stares but proud that she remembered that. Dad explained that the handles in the rakes, the forks and mattocks and axes we were using all came from little seedlings that had grown into big trees.

"See that nut there? That's a hickory nut and that tree there came from just such a nut."

"Look at all these empty hickory nuts," Herbert said. "Did they all make trees?"

"No," Dad replied. "Those were food for squirrels this winter." Sis pointed to a little maple bush and said, "That's like the maple tree in the yard, but it doesn't have nuts."

"Look at those little things under that big maple tree out there. Those things you kids used to pick up and throw in the wind to make them fly," Dad said. "Maple trees grow from them. Time to go back to work." Just then someone found a chestnut that was split and tiny white and greenish leaves were emerging. Under some dried leaves we found some green ones that were larger with budding white flowers of the May Apple plant. Another plant peeping up was Blood Root whose roots and stems bled a reddish color which Dad explained was poisonous, but he said women often used them for dying cloth. "A skunk, a skunk," my brother yelled.

"Where, where?" we asked. "We don't see him."

Dad looked around and said, "There's not a skunk. Look there where he was raking. He hit a skunk cabbage."

Sure enough there was a roundish plant with rather wide greenish leaves that smelled like a skunk. As the plant grows larger and the leaves get bigger and grow closer together, it resembles a garden cabbage. Other little plants started to peep up which we did not know, and if Dad did not know them, he'd say, "Oh, that's just a weed." Then we found some beautiful wide, almost round leaves at the foot of a tree. Dad said they were galax leaves and they were so lovely we gathered some and carried them to the house and kept them for several days.

Sometimes when we were working near the old wooded area, we'd hear the "knock, knock, knock" of woodpeckers boring in a tree for insects, grubs or larvae. We'd stop and try to locate them. The redheaded ones were always easier to see and the prettiest. The grays and black mixed were hardest to see against the dark gray of old or dead trees. Once while working near a partly dead tree a screech owl was aroused from his nap and with a screech flew to find another resting place. Cardinals, blue jays, wrens and other birds could be seen and heard as they swooped down for worms uncovered from layers of dried leaves by our work.

Then we'd stop at the sound of a squirrel scolding from the opening of a smoothly worn round hole in a tree or from the big twig and leaf nest high up in the fork of two limbs, as if saying "What are you doing here? You're bothering my sleeping babies." Birds, too, twittered and scolded, flying around as if aiming at us for being too close to their nests and trying to drive us away. We'd try to locate their nests and at times there would be an egg or two on the ground, likely blown out by wind or dropped by a predator. Also there were empty shells that had hatched and those pushed out by the mother bird. Then Sis and Herbert would recall snatches of a poem in their school reader by Lucy Larcom:

THE BROWN THRUSH

There's a merry brown thrush sitting up in a tree,
He's singing to me! He's singing to me!
And what does he say, little girl, little boy?
"Oh, the world's running over with joy!
Don't you hear? Don't you see?
I'm as happy as happy can be!"

And the brown thrush keeps singing,
"A nest do you see,
And five eggs hid by me in the juniper tree?
Don't meddle! don't touch, little girl, little boy,
Or the world will lose some of its joy!
Now I'm glad! now I'm free!
And I always shall be,
If you never bring sorrow to me!"

And each stroke of the rake or mattock seemed to reveal something of nature; beetles, large beetles, small beetles, brown beetles, black beetles scurrying here and there — some of which we recognized and some our father didn't know. There were worms — earth worms, grubs, measuring worms, "thousand leg worms" (I'm sure not that many, but people called them that), caterpillars, insect eggs, larvae and worms we'd never seen before. We did not have bird, plant and insect books to help identify these things. My brother had learned the calls of both the male and female partridges or bob whites and could lure them closer and closer. He also would imitate the "hoot, hoot" of the owl and the call of the whippoorwill.

These and other observations Dad allowed us to stop work and see, examine and talk about and were perhaps some of our best science lessons.

By the middle of last week of April, Dad decided that the site could be plowed. He used a large heavy steel plow which was called a "turn plow" and was pulled by two horses. The plowing was hard and slowed by occasional tree roots that made the team stop when the plow did not break the root. The mattock had to be used to cut the root away. Then, too, a large rock would stop the plow and might require the use of the mattock, iron or wood lever to dig or pry the rock out. These obstacles slowed the plowing process. Of course large roots and rocks had to be carried off the field and this was done mostly by us children as much as we could do. The steel plow blade was invented by John Deere to replace iron blades as sticky heavy soil tended to stick to the iron blades but would roll off the steel blades. The first plowing with all the difficulties required almost two days to complete by a tired operator and two tired horses.

After arms, legs and back recovered somewhat from handling the heavy plow, guiding the plow and horses, Dad would start harrowing to break up clods and lift weeds and small roots to the top of the soil. Too, little roots appeared on the surface. We children were kept busy gathering these things and carrying them off the patch. The harrow was a wood frame probably four or five feet square (probably made by my father) made of 4 × 4s or 4 × 6s and held together with pieces of the same size wood with iron teeth protruding several inches underneath the bottom of the frame. It, too, was pulled by two horses. The first harrowing took most of the day to complete. A week or ten days later the harrowing was done again, this time with a rock or log to hold the teeth deeper in the soil. Another harrowing would be done before planting.

Corn was to be the main crop. Now a much smaller plow pulled by one horse was used. A lighter frame held the small plow blade with a sharp point on the end of two winglike sides to spread the four or five inch furrow apart with newly turned up soil to cover the seed. (This plow was called a "lay off plow.") I was always amazed at the way a farmer could handle a plow, guide the horse and make rows 24 inches apart up and down little hills and around curves.

My sister who was 13 or 14 years old was always the one to drop the corn in hills about sixteen inches apart — three or four grains in a hill. Depending on the almanac forecast and weather knowledge of elderly people for the season, Dad might tell Sis, "Drop four grains, one to push, one to pull and two to grow." I followed with climbing or running beans to be dropped by the corn grains. Herbert followed with a hoe to cover the seeds. If the weather was predicted to be cool and damp, he was to cover only three or four inches of soil so the seed would not rot. If the season was expected to be warm, he was to cover deeply to hold in dampness so the seed would germinate. He carried some pumpkin seed in his pocket which he was to drop in each fourth or fifth hill. I sometimes cheated when dropping two beans in a hill and might drop five or six. Either I was lazy or remembered that the more I dropped, the more beans to pick in the fall.

After the corn, bean and pumpkin plants were about four inches tall, hoeing began. This time a cultivating plow was used on the small frame of the "lay off" plow, except now three small plow blades, in a space of about 12 inches, were used to break up the soil between the rows. This space was called "the balk" and meant the plow must go twice between the 24 inch rows to a depth of three or four inches to soften the soil for hoeing and lifting the weed roots out. Hoeing was slow and difficult since grass and weeds grew in the hills along with corn and must be pulled out by hand to prevent cutting the plants. Any weeds not loosened by the plow must be dug out and fresh soft soil pulled up around the plants. Dad would stop and inspect our work and if we had not done it properly we had to do it again. The hoeing had to be repeated in about ten days or two weeks until the corn was about two feet tall. We children looked forward to the time when the corn was "laid by" (did not need to be hoed any more). Then each year the whole process became less difficult and after four years the area was seeded with grass and looked as if it might have been part of the adjoining fields.

Teams

Grandpa Barker had two horses that I remember, Dixie and Fannie (Fan). They were both roan in color (reddish-brown with gray and white sprinkled in) and always teamed together. (We tended to use the word "old" before the name of any animal of several years in age.) Old Dixie was a gentle horse, considered safe with children as well as with adults with a rather slow plodding walking gait. Old "Fan" was quite "spirited" especially when being caught and bridled out in the pasture, and was known to bite the arm of those putting the bridle bit in her mouth. Being bitten by a horse could be very painful and usually left the imprint of teeth on the spot. But Fan had a faster and lighter gait and was more often used for riding than Old Dixie.

My brothers were in school and Dad needed to haul some trees to replenish our supply of winter firewood. He hitched Old Maude to the farm sled and went to the woods to get the downed trees. After the chore was completed, and Dad had been sitting quietly for some time, all at once he said, "That Maude is worth her weight in gold!"

"Why?" we asked.

"The second I said 'Whoa,' she stopped stock still in her tracks while I straightened the front of the sled to keep it from getting caught around a tree. Trees in woods are not in straight rows as if planted by people. And it's dangerous getting logs or sleds around trees. I could get a leg broke or even get killed if Maude didn't mind so good!"

Horses had different gaits according to breeds. Work horses tended to have walking, galloping and trotting gaits, while the more slender and lighter weight breeds had comfortable trots (rapid two-beat gait), the pace (a faster two-beat gait), a canter (an easy rhythmical riding gait classified as an easy gallop).

Farmers had to have some means of pulling equipment for plowing for crops to feed the family and animals, for cultivating, hauling in crops, hauling trees for firewood, pulling wagons or sleds to carry farm products to market and to pick up heavy items from stores or depots to homes. A yoke of oxen (two steers) might be the first team a beginning farmer would likely have. His parents or a neighbor might have two male calves he could buy cheaply or pay for when he could. I was told that my father's first team was a yoke of oxen. I remember seeing oxen teams of some neighbors. One sawmill man had two oxen teams which he used to haul logs from the woods to his mill and to haul lumber away from the mill site. Sometimes he would use both teams to pull very large logs up steep hills and heavily loaded wagons of lumber.

Oxen did not wear harness as horses wore but a yoke which was a wooden frame that went over the necks of both oxen and their heads put through two bow shaped pieces underneath the frame, thus holding the two animals together. Oxen could be quite "ornery" and not respond to spoken or "yelled" directions of "Gee" (right turn), "Haw" (left turn), or "Whoa" (stop), as horses did.

Another team my father had (I was told) was a team of mules. Mules, too, had a reputation of being stubborn, and when he could afford it, Dad sold the mules and bought a team of horses. The fact that the mules ran away with my father in a wagon and dislocated his shoulder may have strongly influenced this decision. A number of farmers at that time would have a team of mares (female horses), to raise colts to sell or keep to replace an older team later.

Someone would have a stallion for breeding the mares of those who wished to raise colts. Uncle Roby had a big glossy black stallion which he rode to the farms on demand. We could tell when Uncle Roby was near our place. Before he was in sight, we could hear Big Dan's deep shrill neigh, followed by several snorts. Whenever they came into view, Dan was prancing and pawing with his big front feet which looked to me as if one of them, if it came down on a giant could crunch him to smithereens. Big Dan wore a heavy leather bridle with a large bit between his jaws to help control him. He also wore a leather halter which, I understood, was worn all the time, even when he was in the stable, tied to a strong post in order to reach his head without having to go into the stable to put the bridle on. Uncle Roby carried a leather plaited whip with a fringe at the end. I always hoped I would not meet them when I was walking in the road.

A day or so after colts were born they could walk, if you could call it walk. They looked to be all legs under a body that appeared to be much too small for such long spindly pins. A newborn colt of ours was following his mother and his wobbly legs kept him from going in a straight line and he pitched into a cross-cut saw hanging in the woodshed and received several abrasions and small cuts. The legs of young colts did not grow longer in length in comparison to the rest of the body as it grew and matured. The height of horses was measured in "hands" a hand being four inches and is the measure from the ground to the top of the ridge between the shoulders.

Our first team of horses were rather heavy work horses. People called them Percherons, but from pictures and materials I have read, I don't think they were purebred Percherons — maybe part Percherons. Later, we had one horse at a time who could do light farm work, but was mostly for riding. The first one I remember was a lightweight black mare named Kate. She had slender legs and would usually change from a walk to a comfortable pace or canter. Then we had Fred, a bay male with a white blaze in the front of his face and with white "stockings" on his legs just above his hooves. Fred was very particular about his body. He would not lie down in his stable if the straw was wet or dirty. He would climb the bank of the road rather than step in a mud hole. He held his head high and used a comfortable gait.

Fred was such an elegant horse and so comfortable that we were always glad when we could ride him. I had a dental appointment with Dr. Weiss at Mouth of Wilson, who had an office upstairs over the Fields Store. When Dad rode Fred, he would often stop at Uncle Iredell's to talk for a while. Uncle Iredell would walk out to the big front gate and Dad would just pull up, stay seated on Fred while they talked and Fred assumed that every time he passed there he was supposed to stop. On this day, Dad told me to have Fred in a fast run so he would not try to stop there. Our dog, Bill, hated to see a horse running and he would bark and run toward the road as if to say, "Walk, don't run." He never offered to bark or run toward horses walking along.

That particular morning, Dad had whipped Bill for something he had done or not done and Bill left home. I had ridden safely by Uncle Iredell's without stopping, but a little farther on, all at once Bill ran out of some bushes barking at Fred. Fred and I were both surprised and frightened at this sudden incident and Fred reared up on his hind legs and I went off and under Fred. I remember seeing his front legs swing around over me rather than coming down on me and then he ran. I thought, "This is the end of my dental appointment." Fred ran a short distance, stopped and looked back at me, stood there and let me catch him and on we went "no worse for wear."

Old Byrd was a brownish work mare which we had had for a long time. If I were sent to catch her in the field, when she spotted me coming with a bridle, she'd look for a grass hummock or high spot, get on it and show her teeth as if daring me to come closer, but she never did any harm. Once I was to ride Old Byrd to a store in Rugby. On the way she stumbled on rocks or rough places in the road. My shopping list called for oilcloth for the kitchen table which the merchant rolled rather than folding it, some window shades or blinds and other things. The bundles were bunglesome and hard to carry and I really had to use both hands with them rather than guiding the horse. She seemed to understand my predicament and on the way home, she carefully walked around the rocks and ruts in the roads.

Horses had to be groomed often when kept in the stable and lying on dirty wet straw. A curry comb was used to remove knotted or tangled hair and followed by a brush to remove the loosened dirt, smooth the coat and bring out the gloss. The curry comb was a 4½ or 5 inch squarish piece of metal with thin wires pointed at the ends and in rows under the backing similar to a hair brush, with a wood or metal handle about six inches long. The brush was about the same size as the curry comb with a wood back filled with bristles and a leather strap across the back to keep the user from dropping the brush. Grooming was not needed as often in summer when the horses stayed outside in the fields. Sometimes they would find a very grassy spot, lie down and roll over and over with their four long legs waving back and forth in the air.

In winter horses were fed corn, oats and hay, but in summer they ate grass. They used their lips to gather the grass to their mouth and nibbled it close to the ground. We did not have a lawn mower and the horses were turned in to the fenced-in yard when the grass began to get too high and in a couple of hours they had the yard mowed.

Horseshoes were replaced when the old shoes became worn from frequent use on rocky roads and fields and all the work they had to do. Most farmers did the shoeing themselves. Local stores carried a few horseshoes and men would carry an old shoe to the store or blacksmith shop to make sure of the right size. It was not unusual to find a horseshoe that had fallen off. But in shoeing, the old shoes were pried off after the old nail heads were cut off with cutters. The hooves were smoothed with a whet stone or rasp (a coarse file with pointlike teeth — much as we file our finger or toe nails). Sometimes the hoof had very rough parts which had to be cut away with a drawing knife (a blade with a handle at each end and used to shave away rough surfaces). Then the shoes were nailed on with new horseshoe nails, nailed at a slant through the holes in the shoes into the outer part of the hoof. Any nail points that came completely through the hoof were cut off with nail cutters. Those who never learned to shoe horses would take the animals to the blacksmith or get an experienced "shoer" to do the work for them.

The father of one of my very close girlfriends was a pastor of the Baptist Church at Crumpler very near the North Fork of New River. She and I were to accompany him to fulfill his appointment one weekend, when he would hold services Saturday morning and again Sunday morning. The three of us rode horseback a distance of about 6 or 8 miles and probably took 1½ or 2 hours. My father had told me to tell our host how much feed to give my horse.

After the Sunday morning service we were invited to have noon time Sunday dinner with a different family and we had to ride through the river. After lunch, an electric storm seemed imminent so we started home. Again we rode through the river and since the storm was moving quite rapidly, the minister suggested we ride fast to the round house beside the road where we would stop to be out of the rain. We got to the house just as the rain was beginning. Men rushed out, took the saddles off our hot horses to keep them dry. After the rain stopped we started home.

Everything seemed all right until we were about a mile from my home. My horse began to droop her head and kind of stumble along and go very slowly. After I got home and Dad unsaddled the horse and took her to the barn, she lay down. Of course Dad wanted to know if I had explained the feeding and I had.

Baffled, he got out the book he had about illnesses and treatment of animals. Soon he said, "She has pneumonia." With that he had the whole family on detail. "Heat lots of water. Find eight or more gunny or other large sacks. Get large towels or large rags." Everyone was feverishly scurrying around as fast as we could and I was feeling very guilty. "Wring three or four sacks out of water as hot as the hands can stand. Spread them over front and back legs and the side and back." (She was lying on her side.) As the sacks cooled, other hot ones were to be ready. After nearly an hour she began to move some and attempted to get up. Then we took the dry towels and rags and rubbed the wet areas until completely dry. After a while she stood up. We continued to rub her, talk to her and watch her for several hours but she seemed good as new the next morning. Going through the river, getting very hot from running, and cooled too quickly from the shower was too much for her. But it was good that my father found out what to do.

My father would take the wagon and go to Troutdale at times for a number of things needed which were not carried in the local store, and my mother, sister, brother and I would go along to Volney to spend the day with Aunt Ellen. Instead of going by way of Mouth of Wilson, as we do today, there was a shorter route by way of Reeves Hill which came out at Volney.

Part of the road nearest Volney was very steep and I was always scared of that section. The wagon had brakes for going down steep grades to keep the wagon from pushing onto the horses and causing them to run away, but the wagon brake was not enough on this particular piece of road and my father would take a 4-foot length of 2 × 4 or a wooden pole which he would put between the spokes of one front wheel to keep it from turning and this would keep the wagon from going too fast. Of course, coming back up this hill meant hard pulling by the horses.

Sheep

We kept a small flock of sheep — 15 or 18 ewes, female sheep. Grandpa's ram (male sheep) was turned into the field with our flock two or three days at times. Grandpa told of how one ram would follow him around until he bent over to crawl through the fence into another field or go through a gate. Then the ram would lower his head and send Grandpa sprawling onto a rail or through the gate landing flat on the ground. When this ram was in our field, Dad and Herbert learned to be on their guard.

Around February or early March was lambing time. The little lambs would amuse us with their running games and playful frolics. One ewe which had twins rejected one baby, so Dad brought this one to the house, put it in a large box until it learned to drink milk, then turned it out in our fenced-in yard. He said, "Now, Zetta, this is your sheep! You are to feed it, give it water and take care of it." I was so happy to have a lamb for a pet. I had a light blue glass bowl which

I liked so much, but now I used it for "Lammie's" milk, water and feed. When he was old enough to join the flock, somehow it was forgotten that he was "my sheep."

One night we were awakened by Dad who was up and hurriedly putting on his clothes, dashing to the phone and calling Mr. Sexton, to tell him that dogs were after the sheep. Mr. Sexton, too, had sheep in an adjoining field. Dad grabbed the shotgun, a handful of cartridges and left the house. Mr. Sexton and a couple of his oldest sons met him and they let go a few shots into the air from the guns along with whoops and hollering, hoping to frighten the dogs away.

Even if the dogs did not kill some of the sheep, there was danger that the frightened sheep running hard on their short legs on steep hills might be badly hurt or even killed by running into trees, fences or each other. Dog gangs were the dreaded enemy of both farmers and sheep. In fact this was a situation which led many local sheep owners to give up raising sheep.

When the cold weather was thought to be over in the spring, it was sheep "shearing time." My father and the neighbors we knew of did their own shearing with hand shears — a scissor-like instrument with two long blades. It was a slow procedure and might take several days, being careful not to clip the skin and to cut the wool as evenly as possible. As each sheep was sheared and let out it looked so funny and bare, and, too, some would show where each clip of the shears had taken place. The sheep would be more comfortable in the hot summer and the wool sold.

We had one black sheep which we called "Blackie." One day Blackie was not with the flock. My father and brother looked and looked for Blackie to no avail. When Dad was not involved in a farm project that required his total time, he'd try to go over the farm to check animals, fences, crops and anything that needed attention. I was with him on one of those inspections and as we were going into another field, we climbed the rail fence and sat down on it to rest a bit. Dad happened to look at the ground before jumping down, "There's Blackie," he said in surprise. Sure enough, evidently Blackie had fallen with his back against the fence and his feet lying uphill. He had been unable to get up and had died. Dad said, "I sure hate to lose Blackie. He always seemed to be a leader, calm and sensible, and the other sheep seemed to follow him."

Sheep provided a money crop for farmers when all went well. Wool to sell each year, lambs to sell and while we never butchered a sheep, many people did. Mutton was a special meat for a lot of people and for special occasions. Sheep skins were often dried and used for rugs and rocking chair mats.

Then there was the convenience of having a nearby market for wool, as well as a place to buy or trade for woolen cloth and blankets. Bettye Lou Fields in her published account, *Grayson County: A History in Words and Pictures,* reported that a factory was started at Mouth of Wilson, Virginia, in 1884. In the early part of this century, after changing hands, it was owned and operated by the Fields Manufacturing Company, just four miles from Grassy Creek.

Ginseng

Ginseng ("sang") was hunted in wooded areas and in old overgrown spots as it brought the highest price of any herb or root people gathered to sell. Ginseng was quite scarce — it just did not grow as prolifically as many weeds did, and when someone found a spot where "sang" was growing, they marked that spot so it could be found and watched. Mr. Sexton had a sang patch in his woods. He made a little fence of brush and sticks around it so it would grow and become heavier, drop seeds from the bloom to make more plants, and he could find it easily. But these patches were kept quite secretly for folk knew of the demand for and price of "sang." Mr. Hart, in 1985 or so, told me, "Someone has stolen my sang patch."

Today, pharmaceutical companies, not only in our own country, but in China and other places are paying high prices for ginseng for making medicine. The variety grown here seems to be the preferred variety for some illnesses and is in great demand.

Ways of Earning Money

Heads of households were always looking for ways to have some cash to buy the multitude of items which the farm and family always seemed to demand. Farmers tried to have cattle, calves, lambs, pigs, wool, turkeys and other poultry, and perhaps a horse or colt to sell. Men and boys who were not completely occupied with farm work would do a day's work for those who could pay them. Housewives banked on having eggs, chickens, butter, dried apples, and hopefully a calf or two and maybe the turkey money — at least some if not all. Then there were herbs and roots that could be sold. Those who did not have animal or poultry products to sell, depended heavily on gathering herbs and roots and working for people.

Some women and girls did housework for others. We children wanted more clothing items and things than our parents could afford and we relied on gathering and drying herbs. There was a market for oxeye daisies, peppermint leaves, spearmint leaves, elderbloom, dock and burdock roots, lobelia seeds, blood root and clover bloom. We had to have permission from our father to gather clover bloom. One year when we did not make molasses, he let us gather clover bloom which he took to Lansing for us and bought a case of syrup (which we liked far more than molasses).

One year when I was in high school, I gathered oxeye daisies and clover and mint leaves, enough when dry, to fill two large gunny sacks. I carried one sack on each shoulder and walked across the hills to a store in Sussex, a distance of at least two miles. But I had enough from the herbs to buy cloth for four school dresses which my stepmother made for me.

Tan Bark

In the period of the teens and twenties, gathering bark for sale was a rather lucrative activity for some families and, especially for grown children who wanted to earn money for themselves. This was a time when lumbering in this area was at its height. Ten or more train loads of lumber left Troutdale, Virginia, daily to be shipped to cities all across the country, and the same was going on in Ashe County. From the cut trees for saw logs there were left large branches or tree limbs. Also, in the wooded areas of some family farms, trees were cut for private lumbering and for home heating. There was a demand for acid from the bark of oak, chestnut, willow, hemlock and spruce trees to be used in tanning or changing rawhide into leather hence the name "tan bark." This same acid is sometimes used in making ink, a few medicines and in dyeing to set colors.

The bark from these logs and limbs was stripped and dried and sold to private and wholesale dealers. It was a common sight to see a wagon or truck carrying a load of tan bark on the way to market.

Haying

People in our area needed hay for winter feed for cattle, whether they only had one cow, an ox team, a horse or a large number of cattle or other farm animals. Hay was used for feed and for bedding in the barn for the horses. Of course, winter feed was supplemented with corn, oats and bran.

My father always had five or six acres of grass land to be mowed for hay for four milk cows, a few head of cattle to be sold and our two horses. He grew mostly red clover, timothy and what was called orchard grass. The red clover and timothy seeds were ordered at times from T. W. Woods and Sons in Richmond, Virginia, to be shipped to Troutdale in Grayson County. When notified that the shipment had been sent, Dad would allow a few days for them to arrive and went in the wagon to pick them up and the items on the list that had been made all along to get on the next trip to Troutdale hardware stores.

Farmers tried to select a time when a rain shower or a light snow was expected to sow the precious seed rather than in a dry season when the seed might not have a chance to germinate or the birds eat them. A field of red clover is a beautiful thing, even the leaves are beautiful but a field of the red bloom atop the heavy crop of two-toned green leaves is an unforgettable picture.

When the bloom of the grass turns brown it is time for mowing. In the meantime the mowing machine is made ready. The grass is cut by sharpened steel plates which move back and forth in a cutter bar on one side of the mower. The cutter bar was probably 4½ to 6 feet long and turned by the movement of the horse drawn machine wheels. There was a seat for the mower to sit on as he drove the team. When my father was mowing and at the end of a row when turning the machine, I was so scared when the mower went backward instead of forward,

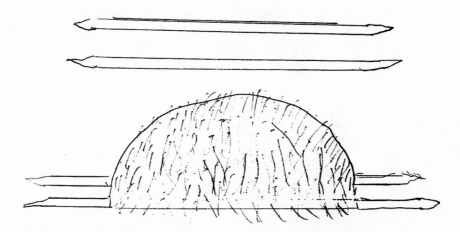

Top: Hay poles used for carrying hay shocks. *Bottom:* Shock of hay to be carried to hay stack.

I thought the horses could not control the machine, but now I understand that Dad had it go backward a bit to have the mower pick up the start of the next row.

A day or two of sunny weather, we three children and probably Dad went through the field with pitch forks and turned the grass over to be dried on the opposite side. If there were rainy or cloudy days we might have to turn the grass several days before it was raked into windrows. If grass was not completely dry before being shocked, stacked or stored in the hay loft, it would mold and be unfit for feed. When the grass was ready, it was raked into windrows by the horse-drawn hayrake in much the same way as is done today with tractor drawn rakes. But the next step was done differently from the way it is done today. With pitch forks, the grass was made into piles or shocks. The sizes of the shocks were determined by the workers as we knew we had to carry those shocks to a place to be stacked.

Some of the dry hay was hauled on a sled or wagon to the barn, where one person pitched forksful to a person in the loft or hay mow (pronounced to rhyme with "cow") to be spread until the space was filled. The rest was carried on poles to stack poles already firmly placed in the ground where it would be stacked. Rather than making stacks close together, they were placed in different spots where feeding would allow several places to benefit from dropped seeds and bits of hay fed into the soil.

Poles for carrying shocks of hay had been cut from tall slender hardwood trees about seven or eight inches thick and eight feet long. The bark was removed and the poles allowed to dry and sanded to be absolutely smooth to slide under a shock of hay. Both ends of each pole were shaved to a slant end about eight inches long to be comfortable in the hands. Two of these poles were slipped under a shock of hay and carried by two people to be stacked. They were dropped

to the ground, then the poles slipped out to carry more shocks. In the meantime two other people started a hay stack. One person stood on the ground and
pitched forks full of hay to the other person who began placing the hay around
the ten foot tall pole and in about a radius of four feet around the pole. When
the stack was probably seven feet high, the stacker began to narrow off the top
so rain or snow would run off.

As hay was stepped on and thrown from the loft, seeds from the dried
blooms fell out on the loft floor. In the spring, Dad would gather all the fine bits
of hay and haul it to the grass fields to replenish grass for another year. Also the
thick bedding hay in the horses' stalls was shoveled onto the farm sled along with
the manure and spread over the hay fields.

Spreading the brand new grass seed, Dad would broadcast the seed by hand
from a peck size zinc or wood pail.

Gourds

We grew gourds, not for food but strictly for utility use. In doing research,
I found that there are a number of varieties of gourds grown throughout the
world for foods, decorations and for their adaptability for many usages. I cannot find gourds as such listed in my seed catalogs. It seems that gourds are
classified into two groups — soft- and hard-shelled. Many people grow the small
colorful soft-shelled ones for show only as most of this variety is not edible and
cannot be dried. In fact, a few weeks after picking, they begin to disintegrate.

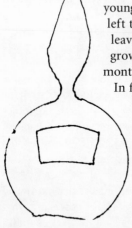

The hard-shelled types are mostly grown in our area and
in nearby border states. Gourds grow on vines much as cucumbers and squash. Some are used as food if picked when very
young, peeled, cut in small chunks and cooked. But we always
left them on the vine until the vine had turned brown, the
leaves dropped off and the fruit had hardened. Not as fast
growing as summer squash, gourds may need four or five
months before being gathered and the skin fully hardened.
In fact, after gathering them, we'd usually store them in a
dry place in the granary or other outside building for a
few weeks. I only knew of two of three types of hard-
shell gourds, the hour-glass or bottle type and medium and long handle dipper variety. We usually
grew the medium length handle kind but some
friends from West Virginia would bring us some
with handles as much as 20 or 24 inches long.

About mid-winter or early spring, someone with
a very sharp pocket knife might spend the greater part
of a day, opening the gourds, removing the seeds and
inside dried fruit, and carve openings for summer

Bottle or hour-glass gourds,
used to hold small items and
some substances

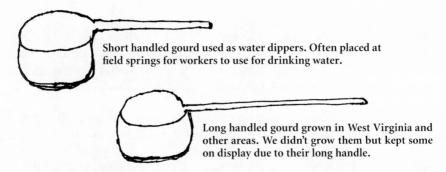

Short handled gourd used as water dippers. Often placed at field springs for workers to use for drinking water.

Long handled gourd grown in West Virginia and other areas. We didn't grow them but kept some on display due to their long handle.

use. The large hour-glass type had a variety of uses. Aunt Lona always kept one hanging in the spring house with salt for butter when she churned. Dad would fill one with salt to carry out to the fields to salt the cattle. They were fastened on poles for bird houses and nests. Some were hung at the granary to hold little nails, screws and other small items. But we children always hid two or three to make sure there would be a gourd dipper at the springs in fields where we would be working so we would not have to carry jugs of water for the workers. One field had two springs, which we counted as a blessing. One of those came out of a bank onto a rounded rock about 20 inches above the ground. The other was in a low spot with water bubbling up from under the ground.

After Grandpa Barker was no longer doing farm work due to age and rheumatism and had left this responsibility to his sons, he certainly was not idle. He always found things to do, such as searching for the right sprouts to make walking canes for neighbors and friends, carving wood combs, gourds and making fly swatters. He died in 1932. Forty years later, 1972, when I was visiting Aunt Lona and we were looking through a pantry, I saw an hour-glass gourd. "Tell me about this." Aunt Lona replied, "Why, it's one that Pa had fixed and we just haven't used it for a long time."

"May I have it?" I asked.

"Why, yes, I reckon so, if you want it."

At least sixty years since Grandpa carved an opening in that gourd, it hangs in my kitchen to hold book matches which I have collected over the years. Many of the matches will not light, but that gourd still faithfully hangs on a nail by the string Grandpa inserted in the stem end of the gourd!

Sorghum (Molasses Cane)

In early spring, the cane pods which had been saved for seed were taken from the bag or box and rubbed by hand over a container to remove the seed that had not already fallen out in the storage bag. Then they were sifted through a screen sifter to remove any husks or trash. When planting time came, six or more seeds were dropped in hills about two feet apart. As the cane began to come up, it resembled the blades of new grass and it was difficult to tell which was cane and which was grass. It was allowed to grow a couple of weeks before hoeing to better determine which were cane plants. As grass was pulled out, cane was thinned to three of four stalks in a hill. Four of five hoeings were needed to remove grass and weeds in order to let the canes grow and mature in about three months.

A short story illustrates the importance of sorghum. One September morning, earlier than usual, Sis opened the room door and called, "Zetta, get up. Get up right now!" I pushed the bed covers down a bit, felt chilly air on my bare arms, quickly pulled the covers up around my neck and slipped further down in my warm spot. A few minutes later, Dad opened the door, "Zetta Rose, get up. Get up right now!" From the tone of his voice I knew he meant right now! I slipped out to the floor and pulled my dress on over the petticoat I had slept in, and the long-sleeved apron (or coverall) on over the dress and buttoned the back as far as I could reach. I hurried to the kitchen to stand by the cook stove to get warm. Dad was stirring flour in the bacon drippings and letting it brown before adding milk for the gravy. Mom slipped the pan of biscuits into the oven, wiped the sides of the wooden bowl with her hand, emptied the extra flour and dough crumbs into the sifter, sifted the flour into the flour bin and dropped the lumps into the pig's bucket.

"Go wash up, Zetta." I went to the back porch and poured cold water into the tin wash pan, rubbed a couple of handfuls over my face and washed my hands. After drying, I hung the towel back on the nail over the wash bench.

In the kitchen, Herbert was filling the water tank of the stove and the tea kettle and hurrying back to fill the water buckets on the back porch. Sis was setting the table, clanking the plates, knives and forks down on the oilcloth covered wooden table as she hurried. Then she brought the butter dish, molasses pitcher, jelly glass and apple butter dish from the cupboard and set them on the table. Soon the gravy and biscuits were done and everyone sat down. Dad and Herbert took two biscuits each, split them open and covered them with gravy. Mom, Sis and I took only one biscuit. My parents ate some of the fried middling meat, but we children thought it was too fat. Them Mom took the biscuit plate and refilled it from the pan which had been left in the warm oven. Now everyone split hot biscuits open, buttered them to eat with molasses, apple butter or jelly. Between biscuits and sips of coffee, Dad began to assign jobs. "Herbert, you slop the hogs, turn the chickens out and hunt up the corn cutters and bring them to the grinding stone."

"Sis, you wash the dishes and make the beds."

"Zetta, hurry and eat and go drive the cows down so Mom and I can milk."

"Mom, after you finish straining and putting away the milk, we'll need a couple of large knives to sharpen."

He finished and said, "It'll frost tonight and we've got to get that cane cut and in from freezing or we won't have any molasses."

"Why?"

"If the cane freezes" he answered, "the molasses will be so dark and strong we can't eat them. And we've worked too hard to get that cane ready. Now, hurry up everybody! We want to get done before sun down."

As all started to their jobs, I went slowly to see where the cows were. And wouldn't you know it? They were all still lying down on the ridge of the upper field! I wished I had my old shoes on. There was no frost but the dew on the grass was cold.

"Why those old cows couldn't come down to the gap where they were always milked." I called, "Sook cows. Sook cows." But the cows never budged. I picked up a little stick from the ground. The newest cow, Koonie, was the first cow I reached. I prodded her with the stick a bit until she reluctantly got up. Old Roan was the last one and her joints creaked as she got to her feet. As each one got up, I stood where they had been lying to warm my feet and, oh, how good that felt. The sun had reached most of the hill by now and the trip back down was not as unpleasant.

Dad was at the grinding stone after the milking was finished. "Zetta, bring some water and pour it into the grinding stone box under the big round stone." The stone had to be kept wet as it turned to make a smooth edge and not ruin the implement being sharpened. A rod through the center of the stone had a handle for turning it and if Herbert was busy, it was my job to turn the stone. It seemed to me that it always took Dad an awful long time to sharpen things. Now he was grinding the blades of the corn cutters to be ready to cut off the canes after they were stripped and topped. Then the medium size butcher knives had to be sharpened.

Herbert and Sis were to strip the long narrow green leaves from each stalk. Dad showed them the brownish leaves of the canes near the ground and that they were not to be left with the green leaves, but I was to pull them off so the canes could be cut longer. Starting at the top of the canes, both hands were used to pull the leaves down and lay them between the hills. I began to pull off the brown leaves as Dad watched to make sure I got them all. I wondered why I had to do this instead of what Herbert and Sis were doing. Dad explained, "You're too little to reach the tops of the stalks, and you're close to the ground and don't have to bend so far."

In the meantime, Dad was collecting some boards and arranging a spot off the ground in the hallway of the barn to hold the cut cane until molasses making time. After the stripping was finished, Dad showed Herbert and Sis how to use the sharp knives to cut the seed tops off. As

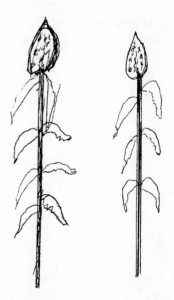

Cane stalks with seed pods

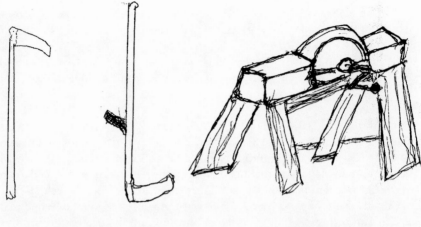

Corn cutters   Grinding stone

they started the stalks were bent over the left arms and the tops sliced at an angle and allowed to drop to the ground. In this way as one hill of cane was cut, the next hill was already starting to bend under the arm and the process went quite rapidly.

Time for lunch! Mom had lunch on the table as the workers washed their hands at the wash bench on the back porch. After lunch we rested a spell, then back to the job. Now all three began to cut the canes with the corn cutters and lay them in piles on the ground. After a few rows were cut, Dad left Sis and Herbert to finish the cutting while he got the horses harnessed and hitched to the sled, and began loading the canes and hauling them to the barn. After all were inside, an old quilt was placed over them to keep them clean and from freezing. When the evening chores were finished and supper over, no urging was needed for tired bodies to fall in bed.

The next day, Dad selected pods to be saved for seed for next year. Then, the children had to pick up the rest of the pods, carry them to the granary to be fed to the chickens later who liked to pick out the seeds to eat. The green leaves were picked up in bunches, tied at one end with one of the leaves and carried to the barn to be used as fodder for cattle.

Sometimes, we children would sneak out, cut off a piece of cane and chew it for the sweet juice.

Making Molasses

Grandfather already had a furnace for boiling molasses and two or more families might decide on a time to make molasses together. The furnace was made of field rocks held together with mud for mortar, was four or five feet long and about three feet wide. An opening was at the front of the furnace where wood was fed for the fire and a small opening at the back for a chimney to let the smoke out.

The cane mill was set up close to the spring and a small stream. The mill had two upright metal cylinders side by side through which five or six canes were fed at a time to press out the juice which ran into a clean white bag in a tub or large container. The pressed out canes came out on the opposite side to be moved to a spot where they could later be used for animal feed or spread over bare spots in fields. A long wood tongue was attached to the mill to turn the cylinders and was pulled in a circle round and round by a horse. Grandpa's Old Dixie, a gentle old horse, was used to operate the mill. Old Dixie, was old indeed, and she didn't think much of this plan. She would get lazy or disgusted and tend to stop so I was put on Dixie to keep her going.

After several gallons of juice was collected, it was poured into the boiler over the fire. Skimmers (a kind of metal box with holes in the bottom) were used to remove impurities as they rose to the top; these were emptied into pails to be poured into the little stream or given to the hogs. After the juice was cooked and boiled, stirrers were used to keep the molasses from sticking or burning on the bottom of the boiler. Usually two experienced people cared constantly for the boiling juice to make the finished molasses as pure and good as possible. The gadgets for skimming and stirring were homemade of metal with holes in the bottoms so the juice could pass through, and were fastened to roundish wood handles about three feet long.

After four of five hours of cooking, most of the water had evaporated and bubbles or "frog eyes" appeared on the surface, the human stirrers would lift the metal stirring gadgets to let molasses drip off to estimate if thickening was about right. A small amount would be put on a saucer or plate to cool. Then everyone checked and gave their opinions. When finished, the boiler was lifted off the furnace by two poles put through metal rings on the four corners of the boiler, the molasses strained again and glass jars or jugs filled and stored for use.

Uncle John Barker had some of his molasses put in a wood keg with a stopper near the bottom to empty the contents when needed. One day as a family member was hurriedly fixing lunch for workhands, she evidently did not get the stopper back in tightly and someone found molasses running out on the springhouse floor. The person who witnessed this catastrophe would not tell me what Uncle John was loudly proclaiming as he was called to try to salvage the situation.

After the boiler had been emptied, the children were all ready with little pieces of cane stalks cut at an angle on one end or a spoon or something to "sop" the boiler before it was washed for another "run."

If some of my sister's and brother's friends had come to the "molasses biling," Mayme might beg some of the new "'lasses" to take to the kitchen, boil them in a saucepan with a bit of butter until much thicker, cool the mixture, and then with well buttered hands, they would have a "taffy pull."

A molasses pitcher always graced the breakfast table to have molasses on buttered biscuits or pancakes. A crock or jar or covered tin usually held "sweet cakes" for hungry children just home from school, work or play. We did not know the term cookie but always called these little cakes made with rolled out dough, sweetened with molasses, and cut out with the biscuit cutter, "sweet cakes." Then a special dessert was a molasses stack cake. A dough was made as for the sweet cakes, rolled out and six or seven rounds cut about the size of a dinner plate and as thin as a sweet cake and baked. After all the layers were baked, a spread of dried apples with sugar and spice, or apple sauce was spread between the layers except on the top layer. This was kept for a couple or three days to let it "meller," as one neighbor put it, before cutting. There was molasses gingerbread and since sugar cost money, molasses was used as a sweetener in many instances.

The Store and
the Blacksmith

Going to the Store

Going to the store could be an exciting venture at times. It was always interesting to look around and see the merchandise — see what new things had been
added since the last visit. The trip meant a walk of 2 miles or a bit more and I
liked it best when my older sister or Aunt Lona went along. The country store
was the gathering place for the men when work or weather allowed them some
free time. Warm days they likely sat on the front porch to talk and spit amber
onto the ground, but other times when sitting around inside the store and laughing, a lone female might feel intimidated wondering whether their jokes were
about her.

Of particular interest were the shelves of bolts of cloth — calico, checked
ginghams, large and smaller checks of red, green, blue and yellow and white;
dimity, voiles and lawn in two or three colors; chambray, denim, khaki, domestic, blue and white striped ticking, and gray and white outing flannel. Nearby
were cardboards of laces and rick rack braids in different colors. On the counter
sat a cabinet with rows of white, black and colors of threads for the sewing
machine to match the materials to be sewed. Packages of needles, for hand
sewing, machine (sewing) and darning: little round balls of coarser thread for
quilt piecing and mending. There were papers of straight pins and those with
colored heads, bone hair pins and fancy, decorative combs to wear in the hair.
Other shelves held canned goods — tins of potted ham, sardines and Vienna
sausage, Garrette snuffs, sweet and regular, in small, medium and large round
tin "boxes," and in glasses with tin covers — glasses usually saved for serving milk
and water. Plugs of tobacco—flat plugs about 3 × 7 inches and ½ inch thick,
Brown Mule and Apple with tiny tin mules and apples pressed in with little
pointed objects on each side, and the tobacco cutter nearby with a sharp blade
to cut the plug in half or quarter as the customer wanted. There were tins of cigarette tobacco— Prince Albert, with a picture of the prince in his long coat, and

R. J. Reynolds bags of Stud, both with attached papers for "rolling your own." Attached to Stud smoking tobacco by R. J. Reynolds Tobacco Company in Winston-Salem, would be two little folders containing 15 papers each with the inscription, "OCB Cigarette Papers roll easily and smoke uniformly. They are of high quality and are made to give full smoking satisfaction." I suppose one bag of tobacco would make 30 cigarettes.

One section of shelves contained health remedies: Epsom salts, castor oil, castoria (for babies), liniments, Raymond's little liver pills, black draught (horrible), turpentine, sulfur, calomel, Vicks Vaporub and mustard plasters. Another section held boxes of soda, baking powder, spices — ginger, cinnamon, allspice, cornstarch, flavorings (lemon, vanilla and peppermint), boxes of cocoa and food coloring.

On the floor underneath the shelves was a 100 pound sack of white sugar. The sugar was in a closely woven white bag with a gunny sack on the outside to protect the white bag from being snagged or torn when hauled in wagons or being thrown around in transportation. Too, brown sugar was carried in bags and measured out in pounds along with the white sugar, coffee beans, rice and dried beans. The coffee beans were usually parched and ready to be ground in the home coffee grinder, but sometimes the merchant might have only green coffee beans if deliveries were late. These green beans were poured into a bread pan and roasted in the stove oven. Also on the floor were wooden buckets of candies — white, pink and red coconut, mouth watering bon bons, different colors of gum drops and chocolate covered "nigger toes." On shelves over the candy buckets were boxes of red and white peppermint sticks, white and yellow lemon flavored sticks, hoarhound sticks, licorice and Long Tom chewing gum. The chewing gum was evidently mostly paraffin. After the "sweetin" was gone the gum was very tough. As I remember, if one wanted to buy 5 or 10 cents' worth of candy, the merchant would pick it from the bucket with his hand into a little bag and weigh it. We didn't think about unwashed hands!

Paper bags were used very sparingly and only for sugar, coffee, salt, rice and dried beans. Other items were wrapped in paper pulled from the big roll on the counter. This paper holder was made of wood and metal with a kind of blade for cutting off the amount of paper needed. Cloth and clothing items were wrapped in paper and tied with string pulled from a round metal holder hanging beside the paper holder that accommodated a round ball of string about five or six inches in diameter.

Depending on what we needed, we might carry a basket of two, three or four dozen eggs, maybe two or three pounds of butter, or chickens. Live chickens were commonly used to buy household necessities. Old hens, roosters or young fryers would be put in a coop for a few days and fed to make them weigh heavier when taken to the store. Usually we sold old chickens which weighed more, but three pound fryers brought a higher price as city folks preferred frying size. A few times I carried six fryers to the store. Each chicken's legs were tied together, then the legs of three tied all together and I'd carry three chickens under each arm. Dried apples were also used extensively for bartering at the stores.

Sitting around on the floor were kegs of nails bought by the pound and widely needed and used in our area. They came in 6, 8, 10 and 16 penny sizes, according to what the need might be. The big 16 penny sizes were used for nailing the rails in fences or for heavy foundation framing. Too, horseshoe nails were in demand as well as carpet tacks and shoe tacks for half-soling shoes. Empty nail kegs made seats for those who spent time in the store telling tales, visiting and playing checkers. Others might ask to have the next empty keg be saved for family use to sit on under the maple shade tree while peeling apples or preparing beans for winter use.

The local stores, also carried "lamp oil," glass globes for lamps and lanterns, as well as wicks and matches, the big matches about 2½ or 3 inches long.

The merchant weighed the chickens, jotted down the weight, cut off the strings from the legs and put them in the chicken coops to await the produce wagon or truck which picked up chickens, butter, dried apples to take to Troutdale or Lansing to be shipped to a wholesale house in Roanoke, Richmond, Baltimore or some city. At the time when trucks became available, Mr. Stokes Vannoy and son, Wick, and Mr. Oscar Burgess and Sons hauled these items to Baltimore, Maryland, to sell and bring back stalks of bananas, furniture and other things to be sold in local stores.

After the merchant figured out the weight of the chickens brought, he said, "You have $2.47. Now, what do you want?"

"5 pounds of sugar, 2 pounds of coffee."

"What else?" he asked.

"Five yards of domestic," I answered.

"Do you want the light weight or the heavier?"

"What's the difference?"

"The light weight is 8 cents a yard and the better quality is ten cents but is the best quality," he answered.

"I'll take the ten cents kind," I said, as I was told to get the better kind to be made into bed sheets.

"Now what else?"

"Two cakes of octagon soap — the middle size. And Dad wants a plug of Apple tobacco. Two boxes of can rubbers and a box of kitchen matches."

"Now, what else?"

"Let me see. A spool of black thread and one of white and three of those little balls. A package of needles and let me see ladies' stockings."

He asked, "Black or ecru color?"

"May I see both kinds?" Maybe we'd like that new color I thought. "I'll take two pairs of the ecru ones."

"Now what else," he asked. "You have seven cents left."

"Give me 2 cents worth of coconut candy and the rest in change." The cloth, stockings and needles were put together and wrapped in paper and tied. The other things were dropped in a paper "poke" and the merchant said, "Thank you. Come again."

A friend had bought an old house and was restoring it about the year 1980. When he was pulling wall paper off the walls, he came across two or three thicknesses of wall paper and newspaper that had been used for wall covering. The section of newspaper he could save was *The Troutdale News*, December 1, 1910. A portion of train schedules was given. There were ten or eleven trains arriving and leaving Troutdale daily at that time. Mr. Charles T. Forrester had a list of Market Produce Prices listed with the notation that prices were corrected every week, and that that establishment was a cash buyer of all kinds of produce, roots, herbs, etc. The following is a list of prices being paid:

> Eggs — 22 cents
> Chickens — old hens — 9 cents
> Chickens — spring chickens — 9 cents
> Chickens — old roosters, each — 20 cents
> Butter — 17 cents
> Turkeys — choice hens per pound — 12 cents
> Turkeys — young gobblers per pound — 12 cents
> Ducks, per pound — 8 cents
> Geese, per pound — 6 cents
> Guineas, each — 20 cents
> Dry hides, per pound — 12½ cents
> Green hides, per pound — 7 cents
> Balm buds — 10 cents
> Prices subject to change without notice.

The paper had a section of Grassy Creek news. Following are a few of the items:

W. W. Spencer went to Troutdale one day last week.

Zeb Phipps and George Martin spent Sunday at the home of L. D. Barker.

D. M. Spencer made a business trip to Independence last week.

Minnie Barker is spending a few days on Silas Creek.

John W. Waddell who has been in Wilkes for a while returned home recently.

Finis Ashley and wife are spending a few days on Grassy.

A number of our folk attended the box supper at the school house Saturday night.

Callie Ballou and Bonnie Sexton attended preaching at Rugby Sunday.

Ezekiel Segraves happened to [sic] a very bad accident last Tuesday night. He and his brother were out hunting when he fell twenty feet. His skull was broken and mashed in very badly. He was taken to Dr. Jones for an operation. His case is very serious.

E. C. Waddell was here Sunday.

L. D. Barker spent Sunday with J. O. Spencer.

Also in this paper were two ads for Dr. Bell's medications.

Dr. Bell's Antiseptic Salve: Is guaranteed for eczema, tetter, ringworm, running sores, chapped hands, and lips, pimples on the face, blackheads, barber's itch, sunburn, insect bites, fever sores, and nasal catarrh. 25c.

Dr. Bell's Pine-tar Honey: Breaks up the worst cold and nasal irritation. This remedy quickly cures coughs, grippe, and all throat and nasal trouble.

When I was growing up, I don't recall seeing tobacco growing except a few people grew a few stalks to have chewing or smoking tobacco. My father chewed tobacco but my mother never used snuff. Two or three people might take turns growing tobacco and dividing with each other. Grandpa smoked a pipe and used home grown leaves of tobacco crushed up when dry. I never knew him to buy smoking tobacco.

For chewing tobacco, the brown, ripe leaves were allowed to become moist from outside dampness or sprinkled a bit with water to prevent shattering when being worked. When the leaves were ready, the center stem was pulled out and four or five leaves stacked together. Beginning with the outside edges the leaves were rolled into a tight roll, making sure the ends held together. The

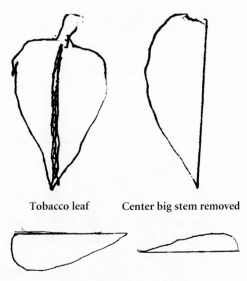

Tobacco leaf   Center big stem removed

Four of five leaves stacked together

Leaves rolled into tight roll

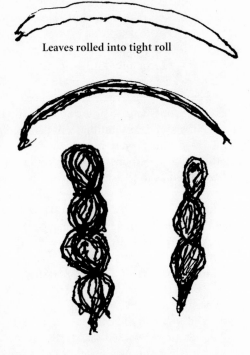

Roll bent in center and made into twist to be cut with pocket knife into a chew as needed starting at small end of twist.

roll was bent in the middle and starting at the center the rolls twisted around each other, hence the name "twist." When used, the user would cut off a "chew" beginning at the small end of the twist and finally ending where the center of the roll began.

The Blacksmith

"In a triangle where two roads met
The village smithy stood."

The village was Sussex in Ashe County. The smithy was Mr. Bob Pierce. The blacksmith shop was a large building with two cupolas on the roof. Villagers and farmers for miles around made beaten paths to this shop. Mr. Pierce made iron utensils for families to use such as skillets, pots, pans, tea kettles and other food necessities to use in cooking over open fireplaces or on cook stoves. He made farm implements — mattocks, picks, shovels, rakes, hoes, andirons, fire pokers, sledge hammers, axes, iron wedges, crow bars, post hole diggers, horseshoes, tires for wagons and buggies and other wheels. Farmers took their broken tools to him to repair. Andirons, for holding logs in the fireplace, often broke from having heavy logs thrown on them while hot, and they were taken to Mr. Pierce to mend. Hoes, mattocks, picks, shovels and chains broke from use in heavy, rooty soil as users grubbed out stumps and bushes to clear land for crops or grazing or hay for the farm animals. Swampy land was ditched to drain for more agricultural use. These ditches were dug by hand using picks, mattocks and shovels to a depth in which the water would easily flow into a creek or branch. These ditches were lined on the sides and tops with oak, chestnut or other wood which could withstand deterioration from dampness or water for long periods of time. These wood linings were made from blocks of wood which had been sawed to lengths of about 18 inches and then split into thicknesses of 2½ or 3 inches. The widths varied as to the sizes of the trees used. Of course, this process required the use of iron tools. To split these blocks of wood, an iron wedge was driven into the block by hitting it with a sledge hammer or a wooden maul. After the ditch lining was completed, the dug out soil was replaced by using shovels and rakes. When the soil settled the land dried and was level and ready to be put in use.

Most tools, after use had to be sharpened — the wedges, axes, picks, mattocks, saws, crow bars and scythe blades and other tools, and for a perfect edge, the blacksmith could be counted on to make it. Some farmers had grinding stones and files and did some of the sharpening at home.

A few people worked for Mr. Pierce and learned some of the smithing and opened small shops. My uncle, Tom Hash, who lived just across the road from Mr. Pierce's shop and helped him at times, learned a number of rather simple processes, opened a small shop and operated it until he moved to Maryland.

These small shops relieved Mr. Pierce of a number of easy jobs and gave him more time for the complicated work.

Some home builders went to a blacksmith to have an iron arm or crane about 20 inches long and a half inch thick made to be inserted in one side of the fireplace (especially in the kitchen fireplace) as the fireplace was being built, to hang pots on for cooking the family meals. Parts of iron cook and heating stoves would break and had to be carried to the blacksmith to be repaired. The blacksmith not only made horseshoes, but was at times called on to shoe horses.

I think it's sad that there are not blacksmith shops, as such, today. I know we have improvements in many areas of our lives and yet, there are memories of some good things we miss.

Roads and Automobiles

Roads

Roads tended to follow streams when possible since streams found the lowest and most level places but high spots separated streams flowing in opposite directions. Then the lowest place between two hills or mountains was selected for walkways and for driving cattle, riding horses, and later for sleds and wagons. Rains and snows let travel turn the roads into mud and ruts. Summer sun and winds meant dust. When mud holes made spots impassable, some residents would go out and with rocks temporarily fix the worst spots. Often a loaded wagon would get stuck so badly the team could not pull it out and a neighbor would take his team and help by hitching another two horses to the vehicle.

I recall that a family received word that their son who lived away had died and, of course, the body was to be sent back for burial. A brother of the deceased went by wagon to pick up the body from the train station or point to which it had been shipped, probably Troutdale, Virginia. Everyone in the community knew of the death and when the body was to be home. Dark came and the wagon had not come and instead of going to bed as early as usual to save heating wood, people stayed up with their kerosene lamps lighted to show respect and sympathy. Someone might go out and listen for the sound of wagon wheels and the thud of horses' feet. Already, just about dark two men with a team of harnessed horses and "single trees" for hooking on waited at the foot of Sheets' Hill to hitch to the wagon and help the bone-tired team pull the wagon with its sad cargo up the hill and through half-frozen mud the rest of the way. When the driver reached the two men and team, he was so cold and tired he was unable to speak for some time.

Finally Grayson County began to allot some small amount of money for road improvement. Some person in selected areas was appointed to supervise the work to be done by hiring residents in the community. They were paid very little for an hour's work but were also allowed to work to pay their county taxes. Workers were to take their own shovels, mattocks, picks and hoes. Sometimes a team of horses was needed to pull what was called a dirt or road pan, used to

224

scoop up dirt and carry it to a place to be dumped in a low spot in the road, or off to the side of the road. Those who had a team to be used in this work received more money than for human work. My father served as a supervisor for road work for several years in a small area of perhaps a radius of five or six miles. My teenage brothers were hired at times and paid ten cents an hour. At times there were large rocks to be moved and dynamite was used to blow the rock apart. Then picks and shovels were used to remove the rocks and they were taken sometimes to a spot to be filled in and covered with dirt. Hard rains eternally washed out gullies, requiring frequent repairs.

Even in the 1970s most of the roads in this area were not paved but had gravel on them. Cars became more prevalent, taxes raised and the demand for better roads resulted in more paving. However there are still unpaved roads which create problems for residents and school buses and utility workers.

After we had a car, a Model T, my father would be driving on rutted roads and see a rut that seemed to be better than the one he was in, and without slowing down he would at full speed bounce over to the other rut. There were many times when cars became stuck in mud holes or deep ruts and the driver would go to a rail fence along the road, get a rail to lift the wheel or end of the car that seemed to be in the most trouble, lift the car to more solid ground and put the rail back where it belonged. I recall a section of road in Crumpler, not far from New River, that was level, had no drainage and stayed very muddy. People just left the road and drove through someone's field alongside the road until the road dried out. Car owners who planned to drive when roads were muddy or slick from snow and ice bought tire chains if they could afford them, and putting these chains on the tires was far from an easy job.

Mr. Arthur Graybeal was our mail carrier for many years. He usually rode on horseback to deliver the mail and had saddle bags and at times a heavy sack such as one might see in post offices today to hold letters, catalogs and parcels. But on days when the Sears, Roebuck or Charles Williams & Sons' catalogs or a lot of packages were to be delivered, he drove a one horse drawn buggy. By riding his horse, together they could pick the best (if any) spots in the road. Horses learned to avoid mud holes and extremely rough places in the roads. On the coldest days, Mr. Graybeal wore a woolen cap that covered his face and head but had openings for the eyes and mouth. Sometimes there would be ice around the opening for the mouth, nose and eyes, especially from frozen breath.

There were always streams to be crossed as there were few bridges. Once there had been a very hard rain and Grassy Creek was swollen and out of the banks. Mr. Graybeal was driving the buggy that day and had to cross the creek to get to the post office. Buggy, horse and driver started to be carried down the creek, but Mr. Graybeal was able to catch on to the foot log or fence and was able to get out of the swift water but the buggy and horse were swept down the muddy, fast flowing stream. Mr. Graybeal followed along the creek, calling to his faithful horse which nickered, but the buggy filled with water which prevented the horse from being able to swim out of the stream and he was drowned.

Ford touring car with tool box on the running board. That is Uncle Aris' son Johnny with his foot on the running board.

Automobiles

The first automobiles in our area were Ford Model Ts which were manufactured from 1908 until 1927 and were open touring cars with two seats, and Ford Roadsters with a small trunk in the back. The only glass in these cars were the windshields with wipers which were operated by hand — quite a job for someone just learning to drive on rainy or snowy days. Under the rear seat of the touring car were four curtains to be put on when the weather demanded them. In each curtain was a small piece of isinglass sewn in the leatherette to let the driver and passengers see out the side. Of course, there were no stop or turn signals on these cars and the signals had to be made by the hand of the driver on the left outside of the car. The hand raised straight up meant a right turn, the hand extended straight out was a left turn, while the hand down toward the ground was the signal to stop. When the weather was good the open cars allowed the air or wind to blow through the car disheveling hair and clothing. So men and boys wore hats or caps while women and girls wore hats or bonnets — hats often held on with long thin veils over the hats and tied under the chin but allowing the color and trimmings of the hats to show. Women also had "riding coats" used for horseback riding on side saddles, and now used in open cars to protect their dress clothing from the dust of the dirt roads.

When the side curtains were to be used, they were hard to put on and especially after they had been exposed to rain or snow and had dried out as they became wrinkled and could never be folded again as before being used. It practically took two people to install the curtains, one to stretch them while another used both hands to put the button holes over one of the small metal plugs and turn the plug to hold it in place.

Each Model T had three pedals on the floor on the driver's side. One pedal was the clutch — the most used and a most important part of the car. When starting the car, a lever put the clutch in neutral and then in low gear to start off and later in high gear and the speed was regulated by the amount of gas fed to the motor. Another pedal was for reverse and the other one for the brake. The pedals had linings and after much wear could be tightened and often were relined. We were on our way to Washington, D.C., on old Highway 11. At the foot of a long steep and curvy mountain, we stopped so the driver could tighten the clutch before attempting the mountain road. If the clutch lining gave out completely or either of the other two linings, and the driver did not have replacements or could not do the work himself, he might be in real trouble.

One time our minister drove a Model T to North Wilkesboro to bring a patient home from the hospital. He had taken the patient's car and found that the clutch was not in good condition. At that time the route to Wilkesboro was old 16 with many steep places and winding curves. On the Wilkes side — about four miles of mountain road — the clutch gave out and he had to drive up the mountain in reverse, no rear mirror, so he had to roll the window down and keep his head outside to watch the road behind them and watch for curves and meeting any vehicles on the road. How tiring and stressful that must have been! The following Sunday he was so hoarse he could hardly deliver his sermon. (Incidentally, the owner's Model T coupe was a later and improved model. Each year something was usually added or improved.)

These earliest cars had to be cranked to start the motor resulting in many broken wrists and arms by the crank flying back before the person could get out of the way after the motor started or the person turned loose too soon.

The tires were small and had rubber tubes filled with air and both the tire and tubes were easily punctured by tacks, nails, sharp rocks or any unkind object in the road. One did not dare venture out on the road without a tire pump, jack, and a kit of flat tire repair items such as patches, glue and a little gadget to roughen the tube to make the patch stick better.

All the cars we knew had a running board on each side to step up on to get into the car, and it was not unusual to see a person standing on the running board as a passenger if the car were full of people.

One family lived at the end of a makeshift road which was used mostly for farm wagons and sleds and passed through two other farms to get to the public state road. There were gates to be opened and closed and small streams to pass through. The father of this family bought a car for the two daughters and the older one learned to drive. The father would go along with the girls to open and close the gates, but he would never ride inside the car but stand on the running board.

The first car I rode in belonged to a Doctor Jones, I believe Dr. Tom Jones, who lived at Helton. Uncle Luther was ill and the doctor was due to visit him one afternoon. I was with my father and brother as they were cutting corn in a field that bordered the road on Sheets' Hill. Dad heard the car chugging up the

Smith Dickson and the author repairing a flat tire on Scott's roadster.

other side of the hill and said to me, "Run up to the road, flag down the car and ride to the house. And here, take this pumpkin to the house for supper." I hurried to the road, and sure enough the doctor stopped, opened the right front door and let me and the pumpkin ride to our house — a distance of perhaps 200 or more yards.

There was an Associational Meeting at Pleasant Home Church one year and since we attended this church quite often we took food to be served at "dinner on the grounds." Foods for all-day events were nearly always taken in trunks since trunks had trays and the foods could be carried without getting mashed and mixed together. We and the trunk went in a wagon drawn by our team of horses and driven by our father. After the meeting had ended, Dad wanted to stay around to talk to people who had come quite some distances and told my brother to drive us home. Two young men in our area had gone away to work and had bought Model T cars and came back for short visits. They were proud of their cars, of course, and attended the meeting and at the end of the day began to drive walkers home. We started home in the wagon and met Garland coming back to take others home. The horses had never seen a loud noisy monster like that coming at them and they ran up a bank, turned the wagon over, broke loose from the wagon and ran away. Down the road about a quarter of a mile away, Willie was coming back in his car, saw what had happened, turned his car across the road, moving it back and forth, and stopped the team, got out and held the team until someone could get the frightened horses. What a brave and dangerous thing to do!

Fields Motor Company, at Mouth of Wilson, Virginia, had the first Ford dealership in the community. My father bought a used Model T from them in 1925. He was taking the family out for a drive on Sunday afternoon and the

Top: Aunt Minnie and Uncle George Plummer and their Velie car. *Bottom:* Art Frazier's new Ford in which Art, his wife Cora, and Gwyn and I made our first trip to Florida during the Christmas school holidays. Art was the manager of the cheese factory.

highway department had begun work on changing the road and had left a large tree root in the road and a front wheel got caught on the root and tipped the car over. Some of the family were rather badly hurt. The accident happened right in front of Grandpa Barker's house and the family was taken in there. My step-mother was hurt and the doctor was called. Kyle had tried to help lift the car and while Dr. Osborne was checking the other family members, Grandma noticed tears running down Kyle's face and asked if he were hurt. He said his arm hurt and when the doctor checked him found that his arm was broken in the elbow. While it was set as best as it could be at that time, he still has a crooked elbow. There was no hospital nearby and very few people here went to hospitals miles away.

Later Mr. Cam Fields was trying to sell my father a brand new Model T car. Dad was taking the three boys and a neighbor to a small carnival below Mouth of Wilson and stopped to talk to Mr. Fields who persuaded Dad to drive a new car on to where the carnival was located. Dad was driving and Harry, the youngest brother, stood in front of Mr. Fields in the front seat. The motor kept stalling and stopping and Mr. Fields was becoming more and more worried about this new car and making the sale! Harry had found a small round knob which he could pull out and push in which happened to be the choke.

Despite the differences in speed, comfort, conveniences and appearance of those cars and the modern cars of today, much of the repair and upkeep of the Model Ts could be done by the owner. A neighbor in Northern Virginia who had moved East with his family, but frequently drove back to Kansas to visit relatives, said, "All we take along in case of needed car repair is a pair of pliers, a screwdriver and some bailing wire!"

The Ford Model A came out after the Model T, had glass roll down windows and a number of improvements that were added with each new yearly model.

Other brand cars and newer models came along but the Model Ts and finally the Model A Fords seemed to be more prevalent in our areas of Ashe and Grayson counties. Along with the two-seated touring car, there appeared roadsters, rumble seats, coupes, convertibles.

My father would buy a few cattle at times and before he had a car, he might call someone to ask if they might drive him somewhere. Young guys who had a car might answer, "I don't know if my jalopy will start or not," or "my junk heap has a flat tire," or one might refer to the car as a flivver or a tin lizzie.

In those days, car salesmen visited prospective customers at their homes, and took them out for a drive or taught them to drive. An elderly neighbor, Mr. Miller, who really wanted to buy a car, told a friend, "I think I could drive the thing if I could learn to treadle it."

In the mid seventies, Grassy Creek was declared an historic district by the State of North Carolina. Historic or not, I can't imagine growing up in a better place.

Appendix:
Neighboring Families,
ca. 1910–1924

Mr. and Mrs. Lee Anderson
Robert

Mrs. Williams
Kyle, Hale

Mr. and Mrs. Preston Haynes
Arthur, Tom, Bessie,
Everett, Minnie

Mr. and Mrs. Lee Reeves
Cleve, Lessie, Mae,
Lula, Vergie, Tom, Blossom

Mr. Robert (Bob) Reeves
Dorthula

Mr. and Mrs. Billie Reeves
Ruby, Hazel, Myrtle

Mr. Bob Peak and family
(Cobbler)

Mr. and Mrs. Arthur Graybeal
Notra, Horace, Paul, Kyle

Mr. and Mrs. Charlie Shelton
Claude, Lena, Bryan, Burl,
Virginia, Kline, Harry
Margaret

Mr. and Mrs. Marsh Sexton
Effie Gualtney

Aunt Martha Davis Francis
Felix & Narcissis Davis
Callie Ballou, Deedie Ballou, Roy,
Georgia, Claire, Bradley
Jessie

Aunt Caroline Davis Peak
Bob Davis & Sue Jones Peak
Alice Peak, Norman Peak
Dean Davis

Mr. and Mrs. Aris Spencer
(Aunt Sarah Ann)
John, Zella, Kate, Vernette,
Tom

Mr. and Mrs. Leonard Reedy
Gilmer, Willard, Don,
Daisy

Mr. and Mrs. William Spencer
Mr. and Mrs. David Spencer
Lutitia (Tish) and Sallie,
wives.
Rebecca Ashley, Mary Ashley,
Wiley, Albert, Fanny Reedy

Mr. and Mrs. Wiley Spencer
(Little Wiley & Mattie Kirk)
Dale

Mr. and Mrs. Lyda Robbins (Rausa)
Millard, Willie, Flossie,
Annie Rose, Carl, Gladys, E. L.

Mr. and Mrs. Millard Spencer
(Mollie)
Mildred, Gilbert, Jessie

Mr. and Mrs. Granville Spencer
(Polly)
Mrs. Lyda Robbins, Sarah Jane
Sexton, Millard, Joe, Gee
Lester, Delila, Deedy Anderson
(Stepson)

Ms. Doda Reedy
Clara, Maude

Mr. and Mrs. Mitchell Spencer
(Dora)
Theodore, Alice, Virginia,
Bly, Hicks

Mr. and Mrs. Bob Reedy (Lue)
Wayne, Dent, Cessie, Ala,
Ruth, Charlie

Mr. and Mrs. John Reedy
Leonard, Winnie

Mr. and Mrs. Wint McGrady
Gladys, Jay, Doris, Clarence,
Kate, Presley, Don, Ruth
Cliff

Mr. and Mrs. Joe Eller
Etta, Elmer, Celia,
Willie

Mr. and Mrs. John Osborne
Monroe, Vick, Mattie,
Ollie, Burl

Rev. and Mrs. David Blackburn
(Jenny)
Molly Campbell (Niece)

Mr. and Mrs. Matt Hart
Claude, Charlie, Virginia,
Pearl, Viola

Mr. and Mrs. Milton Baugess
Flossie

Mr. and Mrs. James Tucker
(Jim and Sis)
Dottie, Wade, Rena

Mr. and Mrs. John Reedy
(Rugby) I believe he had the post
office and a store for a time.

There were Richardsons and Hen-
dersons but I do not know the
given names and different
families. (Rugby)

Mr. and Mrs. Abraham Reedy
(Abe and Frankie)
Quillens' Ridge

Mr. and Mrs. Lee Spencer
Lucy, Nora, Carrie,
Belva, Victor

Mr. and Mrs. Bill Reedy
Lora, Winnie, Lura,
Ola, Charmie

Mr. and Mrs. Irving Reedy
(Lora)
Violet, Fern

Mr. and Mrs. Riley Reedy
(Linda)

Mr. and Mrs. Joe Reedy
(Jane)

Mr. and Mrs. Nathan Reedy
(Ina)

Mr. and Mrs. Vester Reedy
(Grace)
Lily, Kate, Betty Jo

Mr. and Mrs. Robert (Bob) Plummer
Paul, Rausa, Alice, Dora,
Roscoe, Bain, R. L., Roger

Mr. and Mrs. Alfred Brooks
(Alf. and Is.—Probably Isadora)
No children

Mr. and Mrs. Fields Davis
(One daughter) Mr. Davis was a
cobbler.

Mr. and Mrs. Eugene Waddell
and Family

Mr. and Mrs. John Jones
(Connis Young)

Dr. and Mrs. Fielden Osborne
(Betty Duncan)
Vester, Grace, Reeves, Marsh,
Gorman, Ruth, Joe

Mr. and Mrs. Cicero Walton
(Mary)
John and Effie

Tom, Betty and Nelia Walton
(I do not know the names of their
parents)

Mr. Siebert Walton

Mr. and Mrs. John Waddell
(Cansada)
Estel, Flora

Mr. and Mrs. Estel Waddell
(Fannie)
Lola

Mr. and Mrs. Charlie Barker
(Minnie, Etta, Gertie)
Mayme, Herbert, Zetta, Kyle,
Joe, Harry, Wilma, Marie

Mr. and Mrs. Steve Sexton
(Sarah Jane Spencer)
Roscoe, Ernest, Bonnie,
Etta, Curtis, Worth, Clara,
Clyde, Lacey, Bradley, Blanch, Myra

Mr. and Mrs. Troy Halsey
(Lue Delp)
Annie, John, Lessie,
Fannie, Bayard, Walter

Mr. and Mrs. Poindexter Barker
(Catherine Smith)
Ira, John
(Amanda Howell)
Charlie, Lucy, Roscoe, Minnie,
Lona, Luther, Iredell

Mr. and Mrs. Robert (Bob) Spencer
Wiley (Big Wiley), Joe,
Bettie, Bessie, Charlie,
Frank

Mr. and Mrs. Wiley Spencer
(Anne)
Charlie, Bessie, Myrtle

Mr. and Mrs. Arthur Spencer
(Matt)
Garland, DeSoto, LaSalle,
Branson, Edison

There were other families in the area — Mr. and Mrs. Bob Blackburn, other Blackburns, Greers, Robbins, Waggs, Mr. and Mrs. Eugene Duvall, Pughs, Andersons, Blevins — but the families listed were those that seemed to make up our world from about 1910 to 1924. I'm sure there are names that are left off family rosters but I either did not know or have forgotten.

Index